To Prof. Thoma

W. Huang

Institutional Banking for Emerging Markets

For other titles in the Wiley Finance series
please see www.wiley.com/finance

Institutional Banking for Emerging Markets

Principles and Practice

W. Huang

John Wiley & Sons, Ltd

Telephone (+44) 1243 779777

Email (for orders and customer service enquiries): cs-books@wiley.co.uk
Visit our Home Page on www.wiley.com

Other Wiley Editorial Offices

John Wiley & Sons Inc., 111 River Street, Hoboken, NJ 07030, USA

Jossey-Bass, 989 Market Street, San Francisco, CA 94103-1741, USA

Wiley-VCH Verlag GmbH, Boschstr. 12, D-69469 Weinheim, Germany

John Wiley & Sons Australia Ltd, 42 McDougall Street, Milton, Queensland 4064, Australia

John Wiley & Sons (Asia) Pte Ltd, 2 Clementi Loop #02-01, Jin Xing Distripark, Singapore 129809

John Wiley & Sons Canada Ltd, 6045 Freemont Blvd, Mississauga, ONT, L5R 4J3, Canada

Wiley also publishes its books in a variety of electronic formats. Some content that appears in print may not be available in electronic books.

Anniversary Logo Design: Richard J. Pacifico

Library of Congress Cataloging in Publication Data

Huang, Wei-Xin.
Institutional banking for emerging markets / Wei-Xin Huang.
p. cm. — (Wiley finance series)
Includes bibliographical references and index.
ISBN 978-0-470-03076-9 (cloth : alk. paper)
1. Banks and banking—Developing countries. 2. Correspondent banks—Developing countries.
I. Title.
HG3550.H83 2007
332.1′5091724—dc22

2007002349

British Library Cataloguing in Publication Data

A catalogue record for this book is available from the British Library

ISBN 978-0-470-03076-9 (HB)

Typeset in 10/12pt Times by Integra Software Services Pvt. Ltd, Pondicherry, India
Printed and bound in Great Britain by Antony Rowe Ltd, Chippenham, Wiltshire
This book is printed on acid-free paper responsibly manufactured from sustainable forestry in which at least two trees are planted for each one used for paper production.

Each cloud has a silver lining.

Contents

Preface

This is a book of 'principles and practice', as the title indicates. As a rule, a balanced perspective for institutional banking for emerging markets cannot be acquired by studying principles in pieces without referring them to the practice. On the other hand, practice without principles will be a series of accounts with no guidelines. Such a combination of principles and practice will come difficult. But it is inevitable.

The book is an extension of my own career which is in itself a combination of principles and practice. As a career banker, I have been involved in daily banking operational practice especially for institutional banking. This gratifies impulses that arise from my day-to-day operation – to share some of my experiences, right or wrong, with others. In the meantime I have been teaching 'principles of financial management' and other finance courses to MBA students in different universities, some of which have students from different emerging market countries.[1] Questions, experiences and challenges from the students only reinforce my motivation to narrow the gap of principles and practice. To the extent that the gaps can be narrowed, diversity and depth of knowledge will increase.

I have been deeply interested by this subject, as I have spent a great deal of my time in this business. The name of the department for institutional banking in many banks has evolved from 'bank relations' to 'correspondent banking', 'financial institutions and banks' and 'institutional banking'. Whatever the name is, the basic logic is straightforward – a bank needs supporting international networks for business development. It has been my dream for many years to sum up my life of 'practice to principles' and 'principles to practice'. Anyway, a systematic knowledge of banks and countries in emerging markets is helpful for both managers and scholars.

It is noticed that there exists a mass of literature on emerging markets but little on the subject of institutional banking for emerging markets – a subject needed for each and every bank that has an international department. As the ambassador and window to the outsiders of the bank, institutional banking, or correspondent banking as it was called, covers almost

[1] Maastricht School of Management, for example, has students coming from more than 50 emerging market countries.

all parts of banking. Its activities will therefore be related to the majority of the banking activities, especially the international part.

What I have tried in this book is to reduce the subject to the basic organizing principles of the topics, to convey much specialized content in less technical language for nonspecialized professionals, and always to keep the whole picture in mind. The intention is to transfer a practitioner's insights to a wide audience.

The topics dealt with in this book should thus not only be oriented towards specialists but also be of relevance to readers with both academic and practical interests in the subject. What I want to capture in this book is the essence and some highlights of the life of the subject – an integrative type of the book that synthesises the ideas of many practitioners as well as many scholars.

Theories are grey and life is evergreen. This book has the modest aim of summarizing what is happening in real life and discusses the subject in a systematic way. The book is therefore intended for two kinds of audience.

The first is banking/finance professionals in general who have heard of the term 'institutional banking' but fail to have detailed insights in the subject, or, institutional bankers themselves who have daily insights but want to have second opinions or critical views on the subject.

The second is scholars/students who are involved in finance in emerging markets for their teaching/study and research.

Ideally, this should be a fact-finding book for bank professionals and a reference book for graduates (at least for supplementary reading). I have used at least part of the materials for training not only banking professionals but for MBA students as well.

Some of the materials used for courses for MBA students include:

- International Business: Country risk analysis, emerging market country cases, and debt crisis.
- Global finance: Evolution of emerging markets, performance of banks, products of banks.
- Corporate finance: Products of banking, development strategy, financial analysis, trade finance, syndication, etc.

With such an intention in mind, I have arranged some pedagogical aids as the features of the book:

- Summary: Each chapter has its summary to enable readers to reflect the main content.
- Key terms: Basic and important terminologies are highlighted.
- Power Point presentation package: The package consists of major content of the book under different topics separately arranged as aid for teaching and training purposes.

As a textbook to be used with the focus on international business, Part I plus Part III should be more appropriate. If the focus is more on banking, then Part II plus Part III will be more relevant. If the focus is on training institutional banking bankers for emerging markets, Part III will definitely be a must.

It is admitted that some of the readers might disagree with many of my observations. But the book intends to reach at least one target – to stir the interest in this area and ultimately help to better understand this fascinating subject.

The book could not have been written without incorporating the knowledge others have so generously shared with me. The writing of the book reminds me of the discussion and debate with colleagues inside and outside the bank, who helped and contributed to the book. The following list includes only some of them, with whom I have enjoyed working and to whom acknowledgements must go:

Arie Speksnijder
Atilio Pinto
Boudewijn Kunst
Claudine Stelandre
Diane Boogaard
Daan B.H. de Bruin (Deloitte)
Els Boerhof (FMO)
Habib-Mahesh Millie
Leite Edgar
Ertan Aras (Finans Bank)
Frank Haak
François Pierpont
Joop van der Pot
Orkun Ozcan
Piet-hein Ingenhousz
Paulatte Claerhout
Natalia Bodiul
Senol Aloglu (Finans Bank)
Suzan van Toorn (Deutsche bank)
Vivian Wang

Thanks should also go to Charles and Xian-jia both of whom have contributed to some of the charts and tables in the book, and to my family for putting up with many of my days and hours at the writing table. The book is also theirs.

To all, thank you for your encouragement, support and help.

Needless to say, all the mistakes are mine and any critical comments are most welcome. My email is: weixinhuangdr@gmail.com

W. Huang

Introduction

Emerging markets, which tend to have an image of problems, have been attracting more and more attention recently.

According to the *Economist*,[1] there has been a dramatic shift in recent years in the relative economic balance of 'first world' and 'third world' economies. The *Economist* magazine estimates that emerging economies produced slightly more than half of world output measured using purchasing power parity calculations. Emerging markets also accounted for more than half of the increase in global GDP in current dollar terms in 2005.

Not only is the total production impressive but also the speed of development. During the industrial revolutions it took America and Britain 50 years to double their real income per capita. Today China managed to achieve the same in a single decade. More important, this kind of shift in economic power towards emerging economies is likely to continue. Emerging markets are thus becoming the priority of agenda in many ways.

It is therefore not surprising that plenty of books have been published, and will continue to be published, on the subject of emerging markets. But the subject of emerging markets was hardly looked at from the perspective of institutional banking. In fact, a couple of books have been published on the principles of correspondent banking with, however, few daily operational insights. On the other hand, practitioners of institutional banking very often present their job content on individual topics, missing a systematic vision on the subject.

As a matter of fact, institutional banking is both an old and new topic. It is an old topic because it has a very long history. Historically institutional banking, or correspondent banking, was born out of the needs of banking clients for their international business, for example settlement of international trade finance at places where the home bank does not/cannot have branches to realize their request. On the other hand it is a new topic because in this IT era institutional banking has experienced fundamental changes. It now serves not only the needs of bank's clients but also the needs of banks' own business expansion.

The business of institutional banking provides one of the key interconnections among the world's banks and banking systems by facilitating funds transfers, trade finance, loan syndication, risk sharing, etc. These functions may well be handled in other ways, for example within global players that have branches in various countries or through the global payments infrastructure (e.g. SWIFT) and various financial market facilities. People therefore

[1] *Economist*, 'Coming of age', 21 January 2006.

tend to believe that with merger and acquisition in the banking industry and the birth of super global banks, the need for institutional relationship with other banks was expected to decrease. Contrary to this belief, the reality seems to be in the other direction. Today, institutional banking is becoming more and more important in the banking industry.

Before we shift to a detailed discussion on emerging markets and institutional banking for emerging markets, it is interesting to have an overview of the development of the banking industry as a whole.

As we know, in general, banks have played a key role in the financial system by acting as *intermediaries* between ultimate savers and borrowers. They facilitate the circulation of money in the society by channelling surplus fund to deficit units. Banks are also *asset transformers*. They take deposits and add them to the asset side of their balance sheets. These deposits, on the other hand, are also the banks' liabilities because banks must pay back to the people who deposit their money. In this role of asset transformer, banks have engaged in maturity transformation – coordinating the short- and long-term deposits and loans. Their role of facilitating borrowers and savers is also reflected in the fact that they are the centres of the payments system.

If we look back at the history of banking and compare what we have today (for banking service) with what we used to have, we may well notice that either in terms of customer needs (deposit taking and lending) or the basic nature of the banking services they require (banks as financial intermediaries), there are limited changes in the banking sector.

Till today the technology of finance is still very basic, requiring little more than primary arithmetic and minimal literacy. Banks have played and are still playing a key role in the financial system by acting as intermediaries between ultimate savers and borrowers. As *asset transformers*, they have accepted deposits with one set of characteristics and created assets with a different set. They have engaged in maturity transformation with debt contracts on both sides of the balance sheet. However, we must admit that how banks meet these needs of their clients and the environment within which services are delivered have changed beyond recognition in the last two decades.

Banking used to be a comfortable business – so-called 3, 6, 9 business: taking deposits at the interest of 3% pa and lending out for 6% pa and play golf at 9.00 am Sunday mornings. The past two decades evidenced changes in the banking industry, which are largely caused by volatile markets, new technology, free and more powerful worldwide capital flow and deregulation in many countries. Banks nowadays conduct a much wider range of business than simply taking in deposits and making loans. Increased competition among banks and nonbank financial institutions has also made banking a much risky business.

The fundamental forces that have pushed these changes are various. Apart from changes to the economic situation of certain countries we also see:

- Profitability pressure: Despite the fact that the price of banking product is more transparent, shareholders are demanding more return on their investment. Performance based on profitability is pursued by every bank.
- Changes in technology: With e-banking in place, the banking business is reorganizing its internal structure and external relations. Many banks are closing their branch offices and outsourcing their supporting services to countries like India.
- Regulatory changes: The globalization of the banking business forces the regulatory authorities to change the rules and regulations, and the new Basel requirement also changes the regulatory environment. The policy of 'know your customer' and the due

diligence requirements are enforced in many countries. Transparency and disclosure are the key.

- Changes in customer needs and expectations: Clients are becoming less loyal. Banks can hardly have life-long clients. They can easily get access to the services of other banks and they do not passively accept the deposit rate. They request their bank to invent more products, which may give them both flexibility and higher return.
- Necessity for consolidation: With the pressure of competition, banks have to work closely with other banks – to find strategic partners, to take over or to be taken over in order merely to maintain the existence in this competitive market.

In Europe, for example, with the disappearance of the domestic currencies and the erosion of the main source of competitive advantage for local banks, large changes in the wholesale and corporate banking business occurred and Europewide operations started to assume a dominating position. A more integrated government bond and equity market is taking shape.

Thanks to the one single currency, corporate issuance of commercial papers and floating rate notes are having easier access to the financial market based on broader currency area. The international corporate bond market is thus being strengthened.

The future banking market will have to be more transparent. Each and every bank must reposition itself, as domestic strengths will survive only in customer relationships and knowledge or expertise in different parts of the market. By remaining local competitive advantages will be maintained to the extent that there are differences in taxes and regulations.

Under such circumstances we can foresee some general trends in the banking sector:

- Fee income will become more important to banks: Traditional source of income for banking – interest income, that is the margin between the rate of deposit taking and lending – is challenged due to intensive competition among banks and transparency of price. The margin between borrowing and lending rate is thus squeezed. Moreover, interest risk is also increasing. This is because banks are more uncertain about future interest rates facing unpredictable inflation rates and monetary policy of each government. To avoid being committed to both the lending and borrowing side, a floating rate is more favoured. Otherwise banks may end up with negative margins.

  On top of that, traditional banking business has a fundamental shortcoming – the credit risk. With globalization, risk management is more demanding and needs much more sophisticated skills and expertise. It is nearly impossible to hedge against the unforeseen. In the very end, the banks themselves are their own hedgers, and risks can be reallocated only to certain extent. This potential danger of deposit may cause solvent banks to become insolvent.

  Another reason for the pressure for fee income is that bank regulators have tried to reduce overall risk by raising capital requirements. As a result, banks have to move assets off their balance sheets and try to replace interest income with fee income.

  Banks are also making efforts to diversify and redefine their business. They are becoming *traders* of financial products rather than merely lenders and borrowers. Fee income has thus become very crucial and will remain so in the future. European banks have lost a substantial amount of their fee-based income as foreign exchange and related commissions are reduced due to a single currency. They have to develop new sources of fee income by developing more products tailored to both domestic customers and European customers in general. In many countries in the world, the fee income from off balance sheets of banks exceeds income earned from traditional financial intermediation business. This trend is to grow for reasons mentioned above.

- De-regulation and re-regulation: Regulation has a bad name as it has the potential to create and sustain protection. This protection frequently leads to increased costs, excess capacity and strong privileged profits. Historically, regulation has often had the effect of limiting balance sheet growth and the allowable range of business that banks can undertake.

  Since World War II, banks have constantly restructured their operations to circumvent regulation and meet their perceived customers' needs. In response, regulators would step in to impose new restrictions, which markets circumvented again. For European banks, there will be a convergence of regulations due to the integration. In some fields, banks may have more room to manoeuvre. In others they may face the contrary. The universal trend is that public priorities have shifted towards enhancing banking efficiency through competition. Obviously entry barriers in this industry are seen as declining.

  In terms of regulation and supervision for banking, there will be two main concerns. The first concern is the problem of regulation and supervision of different national bodies. The second is linked to the extent of the responsibility of the domestic *lender of last resort* and of the domestic deposit insurance system. Banks are supposed to mobilize their internal and external resources to adapt to the new regulations, especially the capital adequacy requirements.

- Growing consolidation: The need for consolidation comes from the market development itself. The banking industry worldwide has gone through some hard times in the 1980s and 1990s as well. From 1985 to 1992 bank failures in the United States occurred at a rate of over 100 per year. During the same period the total number of banks declined by 3000 – more than double the number of failures. More recent figures confirmed this tendency: the number of commercial banks declined by a little over 4100 in the period 1992–2002. Most of these banks were small banks.

  In conclusion it seems that in the period from 1985 to 1992 bank failures played an important role in the number of declining banks, but since 1992 bank numbers declined because small banks disappeared.[2]

  With Basel II in place in the coming years, banking capital becomes increasingly costly or impossible to obtain. Banks are more motivated to merge. Merger is certainly an expected development for banks to continue their operations. This trend leads to two immediate reactions. For bigger banks, how to make them bigger by taking over smaller banks that have added value, and for smaller banks, how to consolidate their market niche without being threatened by this kind of merger.

  As a result of mergers and acquisitions, people may easily find that the banks are becoming bigger. The merger efforts of banks are intended to create organizations that are both larger and more streamlined. In doing this banks may maintain supremacy in an increasingly competitive market. Such a purpose of becoming a global player can be realized by joint ventures, mergers and takeovers. In this way banks will consolidate their resources with each other in order to become a global player.

  The merger of Japan's Mitsubishi Tokyo Financial Group and UFJ Holdings created the world largest bank with aggregated capital and assets of 58 billion and 1730 billion respectively. This one institution by itself is one and half times the size of all the top

[2] Frederic S. Mishkin (2005) *The Economies of Money, Banking, and Financial Markets*, 7th edition, p. 246.

1001–2000 banks combined in asset terms and six times larger than the 2020 banks. Concentration of assets in the banking industry leads to the fact that the top 25 global banks in the world account for 37.1% of aggregate assets.[3]

Not surprisingly the advent of the web and improved technology is one of the factors driving consolidation of banks. Economies of scale have increased because large upfront investments are required to set up much information technology platforms for financial institutions. Achieving low costs in banking requires huge investments in information technology. In turn, such enormous investments require a business line of a very large scale.

A phenomenon less noticed is that even within banks, people are also facing the issue of consolidation. Banks may prefer to offer their portfolios for takeover. This means that they will have to give up some business sectors to other banks.

With true super banks in our real life, the benefits of bank consolidation for the banking industry have increased substantially, thus driving the next phase of mergers and acquisitions and accelerating the decline in the number of commercial banks.

- Competition on IT: Technology is transforming the fundamentals of banking industry just as it has with many other industries. Gradually but obviously, some of the functions of banks performed by human beings are disappearing, being replaced by ATMs (automated teller machines), point-of-sale terminals, home banking, phone banking, office banking and tele-banking. Automation does not only cover bank-to-customer or customer-to-bank communications. The whole of the business cycle, from customer to enterprise and from enterprise to enterprise, is becoming completely electronic. As banks are treating information about money, this information is no longer materialized on a sheet of paper, on a form or in securities, but becomes an electronic message. IT technology stimulates e-banking which has an impact on the behaviour of banking and raises issues on human resources, education of the market and continuous upgrading of the hardware facility. Access to banking services is made easier. This is particularly true for retail banking.

  Although banks are more than willing to offer a full range of products to their customers, they no longer find it profitable to produce all of them. Instead, they are contracting out business, a practice that will lead to further consolidation of technology-intensive banking business in the future.

  The power of technology has been decisive and it acts both as a threat and an opportunity to banks. The marginal cost of transactions is virtually zero; the distance between consumer and service supplier becomes less important and the costs of switching between competitors are substantially reduced. This is likely to have the effect of eroding customer loyalty and the necessity to have a branch network.

  Development in IT will force banks to move upmarket, avoid the commoditized ends of the business and focus on the value-added business. It will force people to make very clear, concise strategic choices. It has made all information available to anyone at anytime and has made the price of banking product totally transparent.
- Globalization: On the other hand, banking business is becoming more a cross-border game. Globalization facilitates competition among banks on a worldwide level so that not only the size of the bank but also the scope of the bank activities bestrides the world. Banks are more internationally interlinked.

[3] *The Banker*, August 2004.

A fact mentioned earlier is that global banking based on joint ventures, mergers and takeovers leads to the creation of enormous global players. This also implies banks are offering a wider range of financial services to their clients due to the blurring of demarcation between financial functions. The tendency is that banks are more and more becoming 'one-stop' shops.

Globalization brings free and more powerful worldwide capital/information flow and deregulation in many countries. With competition in banking becoming increasingly globalized, the ability of individual bank to stand aside from this general trend is strictly limited. The interbank business market where institutional banking is most active is supposed to grow, so is the need for division of labour in the banking sector.

With the consolidation of the banking industry, we shall see cross-border services develop around a framework of interdependent partnerships, service of integration and joint product development, remote clearing access from centralized processing sites and strongly defined bilateral and multilateral corporate alliances. Banks without the critical mass of technical expertise or desire in the face of competing priorities to develop their own solutions may choose to outsource whole elements of their activities to those better positioned to handle them. The new tendency of cross-selling and outsourcing reinforces the needs for relationship banking.

To stay competitive in the banking sector, banks not only have to offer products at reasonable prices, but also to tailor products to meet individual customer's needs. Whatever the ideal outfit for the banks of tomorrow, whether a large universal bank, specialized boutique bank or standardized MacDonald's bank, we expect a lot of changes still to come under the flag of globalization.

With all these developments in the banking industry, what can banks do?

Banks are facing two strategic alternatives – a relationship-oriented strategy and a transaction-oriented strategy. Whether to adopt a relationship-oriented or transaction-oriented strategy, banks must find their added value and market niche in the new environment.

Institutional banking for emerging markets as a business meets these challenges by adapting their roles and functions – a topic we will deal with in detail in the coming chapters. We will briefly touch upon this issue here.

What is noticed in the market is that banks are growing bigger but are trying not to do everything. The traditional banks are vertically integrated in that they manufacture the products and services they offer to customers and undertake all of the component process of the products and services they offer. But the pattern now is towards subcontracting banking services and processes to external specialist companies with the bank being a manager of a set of internal and external contracts. Outsourcing is becoming a fashion based on the consideration of specialization and cost effectiveness. Banks may need each other more. Against such a background, institutional banking, with its essence of relationship business, is prominent in its role for the expansion of banking business.

To survive in today's competitive banking industry, it seems that banks can have only one option: to consolidate and become bigger. At first glance, this is a logical conclusion. On second thought, you may find out that[4] to become bigger is not enough. To be specialized and offer what others cannot offer is just as important as becoming bigger.

[4] See the interview with Katsuyuki Sugu-ita, President and Chief Executive of Dai-Ichi Bank, p. 293, in *The Future of Banking* by Henry Engler and James Essinger, Pearson Education (2000).

Indeed there is the need to be specialized. There will be no fixed pattern to this development of division of labour. There will be room in the market for various forms of cross-border banking, based on exploiting a combination of extensive branch networks.

Specialization in banking can mean many things. It can be specialization in products or in markets. Naturally emerging markets are part of the targeted area for specialization in geographical terms and in product terms.

As it originally intended, correspondent banking plays the role of 'ears and eyes' of the bank. This kind of business is more often called 'institutional banking' or 'international banking' nowadays. The outreach of banking is the fundamental purpose of correspondent banking. It will enable a bank either to find assets to generate a secure return for depositor's funds or proprietary assets, or to dispose of assets where margins/interest rate exposures/hedges costs may make them no longer interesting.

Today institutional banking can serve the other targets for banks as well:

- To enter a new geographic or product market by physical expansion to new markets.
- To deliver services with cheaper and better technology by outsourcing partners.
- To reduce their risk profile by trading risks among institutional players.
- To cut operating costs by reaching scales.

Emerging markets as a subject is put on the priority list for many banks when the shift of economic power towards emerging economies is a fact.

Many of the financial services and products are unavailable or only thinly available in emerging market countries, and so institutional banking plays a disproportionately large role in this context and remains of considerable interest. Moreover, an emerging market in itself is a kind of specialization for its characteristics.

When asked to answer the question 'what is an emerging market?', an MBA student answered – half-serious half-joking – an emerging market is 'a place where you have blue sky and beautiful beaches'.

He was not necessarily wrong – an emerging market is a market under the process of development and therefore not yet well-developed. Under the globalization tendency, emerging markets are attracting attention because they offer higher return on, of course, high risk.

Institutional banking business can be organized in a centralized way (i.e. institutional banking is centred mainly in the head office) or decentralized way (i.e. each of the branches has such a correspondent function) in a bank. There are pros and cons but one thing is sure – an institutional banking professional as an ambassador of the bank is both product generalist and country and bank specialist. Institutional banking – whether centralized or decentralized – will actively work for commercial development for the bank.

Admittedly, in different banks institutional banking may have different coverage and different functions. The primary focus of institutional banking, however, should be on operational products and the need both to service and to be serviced as regards international payments, clearing, cash management and risk redistribution. These prime issues cause us to reflect on the ability of correspondent banks to support each other – with possible realignment of responsibilities being necessary. It can be valuable as well to consider the complementary prospects for increased cooperation in nonoperational products among correspondent banks. But the function of institutional banking is not only to support. It should also be 'commercial'.

'Commercial' is a word often used in business practice but can be interpreted in many ways. Basically, 'commercial' is what a dog will do if it smells meat. For that dog to run after the meat is 'commercial'.

Institutional banking has the 'smell' function for a bank. As a window for the bank to the external institutions, an institutional banking unit should have an overall picture and overall knowledge of products for the bank. To use their network as 'ears' and 'eyes', listening and watching the development of the market, institutional bankers contact institutional clients for business. Incidentally, they also assist in solving commercial conflicts among banks.

The marketing function or the commercial role of institutional banking is usually not difficult to understand and is usually discussed, measured and emphasized in most banks. The risk management function, especially risk management for emerging markets, is, however, not so obvious and mostly ignored. This seems to be a pity – a pity that may remain in many banks.

Why is the risk management function for emerging markets as important as, if not more important than, the function of marketing?

Making deals for emerging markets is motivated by higher return. But higher return for the business in emerging markets is based on your understanding and mitigation of the emerging market risks. Otherwise what is waiting for you in emerging markets will be disappointments and losses, as will be indicated in the detailed discussion on country crisis and bank difficulties in emerging markets.

Indeed for many businesses including banking business, success in the future for emerging markets will hinge on embracing the opportunities that globalization, privatization and technology offer them. Success will also depend on expertise which has the experience and specialization to understand the risks of emerging markets and emerging products.

Institutional bankers are supposed to be country and bank specialists in this regard. Their knowledge, experience and networking in emerging countries should present their unique value in risk management for the difficult emerging market countries. By offering their insights into the emerging market countries, they will play a role in risk mitigation, risk reduction and diversification.

As far as emerging markets are concerned, another important success factor in institutional banking is the sensitivity of culture.

In many banks, institutional banking is still called 'correspondent banking'. Correspondent, in its original English, is 'communication'. Banking business needs communications that are received, understood and returned with goodwill and the promise of continued interaction. Banking business needs communications that will build enduring relationships. These communications, either for marketing purposes or for risk management purposes, must reach the mind and, hopefully, the heart of the receiver. For this purpose we will discuss at length the cultural aspect of institutional banking.

The book is divided into three parts – emerging markets, institutional banking and institutional banking for emerging markets.

Institutional banking is linked to both country and bank risk. Starting with a general discussion of emerging markets, we first discuss the relationship between bank crisis and country crisis.

As Part I is focusing on countries rather than banks, the principles and practice of country risk management will be presented. Both the history of sovereign defaults and recent cases of country crisis will be reviewed.

Part II deals with the topic of institutional banking itself along with its role as an account manager, a risk manager and a relationship manager. Here bank risk is the focus and methodology for bank risk analysis will be presented. Some recent issues in institutional banking such as money laundering and Basel II are also included.

Part III will further elaborate the marketing and risk management roles of institutional banking vis-à-vis emerging markets. Here some specific banking sectors or skills for emerging markets are to be reviewed – project finance, commodity finance and micro finance. Practical solutions and tools to bank risk and county risk will be discussed with real life cases.

The book ends with some speculation and highlights on the subject of institutional banking in emerging markets.

Part I
Emerging Markets

1 Country Classification: Principles and Practice

1.1 DEFINITION AND SCOPE

How are countries in the world classified, and which part is the so-called 'emerging market'? These are difficult questions, or so it would seem.

Broadly following the World Bank classification, there are six main types of country:

- Main industrial nations such as the countries of Europe, North America and Japan.
- Smaller industrialized countries such as Australia and New Zealand.
- Countries in transition such as those under the former Comecon.
- Newly industrialized countries.
- Less developed countries.
- Emerging markets, which are countries where there is a great deal of incentive and interest to invest.

No doubt a country can move from one type to another over time.

But classification for countries is not so easy because some of the countries may also belong to other categories at the same time. The 'less developed countries' may belong to countries in transition or even newly industrialized countries, all of which are vulnerable to economic cycles.

In fact, in the growing literature on 'emerging markets', one can hardly find a precise definition on what it is or ought to be. 'Emerging market' is still a vague and dynamic concept, a concept that is frequently in daily usage but one that is rarely defined, or the definition, if any, is not universally accepted. Hence the concept of 'emerging market' can mean different things to different people. Ironically, however, this vagueness of the concept does not at all prevent the business community from moving on in their business in emerging markets.

Geographically, emerging markets usually refer to Asia, Middle East, Latin America, Central Europe and Africa. With few exceptions (such as Japan), emerging markets are located in these areas. This coverage implies a wide variety of terms: political, social, economical and financial as well as cultural. By name, 'emerging markets' covers markets that are 'emerging on the horizon'. As such, for many banks the list of emerging markets changes all the time. For example, Poland, Czech Republic and Hungary are gradually off the list in some banks as they are entering the EU.

Many banks try to use GDP per capita as a measurement for being 'qualified' for emerging markets. This, however, does have deficiencies because it ignores the potential. Some banks use the concept of OECD and non-OECD countries, which seems relatively easier. However, countries like Turkey and South Korea were once under OECD but they are still widely accepted as emerging markets by many banks.

A well-established and related concept is LDC – less developed countries. Here per capita real income is generally regarded as one of the main indicators of the socio-economic conditions. A comparison of per capita income of less developed countries with that of the developed countries can be striking, as there is a clear difference between the economically developed countries and the less developed countries.

The question is – if the per capita income of the United States and India are considered and assuming that an average Indian earned about 5 % of the income of an average American,[1] can we conclude that we may have clear-cut categories for countries? In general, is the problem then settled for country classification? No, not really.

First of all, on what terms is income per capita calculated? The per capita real income concept may encounter the issue of foreign exchange rate. The famous purchasing power parity should work if you want to have a precise income comparison, that is the comparison of income in real terms of purchasing power. That is to say the income level is not on a current dollar basis but should be on purchasing power terms. To judge the standard of living is to consider the purchasing power of a country's currency over GDP rather than make a simple conversion of domestic per capita income into US dollars at a certain exchange rate. The per capita real income data converted into foreign exchange rate may not always be an adequate index to measure development in a world of floating rates. The expression of per capita real income in terms of official exchange rates may not be meaningful if such rates remain highly overvalued.

More complicated is that although a growth of the per capita income is supposed to contribute to a general rise in the standard of living of the people, it, however, does not really represent the overall quality of life. Per capita real income as a valid index is thus being challenged. In this regard, Kuwait is often quoted. The real per capita income for a Kuwaiti is impressive but the standard of living of an average Kuwaiti may not be the same as that of an average resident of France. This clearly indicates that per capita real income figures may be misleading because an average figure is obtained by dividing the total real income derived from them by the total population. A country's gross domestic product may grow at a very fast rate but only a small proportion of its population could be the beneficiary of such growth, whereas the masses of its population may not experience any improvement in their standard of living.

What other factors, then, determine the development level of a country? One of these factors is the quality of life. The development level of countries depends on the quality of life and the quality of life is to be regarded as an important index of development. Nevertheless, 'the quality of life' is a composite index with factors other than income such as:

- Life expectancy
- Education and literacy rates
- The level of nutrition
- Proportion of infant mortality
- Consumption of energy per capita
- Pollution index for environment, etc.

In 1990, the United Nations Development Programme (UNDP) published a human development index – a new yardstick that provides a broad method by which intercountry and

[1] Subrata Ghatak (2003) *Introduction to Development Economics*, 4th edition by Routledge.

intertemporal comparisons of living standards can be undertaken. The human development index according to the UNDP comprises GNP per capita, longevity and education.

Despite the already complicated measurement problems, to quantify human development becomes more complex for political freedom, personal security, interpersonal relations and the physical environment.

On the other hand, the human development index did help to understand in a broader way the development level of a country. At that time a comparison of ranking for countries either under GNP per capita or under HDI was made, which indicated the gap between these two concepts (see Table 1.1).

Table 1.1 Prosperity ranked by HDI vs GNP (ranks based on 160 countries)

Country rank	on HDI rank	on GNP per capita	Global HDI	Global GNP per capita
Japan	1	1	2	3
United Kingdom	2	3	10	21
Germany	3	2	12	10
Republic of Korea	4	6	34	39
Singapore	5	4	40	25
Brazil	6	7	59	54
Saudi Arabia	7	5	67	33
Thailand	8	8	69	79
Sri Lanka	9	10	76	120
China	10	11	79	130
Cameroon	11	9	118	88
Tanzania	12	14	126	158
Uganda	13	13	133	141

Source: Based on UN Human Development Report 1992, World Bank, etc.[2]

Obviously it is no easy job to define the development level of a country.

From the very beginning, 'emerging market' is an unclear concept due to its dynamic nature, and so is the definition of an emerging market country. Nevertheless, we may identify some of the other criteria used for country classification:

- Location of the country, income level by World Bank definition
- Political status and economic performance
- Level of inflation, the rate of GDP growth
- The level of budget deficit
- Size of external reserves
- The trade deficit, etc.

It is widely recognized that the so-called emerging markets mainly have at least three parameters:

- Level of absolute economic development measured by GDP, etc.
- Level of relative economic development measured by GDP growth rate, HDI, etc.
- Market management system measured by the stability of the free market system.

[2] Based on a table from Subrata Ghatak, *Introduction to Development Economics*, p. 28.

According to Carl Olsson in his book *Risk Management in Emerging Markets*, emerging markets are 'those countries which have started to grow but have yet to reach a mature stage of development and where there is significant potential for economic or political instability'.[3] Here 'those countries' refer first of all to LDCs – less developed countries.

Two useful implications of emerging market may be distinguished here – potential and problem. That is, for the future perspective, emerging markets are those with potential for development. Those without can be calculated as developing countries but not as 'emerging markets'. In the meantime, emerging markets are markets with problems as well.

Therefore 'potential' and 'problem' are the key words for emerging market. However, economies like Singapore and Hong Kong are questionable when using this definition, although some banks put them under the category of 'emerging markets'.

Undoubtedly some of the less developed countries are picked up and labelled as 'emerging markets' due to their dynamic nature with development and growth potential.

Despite the fact that it is not easy to define precisely an 'emerging market' and that emerging market is a broad and ambiguous term, there is a consensus that the scope of so-called 'emerging markets', traditionally, covers the following parts of the world:

- Latin America (Mexico, Brazil Argentina, etc.)
- Africa and Middle East (South Africa, etc.)
- Subcontinents (Pakistan, India, Sri Lanka, etc.)
- Southeast Asia (Asian countries, etc.)
- Greater China (mainland China, Taiwan, Hong Kong, Macao, etc.)

The *Economist* magazine regularly publish data on 27 emerging market economies. They are: China, Hong Kong, India, Indonesia, Malaysia, Pakistan, Philippines, Singapore, South Korea, Taiwan, Thailand, Argentina, Brazil, Chile, Colombia, Mexico, Peru, Venezuela, Egypt, Israel, Saudi Arabia, South Africa, Turkey, Czech Republic, Hungary, Poland and Russia.

This gives an indication at least as to which are the most 'active' economies that are 'emerging'. Instead of giving various arguments to explain why these countries are put under the category of 'emerging markets', we should examine these emerging markets in political, physical, social, economic and financial terms.

1.2 EMERGING MARKETS: 'SYMPTOMS' AND SIMILARITIES

1.2.1 'Symptoms'

Emerging market countries differ widely among themselves, and no single list of 'typical' features could cover all emerging markets. Nevertheless, we may well notice some of the emerging market features from our day-to-day work, such as:

- Volatility of macroeconomic environment
- Bubble economy
- Frequent government intervention
- Misleading government policies

[3] Carl Olsson, *Risk Management in Emerging Markets*, p. 181.

- Booming real estate prices
- Price volatility of stock market
- Significant debt in foreign hard currencies, etc.

As a matter of fact, most of the emerging market countries can be characterized by at least some of the above 'emerging market symptoms'. We may well identify them by the following similarities.

1.2.2 Similarities

- Political: Politically, the governments in emerging markets are very often labelled as multi-party but the political system is subject to changing factions. Governments in these economies operate with historical legacy. Such legacy is inherited by either colonial past, as many of them were colonies, or by former communist state.

  Transition of power is linked to social unrest, as it is hardly smooth with a potential for violent overthrow. This also implies the danger of war or threat of civil war. In these countries, the government, with the intention to reinforce the ruling party, tends to control or at least influence the public media including the press. In some countries, political power is associated with wealth. Government is operating with corruption scandals, or in the shadow of strong influence of the military. Patronage, cronyism and nepotism are the name of the game.
- Geographical: Geographical characteristics are also worth our attention. Some of the emerging market countries have unfavourable physical environments. These countries, large or small, are located in inaccessible regions or regions where barriers to travel exist. There also exists a distance from developed markets. Some of these emerging markets depend on or have vulnerable to weather patterns – monsoon rains, El Niño effects, hurricane, etc. Sometimes these countries are vulnerable to other natural disasters – floods, earthquakes, tsunamis, etc. Typically their infrastructure – transport, utilities, etc. – is backward or underdeveloped, and their national income, especially hard currency income, comes from a few agriculture and/or primary commodities.
- Social: From a social point of view, problems prevail for language, and population (family planning, health, religion, etc.) due to lack of economic means. In these countries several local dialects coexist but a foreign language (often linked to colony history) is used for international communication. Criminality and ethical problems often hamper foreign investors' ability to protect themselves. Population growth outgrips the economic growth. Nationwide healthcare by the government hardly exists or exists only in name. This results in uncontrolled spread of epidemics such as AIDS. Illiteracy rate is high and education level low.
- Economic: In the economic field, many of these emerging market countries rely on the 'visible hands' for economic development. Government plays more roles in the economy than the market forces do.

  There is a history of extensive direct government control of the economy, including restrictions on international trade, capital movement, etc. State control of large parts of the economy is obvious with limited state sell-out. Government ownership or control of large industrial firms directs government control over internal financial transactions. Governments provide subsidiaries to state-owned enterprises. Prices are under the control of the state and therefore do not reflect the economic costs of producing. Price volatility is high which results in inflation, sometimes even hyperinflation. The economies depend on primary raw materials exports and/or tourism, and foreign workers' remittance as a source of foreign exchange income. Some countries even depend on international aid flows. From time to time IMF/World Bank's support is required.

Due to a lack of competitiveness in the international market, home markets are protected and there is a large 'underground' economy. Some of these emerging market countries are also net oil importers and therefore subject to the vulnerability of the price of oil. High unemployment or underemployment exists with no or limited state support. Poor quality/quantity of statistical data leads to lack of transparency for the economic system. Few large conglomerates operate in many sectors – including banking. Standards of corporate governance tend to be low and company law may be inadequate. Contracts are not always honoured, leaving investors unprotected in the event of disputes. There is a lack of legal framework or laws are in place but not enforced. Corruption may affect the judicial process to the detriment of foreign investors. Regulators are often weak and subject to manipulation and pressure from political or commercial interest groups. Budget/trade deficit is high as a percentage of GDP.

- Financial: Looking further into the financial system of these emerging markets, we find that there is a lack of proximity of financial institutions both in geographic and social and cultural terms. The banking industry is usually underdeveloped with many undercapitalized banks, which may suffer occasional illiquidity.

  Lack of sound capital markets is another shortcoming in mobilizing surplus of funds to those who may need them. There is only a small-scale stock exchange or no stock exchange at all, while trading in a few stocks heavily influences those stocks that exist. The capital market is thus underdeveloped and a limited amount of stocks stay in the hands of the public. Shallow or nonexistent markets lead to inadequate bond market trading for the government or the private sector to raise funds. As a result there is a lack of markets for hedging risks.

  The fiscal situation is nonefficient or primary. Official income for government spending is limited and unstable – tax base is limited and tax avoidance is common either because of loopholes in the tax system or because of a lack of tax discipline.

  For the public, there is limited financial literacy among the people, especially the poor. Segregation between financial players is strict, and correlation between economic struggle and financial stability is noticeable. As we know, a financial system performs the essential function of channelling funds to those individuals or companies that have productive investment potential. In emerging markets, the financial system cannot function efficiently and is even disrupted sometimes. The lack of an efficient financial market leads to a contraction in economic activities.

  Regarding monetary policy, for the balance of international payments, monetary authorities tend to rely on dollarization – the common use of US dollars in lieu of local currency or the establishment of a more formal link between the two. This will result in two-tier exchange markets – official exchange rate goes hand by hand with black market exchange rate. Thus, to ease the management of currency risk, borrowing by the state and private sector is often done in foreign currency. In these countries a high percentage of exports proceeds is committed to financing debt. There is an obvious lack of hard currency and devaluation is regular, or the currency is under the pressure of devaluation due to speculation against the currency.

1.3 SINK OR SWIM: THE EVOLUTION OF EMERGING MARKETS

Emerging markets are the group of less developed countries that 'emerged' on the horizon judged by their development level.

When reviewing the 'decline and rise of emerging markets', a couple of development theories and concepts try to explain and analyse the reasons behind. The discussion on why some countries could emerge while others could not throws light on insights of economic development as well as patterns of development.

1.3.1 The 19th Century

Economic development needs capital. In the 19th century when most of the emerging markets nowadays were still colonies of European countries, the capital needed for development originated mainly in Britain, Germany and France. The United States was the then emerging market.

Like the situation for other emerging markets today, the 19th century saw the turbulence in the economic and financial system of the United States. In fact the United States has had a long history of banking and financial crisis in the 19th century – crises occurred almost every 20 years in 1891, 1837, 1857, 1873, 1884 and 1893. Even in the 20th century, there was the so-called *Great Depression* of 1930–1933.

1.3.2 The 1930s

The Great Depression in US characterizes some of the emerging market 'symptoms': bubble economy, price volatility of the stock market and volatility of the macroeconomic environment. The booming stock market in both 1928 and 1929 was followed by a stock market crash in October 1929. By the middle of the 1930s, more than half of the declining stock market had been reversed. There was a continuing decline in the stock market in the middle of the 1930s.

Together with the declining of the stock market followed a sequence of bank collapses from October 1930 until March 1933. One-third of banks in the US went out of business. The loss of one-third of the banks reduced the amount of financial intermediation and the amount of outstanding loans fell by half from 1929 to 1933. The Great Depression was the worst crisis ever experienced in the United States.

After short recovery from the Great Depression, the United States gradually became a major exporter. Together with Europe, the US emerged as a major capital and industrialized product exporter in the 20th century. Countries, especially those in America and Asia, became recipients of capital and finished products, whereas the emerging market countries exported raw materials.

1.3.3 The 1950s and 1960s

In the 1950s and 1960s, the belief was that developing countries could realize industrialization by substituting domestic manufactured goods for imports. Many developing countries tried to 'emerge' and accelerate their development by limiting imports of manufactured goods, to foster a manufacturing sector serving the domestic market. This belief was, however, replaced by the export-oriented strategy in the 1970s. In that period it became increasingly apparent that via exports of manufactured goods developing countries could achieve accumulation of hard currency capital to realize their industrialization.

The countries that developed under this pattern, especially those in Asia, achieved spectacular economic growth. For some countries the growth rate was at more than 10% per year. The World Bank called these countries the 'high performance Asian economies'. This refers to three groups of country, the 'miracle' of which began at different times.

1.3.4 The 1970s and 1980s

First on the list was Japan, whose growth began soon after World War II. In the 1960s rapid economic growth began in four smaller Asian economies, the so-called four 'tigers' – Hong Kong, Taiwan, South Korea and Singapore. Finally, in the late 1970s and the 1980s rapid growth began in Malaysia, Thailand, Indonesia and, most impressively, in China.[4]

Figure 1.1 shows the growth for seven of these economies in the period 1965–1990.

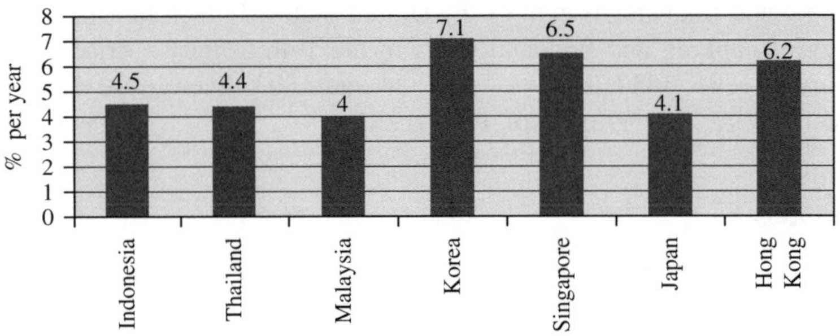

Figure 1.1 Growth of GNP per capita, 1965–1990
Source: World Development Report.

The growth was due to a combination of economic policies, which was by far the main factor that contributed to this fabulous performance. These *high-performance Asian economies* aimed at stability-oriented macroeconomic policies, with the emphasis on low inflation rates and the avoidance of overvalued exchange rates.[5]

There were ups and downs. In the 1980s, developing countries in emerging markets especially those in Latin America experienced massive bank debt rescheduling. The 1980s have seen the debt crises of Latin American countries.

On 13 August 1982 Mexico unilaterally announced that it could no longer service its $80 billion external debt. Although individual countries like Ghana, Turkey and Indonesia had similar situations in the 1970s, these had essentially been associated with hardly any international attention.

The case of Mexico was different as in the second half of 1982 it became apparent that dozens of other developing countries shared Mexico's problems.

[4] John M. Page (1994) 'The East Asian miracle: an introduction', *World Development*, Vol. 22, No. 4, pp. 615–625.

[5] World Economic Outlook (1998) 'The Asian Crisis and the Region's Long-Term Growth Performance', International Monetary Fund.

1.3.5 The 1990s

By the late 1980s, the threat of financial disaster had receded. In the early 1990s, under the concept of 'Washington Consensus'[6] many countries had their policy shift to cater free market approach. The 'Washington Consensus' was endorsed by the US Treasury and Washington-based international institutions such as IMF and World Bank. Ten particular reform policies made up this 'Washington Consensus'.[7]

The focus was the creation of a relatively free market to encourage more capital inflow for emerging markets. Monetary prudence reduced inflation. Fiscal discipline lowered the average budget deficit from 5% of GDP to about 2% and reduced public external debt from about 50% of GDP to less than 20%. Financial liberalization eliminated direct credit controls, interest rates were deregulated and foreign investments were encouraged. Foreign exchange and capital account controls were also removed. More than 800 public enterprises were privatized between 1988 and 1997.[8]

In the early years of 1990s, with the stimulus of the new free market approach, *FDI* (Foreign Direct Investment) into emerging market countries soared. The extent of economic reforms in emerging markets was historical but the economic growth in Latin America was discouraging for emerging markets: real GDP growth in the region was low which was substantially below the rates of 5% or more in the 1960s and 1970s.

Public opinion surveys in the late 1990s indicated that Latin Americans thought their economies were not doing well, and that their quality of life was lower than that of previous generations. Many therefore look beyond the 'Washington Consensus'. Latin American heads of state at their summit meetings in 1994 and then in 1998 broadened their development objectives to include social targets such as poverty reduction, education and good governance. The Mexico peso crisis in 1994 and 1995 brought an unpleasant surprise and the Asian currency crisis later reinforced doubt on this free market approach. Meanwhile, several new emerging economies in Asia such as South Korea, Taiwan, Hong Kong and Singapore attracted attention and they were called as *newly industrialized economies* or NIEs.

These economies are different in their economic structures: Singapore with detailed government direction of the economy, South Korea with growth via the formation of very large conglomerates, Taiwan with flexible small and medium size family-run businesses and Hong Kong with a policy of laissez-faire for business.

The miracle-like growth of these economies set examples for developing countries to emerge as industrialized countries until the so-called Asian crisis in 1997 – the onset of the Asian crisis witnessed the 'sinking' of many newly emerging markets.

A point worth mentioning is the so-called 'flying goose' phenomenon, which emphasizes the function of export. It was argued that countries would develop via export expansion by focusing on their 'comparative advantages'. As a country moves up the ladder of dynamic comparative advantage, the increasing value of its exports contributes all the more to the economy's development. Beginning initially with Ricardo-type exports based on 'natural

---

[6] 'Washington Consensus' is a loose concept, put forward by John Williamson of the Institute for International Economics. The concept represents the conventional wisdom that liberalization and macroeconomic (notably price) stability are key factors for economic development.

[7] (1) The fiscal discipline, (2) public expenditure priorities, (3) tax reform, (4) liberalization of financial marktes, (5) competitive exchange rate, (6) liberalization of trade policy, (7) foreign direct investment, (8) privatization, (9) deregulation, (10) property rights.

[8] Nancy Birdsall and John Nellis (2002) '*Winners and losers: assessing the distributional impact of privatisation*', Washington DC, Centre for Global Development, Paper No. 6.

differences in labour productivity or Heckscher–Ohlin-type goods based on historical factor endowments, the value added in exports increases as the country moves on to skilled, labour-intensive, capital-intensive and knowledge-intensive exports. This implies that the sources of comparative advantage evolve over time, thereby changing a country's composition of trade and its position on the ladder of comparative advantage. At the lower rungs, 'natural' comparative advantages have a cost-based type of advantage. The higher rungs of 'acquired' comparative advantage relate to goods that have a product-based type of advantage.[9]

The evolution of Asian emerging markets explicitly evidenced that less developed countries 'emerged' one by one with a 'leading country' moving up the ladder and 'followers' occupying the vacant rungs. We can readily conclude that export promotion has contributed more to a developing country's rate of growth income than that of import substitution. This has been mainly due to dynamic gains from trade in practice.

The evolution of emerging markets in Asia is particularly relevant to this pattern and the following is a summary of these three rungs of the 'flying goose':

- Japan (R&D and knowledge-intensive; 'acquired' comparative advantage, capital-intensive).
- NICs (skilled labour-intensive; 'natural' unskilled, labour-intensive).
- ASEAN (comparative advantage: resource-intensive, raw materials, low skilled labour, etc.).

The demolition of the Berlin Wall and the overthrow of Eastern European communist governments in 1989 opened the door to countries that previously had been considered off limits to Western countries. These former communist countries, which were under the category of *centrally planned economies* (CPE), joined the territory of 'emerging markets'. Most of those economies were in the process of transition to a market economy. These CPEs include the European (Estonia, Latvia, Lithuania, Belarus, Republic of Moldova, Russian Federation and Ukraine) and Asian parts (Armenia, Azerbaijan, Georgia, Kazakhstan, Kyrgyzstan, Tajikistan, Turkmenistan and Uzbekistan) of the former USSR, plus other European countries (Bulgaria, Czech Republic, Hungary, Poland, Romania, Slovakia, Albania, Bosnia, Croatia, Slovenia, Macedonia and Yugoslavia).

In the late 1990s, the concept of 'social capital' was first introduced.[10] The World Bank defines social capital as the social relationships, networks and norms that shape the quality and quantity of a society's interactions.[11] Various types of social capital are relevant for analysis of country development.

For developing countries, the concept is further divided into 'civil social capital' and 'government social capital'. It was noticed that culture plays a role in development as civil social capital relates to *values, beliefs, attitudes and norms of behaviour*.

Alongside this line S. Gordon Redding in 1993 wrote his book on *The Spirit of Chinese Capitalism* which examined the fundamental beliefs and values, social structures, relationship rules, rules for action and forms of cognition in the Chinese communities in Southeast Asia.

---

[9] Those who are interested in this development model for emerging market are recommended to read a textbook on trade theory, such as the one written by Krugman and Obstfeld (2003).

[10] Coleman and Putman have been the most influential in introducing the concept of 'social capital' although the concept is used differently by sociologists, political scientists and economists.

[11] www.worldbank.org/poverty/scapital/library

His attempt was to explain so-called *Chinese capitalism* in Hong Kong, Taiwan, Singapore, Indonesia, the Philippines, Malaysia, Thailand, etc.

Although it is neither the task nor the ambition of this book to label the emerging markets according to their categories, the review of these concepts and models is, however, helpful to understand the evolution of policy changes.

1.3.6 The 2000s

The 2000s saw the young emerging economies growing up in more than one way. The major emerging markets today are so-called *BRICT* countries: Brazil, Russia, India, China and Turkey, which will be discussed in detail in the next chapter.

Most of these countries have so far embraced market friendly reforms and opened their doors to trade and investment. They catch up quickly by adopting technology and management know-how from the West.

It is nevertheless clear that their development will not be a straight line. It will not surprise us if some of the emerging markets today do sink or 'submerge' in the future while others move on. But the interest in the emerging markets is related to the fact that, despite difficulties and setbacks, the emerging market economies nowadays are truly becoming an exciting and alluring place in which to do business. This is because advances in technology especially in communications and transportation have connected business with additional sources of labour and other resources. Imports and exports are fuelled by the accumulation of capital in many countries of the world.

The rationale for emerging markets to attract attention from the business community is simple and straightforward – the market potential of these markets.

1.4 EMERGING MARKETS: THE POTENTIAL

Emerging markets are interesting because they are now doubling their gross domestic product (GDP) roughly every 12 years according to Daniel Riordan from Emerging Markets Solutions group.[12] In the next decade the collective economies of developing countries are expected to account for over 65% of the world's production as measured by GDP. Add to this growth is a surge in population and continued urbanization. Experts estimate the economic growth will create nearly 50 mega cities in emerging market economies over the next 50 years.

Rapid economic growth in emerging markets also means that their share of the world's economic wealth is growing. As mentioned in our introduction, the *Economist* gave more detailed estimation and statistics – the combined output of emerging economies rose above half of the global total in 2005.[13] The message is that, by one measure at least, the dominance in the global economy of the rich countries since their industrial revolution in the 19th century is over. This estimation is based on the IMF's method of converting national GDPs into dollars using purchasing power parities instead of market exchange rate.

Even when measured by market exchange rates, emerging market economies are also showing growing clout. In 2005, their combined GDP grew in current dollar terms by $1.6

[12] See *Trade Finance* magazine, America's Trade Finance report April 2004.

[13] *Economist*, 21 January 2006, p. 65.

trillion, more than the $1.4 trillion increase of developed economies. This rapid growth will also allow developing countries to narrow the economic gap between the emerging market countries and developed countries.

Today, the G7 countries produce about two-thirds of the world's GDP, feeding 11% of the world's population. In 20 or 30 years' time, this world GDP picture will look very different. A relatively small number of countries which are home to half of the population today will be the main drivers of the world's economic growth during the next 20–30 years. On the other hand, their combination of increased life expectancy and low population growth has created a situation where most developed countries, with the exception of the USA, will be faced with ageing populations and shrinking workforces in the decades ahead. This will put motivation on capital flows around the world, as developed countries with ageing populations seek to maximize returns on their savings by investing in high growth emerging market economies. These emerging market countries – notably China, India, Brazil, Russia, Turkey, etc., will therefore become the focus of economic development.

It is not surprising that foreign direct investment flows to emerging markets also outpaced those to the developed world. In 2004, foreign direct investment flows to developing countries spiked by 41%, reaching an all-time high of $268 billion. In contrast to this, the developed world experienced a 14% decline in foreign direct investment inflows, down to $380 billion – a six-year low. Emerging economies in Asia benefited particularly from this massive shift, taking nearly one in four global foreign direct investment dollars in 2004, compared to only one in 10 in 2000. Asia's inflows reached $148 billion in 2004, $46 billion more than the year before – an unprecedented increase in the region.[14]

This response by international investors to emerging markets is impressive. Asia and Latin America have attracted most of the investment community's attention as compared with Africa. The emerging markets of Asia have attracted almost all the private equity investment from Japan and half of the equity dollars invested in developing countries by the US. Africa and the Middle East remain largely ignored, yet their economies represent around 20% of all emerging markets.[15] Today, China and India combined account for 45% of the region's foreign direct investment.

Foreign direct investments are an important source of momentum for economic development as they create jobs, exports and new industries. They also transfer technology and know-how in ways that have introduced new growth dynamics in these markets and on a scale the world have never seen before. Not only are these emerging markets enjoying robust economic growth, but deep economic structural changes including but not limited to technological transformations that will position them as new emerging centres of future global growth. More interesting is that, some emerging markets, such as China and India, are becoming sources of foreign direct investment themselves.

Together with the shift of wealth comes the rise in living standards in these emerging markets. The rise in living standards naturally implies the rise in purchasing power of the population. This development of new consumer markets provides opportunity for companies as well as for banks. Emerging markets, with both hidden dangers and opportunities, are thus becoming an important and interesting topic to many companies and banks.

---

[14] Paul Laudicina and Jonathan M. White (2005) 'India and China: Asia's FDI magnets', *Far Eastern Economic Review*, Vol. 168, No. 9.

[15] See IFC paper, *Emerging Stock Markets Fact Book*.

On the capital market side, emerging markets are also on the top of the list of the world's best performing stock markets, although the worst performers happen to be concentrated in emerging markets too.

The increased interest by private equity investors has been accredited to the 'push and pull's factors. The push factor is for better profits and more diversification because of the knowledge that investment returns in emerging markets are generally higher than in mature markets, even with adjustments for risks. Increasingly the investment community has recognized a low or even negative correlation of stock markets in the developing and in the developed nations. Therefore investing in the developing world is a means of reducing overall portfolio risk.

The pull factor is a result of wide-ranging reforms, legislative as well as economic, in many emerging market economies. Governments have liberalized or eliminated capital restrictions, improved the flow of financial information and strengthened investor protection thereby earning the attention of the investment community. This helps to attract foreign investment. Investment banks have confirmed that returns on emerging market investments have outpaced those in developed economies.

Emerging markets, at least some of them, are fast growing economies that have benefited from their comparative advantages in low labour costs and corporate taxes and sometimes an absence of red tape.

Alain Bourrier and Plamen Monovski, co-managers of the Merrill Lynch Emerging Europe fund, believe that the central European countries will continue their fast growing trend owing to the convergence with the established members of the EU. Lower interest rates reduce the cost of capital, boost credit growth and the banking sector and raise consumer confidence. 'The success of these countries is the mirror image of the problems in Germany and France', Mr Monovski, who himself was born in Bulgaria, commented.[16]

Although emerging market economies still have income per capita far behind that of the developed world, and the sustainability of recent development tendency for emerging markets can be argued,[17] the fact is that by a wide range of gauges, emerging markets are flexing their muscles. They are the markets that no businessman can afford to lose.

SUMMARY

Emerging market can mean different things to different people. One can hardly find a precise definition of what it is or what it ought to be. It is a concept that is frequently in use for daily work.

Geographically, emerging markets usually refer to Asia, the Middle East, Latin America, Central Europe and Africa.

On the other hand, the concept of less developed countries is well established. People judge the development level of a country by its per capita income, the growth of the per capita income and other measurements such as life expectancy, education level, the level of nutrition, proportion of infant mortality, consumption of energy per capita, pollution, etc. The United Nations Development Program published a human development index under which intercountry and intertemporal comparisons of living standards are to be taken.

---

[16] *Financial Times*, 'An eye on emerging Europe', 19 October 2005, p. 33.

[17] Main concerns are: (a) rising commodity price may favour the producing countries such as Russia, Brazil and South Africa; (b) lower interest rates have reduced debt-service costs especially for Latin America; (c) recent booming of export from emerging markets has been due to America's strong import demand.

Despite these discussions along the development level of countries, the *Economist* regularly follows the development of 27 countries and puts them under the category of emerging markets. These are at least the most active emerging countries.

Emerging markets share a lot of similarities in political, economic and financial terms. There are also common symptoms for emerging markets. The evolution of markets indicates that during the development of many countries they experienced similar stages and similar problems – among which is the twin crisis – (bank crisis and country crisis) – in these emerging markets. But the market potential of these emerging markets has attracted attention both from the business circle and from the academic community.

2

Emerging Markets: The Twin Crisis – Bank Crisis and Country Crisis

2.1 BANK CRISIS AND COUNTRY CRISIS

The discussion of emerging markets is the discussion of their potential and problems. The evolution of emerging markets indicates that these economies are still vulnerable to internal and external difficulties. During the past three decades, at least one country was found in recession if not in crisis. Some economies will inevitably face crisis including *bank crisis*.

In general *country crisis* occurs when there is a disruption in the financial system so that the markets are not able to efficiently channel funds from savers to people with productive investment opportunities. As a result, the economy as a whole contracts.

Country crisis can either be *currency crisis* or *bank crisis* or both. Country crisis can start with currency crisis but end up with bank crisis or the other way round. Currency crisis itself may have an impact on the balance sheet of the bank, thus influencing the performance of the bank.

In emerging markets where domestic financial markets have been liberalized but weak credit institutions often abound, it is understandable that banks are vulnerable. Banks frequently lend funds, which they have taken from depositors, to finance poor or very risky projects. Consequently, banks are constantly in trouble for *non-performance loans*. This may lead to the 'twin crisis': bank and/or country crisis – an interesting phenomenon to be discussed throughout this book.

2.2 THE TWIN CRISIS AND ITS COSTS

Since 1980 more than 100 emerging market countries have suffered, in one way or another, some kind of serious '*twin crisis*'. The damage is substantial if we look into crises all over the world.

During the African banking crisis, for example, five of 20 African countries spent more than 10 % of GDP to repair the damage. In Eastern Europe, banks in almost every country ran into trouble. The Asian financial crisis in 1987–1988 caused many bank crises in Thailand, Indonesia, South Korea, etc.

The Bank of England has estimated that a full-blown bank crisis costs the country concerned an average of 16 % of GDP (see Table 2.1). In the past, countries like Sweden, Turkey, Czech Republic, Argentina, South Korea, Indonesia and Japan have had such crises and suffered damage.[1]

[1] *Economist*, 'A survey on "International Banking"', 21–27 May.

Table 2.1 The cost of rescuing banks in several countries

Date	Country	Cost as % of GDP
1980–1982	Argentina	55
1997–	Indonesia	50
1981–1983	Chile	41
1997–	Thailand	33
1997–	South Korea	27
1997–	Malaysia	16
1994–1997	Venezuela	22
1995–	Mexico	19
1990–	Japan	20
1989–1991	Czech Republic	12
1991–1994	Finland	11
1991–1995	Hungary	10
1994–1996	Brazil	13
1987–1993	Norway	8
1998–	Russia	5–7
1991–1994	Sweden	4
1984–1991	United States	3

Source: Daniela Klingebiel and Luc Laewen (eds) (2002) 'Managing the real and fiscal effects of banking crises', World Bank Discussion Paper No. 428, Washington: World Bank.

2.3 BANK CRISIS AND COUNTRY CRISIS: MAJOR UNDERLYING FACTORS

Vulnerability of banking systems is not exclusively for emerging markets. Banks, as part of the financial system, which has a function to channel public funds to the most profitable projects, are vulnerable anyway. The notorious lesson for Leeson in ex-Britain's Barings, a property lending fiasco in Scandinavia, America's $150 billion S&L disasters, Crédit Lyonnais $4 billion loan losses are only some of them.

Although bank crisis may occur in the mature markets as indicated above, the financial system there and strong base of financial resourses from the government may prevent the crisis from being a nationwide country crisis. Bank crisis is therefore more harmful to emerging countries where banks remain the main source of finance. This is because other alternatives for financing are often underdeveloped.[2]

Underlying factors of these crises are many. In the banking sector of emerging markets, connected lending (e.g. internal lending to the shareholders or the parties who have vested interest in the bank), low profit orientation, poor lending decisions and poor loans management, limited product innovation, weak corporate governance, less transparency for financials, etc. are evident. Many of the loans are made on the basis of personal connections rather than prospective returns/risk credit criteria. With weak bank supervision and loose

[2] There was research on *'The unbanked in Mexico and the USA'* by Tova Maria Solo of the World Bank, Professor John Caskey, Swarthmore College, and Professor Celemtine Duran, Universidad National Aotunoma de Mexico, which mentioned the percentage of unbanked in Mexico city was 75 % whereas in USA it was 9.1 %. See Conference paper from World Saving Banks Institute/World Bank on 'Access to Finance', October 2004 (www.savings-banks.com)

discipline in the banking industry, it happens often in emerging markets that one bank's failure triggers a chain of similar collapses through the financial system.

Not surprisingly, the emerging market banks in general have fundamental weaknesses. Among these emerging market economies are so-called *ex-centrally planned economies* such as economies in Eastern Europe as well as China and Vietnam. It is due to historical legacy that these economies share their own characteristics which give internal structural vulnerability. The fundamental weaknesses of their banking sector were due to their unique banking system under the communist regime of the past:

- Relationship between banks and the government: There was no clear separation between the government sector and the enterprises, and between the government sector and the monetary sector. In many cases, the monetary sector was dependent on the government sector.
- The functions of the banks: Given the situation mentioned above, state banks had a monopoly position. They were organs of central government and had unlimited capacity to create money and to obtain credits, because they did have unlimited capacity to create bank deposits. In the case of China, the People's Bank of China, now the central bank in China, was the only name for taking deposits and extending loans before the economic reform started.
- Credit allocation: Credits were allocated according to plan targets rather than on a commercial basis. The plan targets were first decided and credits were then allocated to these plan target-related enterprises. Those enterprises, which were on the priority list, would have substantial credit with low or even zero interest. There was no importance of interest rate, no consideration of default risk, maturity and expected profitability. This kind of credit allocation resulted in low motivation for efficient use of the credit. Banks were mere administrative agencies rather than commercial institutes.
- Flow of funds: Flow of funds was centralized and there was less flexibility for flow of funds among local banks. Interest rate was not an indication of availability of funds. This led to misuse of funds because the enterprises given the credit might misuse their privilege by allocating their credit to the projects not directed to the target, for example buying resident houses instead of storage houses.
- Foreign exchange: The foreign exchange sector was monopolized, so was the determination of the foreign exchange rate. There existed a two-tier foreign exchange market: a separation of domestic and foreign markets, and the currency was nonconvertible and usually overvalued.

The consequence under such a financial system is obvious: instead of channelling funds from savers to those with productive investment opportunities, the funds were allocated by the planning authorities without consideration of profitability or risk. The function of the financial institutions was thus simple – to carry out the plan of the planners. The instruments were simple as well because there was no demand for diversifying instruments.

The whole economy was organized by efficient areas (more profitable sectors of the economy) being drained to support inefficient areas. There was no stimulation for savings due to lack of competition. Further, there was no connection between savings and credit placement.

The vulnerability of the banking system in other emerging markets can be caused by many other factors.

In some of the emerging markets, reckless lending has left banks with unrecoverable loans that far outstrip the shareholders' equity. In others, a sharp sliding of assets price or a sudden loss of confidence that lead to runs on the banks are causes of bank failures.

It is interesting to have a systematic look at many macro-factors that can explain the fundamentals of banking crisis in emerging markets:

- The strength of the economy: The fundamental weakness of emerging market economies is one major factor in explaining frequent banking crisis. A sound economy will ensure a healthy environment for banks to function, and to ensure sound banks are needed to run a sound economy. If an economy is struggling with wild swinging in asset prices and exchange rate fluctuation, it will make banks' survival more difficult.
- The supervision capacity: Lack of supervision capacity and instruments raises questions about bank discipline and opens the door for bank problems. In some emerging market countries, some bank rules are in place, for example to maintain the minimum equity threshold and to limit a bank's exposure to any single borrower to a fraction of its capital base (10 %–25 %). But emerging market banks may play games with the rules if the regulators have no capacity to manage. The banks may find loopholes, use dumpy accounts, offshore operations and borrowers with fictitious names to escape the regulator's attention, especially in better times.
- Government's unwise intervention: Governments in emerging markets have great influence on the banking sector and political meddling is everywhere in banking practice. Unwise intervention from the government may distort good market practice. Governments often influence state banks which are neither efficient nor prudent to plug gaping fiscal holes and to finance dubious projects. This leads to an increase in nonperformance loans.
- Pressure under globalization: Globalization requires liberalization. Many emerging market governments, especially those in Latin America which follow the policy of financial liberalization, have a low threshold for minimum capital requirement and allow aggressive expansion of bank assets. Such liberalization exposes banks to new risks.

  Financial liberalization may give benefits in the long term but cause short-term pain. Without proper precautions and pre-training, it will nevertheless make a crisis more likely. Increased competition under globalization forces the emerging market banks to passively follow the practice.

  On the other hand, the introduction of foreign competitors intensifies the mutual influence. Such globalization of the financial industry has resulted in banks facing competition from a variety of sources including nonbank sources. Those banks, often unprepared or not ready for such competition, will suffer due to pressure on banks' existing earnings. Very often the competition tempts them to finance ever-riskier ventures to try to match the easier profits of the past. Eventually, nonperforming loans surge and banking scandals and collapses become commonplace.

SUMMARY

Bank crisis is not exclusively for emerging markets. But the financial system and strong base of financial resourses from the government may prevent the bank crisis from developing into a country crisis. This is evidenced in developed countries such as Japan,

Sweden, the United States, etc. But banks in emerging markets are more vulnerable to internal and external difficulties. Under the circumstance that financial markets are liberalized for free competition, financial institutions in emerging markets are weak in credit risk control. Therefore in the banking sector of emerging markets, connected lending (e.g. internal lending to the shareholders of the bank), low profit orientation, poor lending decisions and poor loans management, limited product innovation, weak corporate governance, less transparency for financials of banks, etc. are evident. Banks tend to be vulnerable and the banks are constantly facing problems with nonperformance loans.

The twin crisis phenomenon is explained by the fact that country crisis will lead to disruption in the financial system and thus further contract the economy. A contracted economy will squeeze the banks. Bank crisis and country crisis, which may come together in emerging market countries, are the so-called twin crisis.

To rescue banks in crisis is no cheap task at all. An average estimation is 16 % of GDP. For this kind of twin crisis there are many underlying factors rooted in the nature of vulnerability of banking systems in emerging market countries. For those economies in transition from centrally planned economy to market economy, lack of efficient market mechanism and lack of market-oriented mentality can all contribute to bank crisis.

In general, weak macro-economy, weak supervision capacity, inconsistent government policy and competitive pressure under globalization can all be added to the list of factors that may impact on banking problems in emerging markets.

3
Emerging Markets: The Culture Outline

3.1 CULTURE AND IMPORTANCE OF CULTURE IN BUSINESS

In our daily life, we tend to have a human instinct to believe that all people are the same – but they are in fact different. When our businesses trade in other countries, we tend to believe that people all over the world are the same – but they are definitely different. There are chances that we may make some very bad decisions due to lack of cultural awareness.

The culture value system says a lot in business, especially for emerging markets. That is why cross-culture consumer behaviour has received growing attention from both academia and the business community.

Geert Hofstede, Emeritus Professor of Maastricht University, said:

> *Culture* is more often a source of conflict than of synergy. Cultural differences are a nuisance at best and often a disaster.[1]

For those who work in cross-border businesses, it is sometimes amazing how different people in other cultures behave. Insights into culture will enable us to be more effective when interacting with people in other countries. It is critical to understand other cultures you are doing business with.

Definitions of *culture* are many. A number of specialists in this field have made efforts to give an exact meaning of culture. Culture is that complex whole which includes knowledge, belief, art, law, morals, custom and any other capacities and habits acquired. Culture is a system of socially transmitted behaviour patterns that serve to relate human communities to their ecological settings.

The culture issue is more apparent in emerging markets, with all their diversity. Managers may easily be misled when considering specific business practices to use abroad and get a *culture shock*.

Culture shock is the dramatic difference between the things you see in a foreign country and those at home. In business, awareness of cultural difference will enable a manager to adjust the business plan accordingly to ensure success. The more countries you intend to do business with, the more cultural nuances you may have to consider.

There is no denying that not all countries have been studied extensively in terms of attitudinal variables, which may have different effects on the efficient conduct of business, and those that have been studied may not offer standard answers to the questions of culture value systems. Nevertheless, for banking business, especially for institutional banking which is international by nature, banks must be concerned with a wider array of cultural relationships.

---

[1] See www.geerthofstede.com

The more foreign banks you intend to establish a client relationship with, the more cultural differences would be encountered and the more training and exposure would be needed in order to be successful in business.

Some countries can be well grouped together in cultural terms as having similar attitudes and values. In many banks, emerging market countries are very often grouped into several parts in geographical terms: Asia, the Middle East, Eastern Europe, Latin America and Africa. Although such grouping is mainly for geographical consideration, it has been noted that such a grouping may also have cultural relevance.

An interesting example is Asia. Asia, especially Southeast Asia, is sometimes nick-named as a region of *Three Cs*: chopsticks, corruption and Confucianism. In Asia common cultural background does have impact on consumer behaviour, executive decision making, negotiation, etc.[2] In terms of culture countries in these regions share more similarities than those in other groups. Economies like Taiwan, Hong Kong, Malaysia, Singapore, Vietnam, etc. share more cultural similarities than Arabian countries like Abu-Dhabi, Bahrain, Kuwait, Oman, Saudi Arabia and United Arab Emirates.

Culture element is important as it is usually easier to adapt to things that do not challenge your own cultural value system than to do things that do. For example, it is usually easier to decide on drinking either red or white wine than drinking no wine at all. You may encounter this 'wine issue' when you arrive at the airport of some Middle East countries. You will also consider twice about 'paying' government officials to achieve your own ends – actions that would require moral adjustment if you do not do them in your own country. The more a change disrupts basic values, the more likely people will resist it. Accommodation of a different culture is easier if the adaptations needed do not interfere too much with deep-seated customs of your own culture value system.

However, cultural awareness can hardly be achieved only by reading books or attending training courses. It is a combination of knowledge and skill, which can only be accumulated by experiences in and exposure to the practice of business-doing in emerging markets over many years. Cultural consciousness is not only to know 'how' and 'what'. It is more important to understand the fundamental 'why'.

In the early 1990s, when the business community intended to do business smoothly with the Japanese, many training courses on 'How to do business in Japan' taught businesspeople the 'Japanese way of bowing'. Needless to say, the 'Japanese bow' does not guarantee every business success in Japan. Culture is much more than just behaviour.

Another misconception of culture in emerging markets is to judge cultural value systems only by geographical location. It is not always that countries near to each other are also closer to each other in terms of cultural values. People can easily find that the culture in Belgium is quite different from that in the Netherlands although these two countries are indeed neighbours. Similarly, Japanese culture is different from that of Chinese or Korean, although these countries are all neighbours to each other as well.

---

[2] Hirschman looks at Jewish ethnicity; Mehta and Belk address the consumer behaviour of Indians; Ellis *et al.* (1985) and McCullough *et al.* find that cultural differences affect advertising. Tse *et al.* relate the cultural differences to executive decisions making. Graham *et al.* examine the cultural influences on the negotiation process.

3.2 DIFFERENT DIMENSIONS OF CULTURE

Culture is something concrete. It can be reviewed and discussed from different dimensions. A closer look into different cultural value systems will discover several composite elements of culture.

In fact, different cultural value systems can be examined and compared with different perspectives. Some of the following aspects, which will be used as an outline for the discussion of cultural code for different countries throughout the book, are introduced for the convenience of discussion. They are not exclusive nor are they necessarily perfect.

- Individual vs group: In some societies, such as that of the United States, the value of an individual person is accepted and promoted, that is an individual's competence is recognized and rewarded. Ethics are characterized more by competition than by cooperation. Such an attitude may be viewed as selfish in Asian eyes. The Orient in general may be labelled as a group-centred society. That is perhaps why 'I' in English is a capital letter whereas in ancient Chinese 'I' is always a small letter. In the Orient ideas and actions are considered in relation to how they are perceived by the benefit of the larger group. A 'group' can mean family, company, business, etc. In some cultures, an individual's acceptance in society is largely based on the family's social status rather than on the individual's achievement.

  Group culture emphasizes harmony – a person can belong to any one 'group' but consensus in decision making is critical to promoting harmony and maintaining it. This is contrary to Western-style individualism. Asians usually take great pains to achieve and maintain group harmony, among subordinates, peers and superiors, at all costs.
- Formal vs informal: This is certainly linked to business behaviour code: for example how you should address and be addressed, how you dress yourself in meetings with your counterparts, etc. It is also related to communications: schedule of meeting, status/position check before meeting. The Japanese, British and Germans are supposed to be formal.

  In fact the Orient is in general formal for business behaviour and the code of conduct must be strictly observed. If you are marketing in Asian countries, in addressing the people you are dealing with, you have to use their position titles or Mr, Mrs, etc. In some places such as Taiwan or Japan, it is so formal that you have to say the family name and the title together. This sounds awkward in the West.

  'Formal' is also related to dress. In Korean banks, I once saw a unique profession – to shine the shoes for the banking staff. It is one person's daily task. The 'shoe-shiner', so to say, comes to the bank to collect the shoes and returns them after cleaning to the banking staff. This indicates the formal style of dress in the bank.

  James David (1995) has ranked the formality of countries discussed in his book *Asia Pacific Communications* (see Table 3.1).
- Vertical vs horizontal society: Whether a society is vertically or horizontally organized indicates the nature and structure of the society. A flat structure usually gives a more relaxed style between the bosses and their subordinates whereas a hierarchy structure demands a more strict reporting flow under different tiers of the hierarchy.

  The Orient is usually characterized by a more vertical social architecture whereas the West is the horizontal. Age-old hierarchies, for example, stratify India. Although discrimination on grounds of caste is now illegal in India and a huge affirmative-action scheme covering places in colleges and civil service jobs is written into India's constitution, the

Table 3.1 Formality ranking in Asia Pacific

Country	Ranking	Formality factor
Japan	Most formal	very high
South Korea		high to very high
Indonesia		high
Malaysia		high
China		moderately high
Vietnam		moderately high
Thailand		moderately high
Singapore		moderate
Taiwan		moderate
Hong Kong		moderate
Philippines		moderate
New Zealand		moderately low
Canada		moderately low
United States	↓	low
Australia	Least formal	very low

Source: based on *Asia Pacific Communications*.

tenacity of the caste system is still so popular that many parents expect their children to marry within their caste.

In the hierarchy structure, attitude towards age plays an active role. Some cultures assume that age and wisdom are correlated and the hierarchy often consists of a seniority-based system of advancement. Western citizens, especially the Americans, boast a roughly flat social structure with a large middle class buffering the vast differences between the rich and the poor. The Orient, conversely, is characterized by a more vertical social architecture with an established hierarchy and sincere loyalty to this structured system.

In the extreme of this system, it is very similar to a military hierarchy where rank is a key determinant. Therefore power distance plays a more essential role in the East than in the West. If you visit bank executives in the Philippines, you may find out that these executives will even have their own separate elevators to their offices.

People may move up or down within the hierarchy but whatever position they may occupy carries a rigid, Confucian-based code of conduct, which must be strictly observed. Individuals must show respect and use proper honour when speaking with those above them in the chain and may use less formal or even less respectful terms to those below them. This tendency is clearly indicated in the Japanese language where two tiers of language are used when addressing seniors and nonseniors.

This culture orientation has practical implications. In marketing your products to the Oriental countries, you have to guess the hierarchy structure and see the ladders of decision makers. In some Japanese banks, it is said that you may not leave the office (even if you have finished your daily work) before your superior leaves.

- Personal contact: A linked issue is the importance of personal contact. Personal contact is important in every business. But, without a doubt, the individual network of relationships determines business success more in the vertical society than in the horizontal society.

  When you hire a person in an Oriental society, his/her social profile is as important as, if not more important than, his/her professional profile. The person you hire may allow you to get access to special layers of a hierarchy. This should be borne in mind for institutional banking business, as it is a relationship business.

Relationship – the weapon for selling – is developed slowly over a long period. In this way, when one member of staff leaves the bank, he/she may bring away contacts and clients. It is not surprising that personal and professional relationships are closely intertwined in the East whereas they are normally separated among Westerners. In the West, true friendships are often formed based more on personal attractiveness than on advantage or hierarchy.

In some societies where there is low trust outside the family (e.g. among overseas Chinese and Italians in southern Italy), family ties are so strong that there also may be a compulsion to cooperate closely inside the family unit distrusting links involving others. Contact with one member of the family will lead to access to the business circle. In Southeast Asia, you may find many 'family-run banks'. Relationship with the important member of the family will indicate your access to the business of that bank.

- The implicit vs explicit: The implicit or explicit expressions of opinion are sometimes called the 'spoken' and the 'non-spoken'. This is also an important cultural code in conducting business for institutional banking. Admittedly, nonverbal clues form a part of unspoken communication for every culture, East or West. In some cultures, to say 'no' directly is hardly possible. You have to understand the unspoken 'no' by using body language.

  To understand the unspoken is indeed a challenge, it is, however, also a skill that pays big dividends for the correspondent bankers who can develop and utilize it effectively while marketing their products. In Asia Pacific it is important to be sensitive to subtle messages and not to expect to reach agreement within minutes.
- Male vs female: Gender in some cultures is a very important aspect. There are strong country-specific differences in attitudes toward males and females. The Chinese and Japanese, for example, are supposed to have degrees of male preference.[3] In male-oriented society, you may notice that senior staff are usually men. A random investigation was done on bank annual reports and it was noticed that among 28 Asian banks, women represent only 3% of board members. In countries like Japan and Korea, you can hardly find any female board members. In countries like Thailand, Vietnam and to some extent China, you may sometimes find one female board member. In the Middle-East, you seldom find a woman in a senior position. In the extreme cases in the Middle East women are legally prohibited from driving and socially restricted from riding a taxi without a male relative.[4] Failure to consider this male/female issue will result in low efficiency of your business development efforts.

Apart from the above-mentioned aspects, we may also identify some other important cultural aspects such as:

- Value of education: How important education is in career development.
- Family value: How people respond to the role of family as a cell of society.

---

[3] One is the desire to have a son to carry on the family name in the Japanese and Chinese communities.

[4] See Johan D. Daniels and Lee H. Radebaugh (1998) 'International business', Chapter 2 in *The cultural Environments Facing Business* by Addison-Wesley.

- Face: Whereas every culture respects 'face', in some cultures face is given more weight than in others.
- Name: How you pronounce a name correctly.
- Title: What a title may imply.
- Religion: How sensitive religion is in the country, etc.

Of course, in big countries (sometimes in small countries too), regionalism and dialect can also make a difference for cultural subtleties. That is to say, there is a subculture under general culture.

In his book *Riding the Waves of Culture*, Fons Trompenaars mentioned the dimensions of culture using America and Asia as a comparison[5] (see Table 3.2).

Table 3.2 Dimensions of culture

Rigidity
AM: Following the rules tends to be more important
AS: Flexibility is likely to be avoided depending on circumstances, relationships or obligations
Individualism
AM: Primarily individually focused
AS: The group may have more importance than the individual, especially family
Objectivity
AM: Emotions often avoided
AS: Emotion may be important but will rarely be openly expressed
Relationship
AM: Focus on the task first. Relationships may follow but are not essential
AS: Doing business usually starts with building relationships. Handshake is seen as important as a formal contract
Merit
AM: Promotion should be based on results
AS: Family, school and other connections of prime importance
Time:
AM: Forward looking. Much less focus on the present or the past
AS: More equal balance between past, present and future orientations
Influence
AM: Believe the environment can be changed
AS: More fatalistic

AM = American AS = Asian
Source: based on *Riding the Waves of Culture* by Fons Trompenaars.

3.3 CULTURAL CODE IN SOME COUNTRIES

A summary of the cultural code in some of the emerging markets is presented here. The summary is made from an investigation of people who can meet two criteria: (a) they come from that country and (b) they have overseas experience so that they are culture sensitive.

[5] See 'Culture and language', p. 189 of Carl Olsson's *Risk Management in Emerging Markets*.

It is not surprising if you disagree with some of the observations even if you come from the same country. The intention here is not to give a comprehensive guidance on cultural issues. Rather, the summarized cultural codes are only a reference map for dealing with the countries mentioned.[6] Brazil, Russia, India, China and Turkey will be treated separately in the next chapter.

Austria

- Individual vs group: Group, as saving face is important.
- Formal vs informal: Formal, as the title is very important (we call a person 'Dr Schüssel').
- Vertical vs horizontal: Vertical, as a lot of companies have a strong hierarchy.
- Personal contact: Austrians are searching for personal contact, as in Austria there large number are of festivities.
- Explicit vs implicit: It is important to speak explicitly. We are counting on facts and want to have clear results after negotiations.
- Male vs female: Male, results should be clear.
- Family: According to the latest studies Austrians are now again focusing on family as there have been new laws and changes in the tax system, which encourages women to stay at home with the children.
- Education and age: Education has a very strong value. In 2006 there was the greatest percentage of graduates in secondary school. Regarding age it can be said that the elderly are respected and valued.

Ecuador

- Individual vs group: More group oriented. It can be observed that Ecuadorians prefer to work and perform any type of activity within a group.
- Formal vs informal: More formal oriented. In terms of clothing and behaviour the culture is more formal oriented. Formal treatment can be observed even within families. For example, children have to conduct themselves in a very formal manner in the presence of their parents or grandparents.
- Vertical vs horizontal: Vertical society. In most companies the organizational structure is vertical or hierarchal.
- Personal contact: Personal contact between friends and family is very high. People in Ecuador are very social; friends and family are highly valued.
- The explicit vs implicit: Implicit expression. Ecuadorians understand each other through nonverbal communication. For example, there are many different hand movements which can express a special meaning.
- Male vs female: More male oriented. In many organizations, it is observed that CEOs, managers and upper level positions are occupied by males rather than females. Not only because there are more males than females but because people still believe that males are stronger and wiser than females.

[6] Thanks to the participants of Intake 2005 of an MBA course in the Maastricht School of Management. This part of the summary would not be possible without their contribution and cooperation. Except for some grammar corrections and obvious mistakes, efforts were made to keep the original sentence from the people coming from that country. Some countries are not necessarily emerging market countries but their comments are also kept for reference.

- Family value: Family values are very important. It can be observed that children live at their parents' house until they get married. It is also very common to see families organizing activities together. Ecuadorians perceive their families as the essence in life.
- Education and age: The level of education is low and not economically available for everyone. In terms of age, Ecuadorians respect older people.

Ethiopia

- Individual vs group: Group.
- Formal vs informal: Formal.
- Vertical vs horizontal society: Horizontal.
- Personal contact: Important.
- The implicit vs explicit: Nonspoken.
- Male vs female: Male.
- Family value: Very important.
- Education and age: Education is important for social status and there is high respect for the elderly.

Georgia

- Individual vs group: Georgians are more individualist than group workers. In the positions in which I have worked, many things were dependent on the abilities of the boss, in organizing and managing groups. When the boss was week in those abilities, achieving group task was always hard, because each group member tried to implement his/her own ideas and paid less attention to others' ideas. Not because they were bad people, but because they did not know how to work in a group, it was not in their character.
- Formal vs informal: Informal relationships are preferred to formal relationships in Georgia. This is mostly because of a high appreciation of personal contacts.
- Vertical vs horizontal society: Georgia definitely bears characteristics of a vertical society. People believe in the central role of a person (individual) and even their families are built around the central figure.
- Personal contact: Personal contacts are highly appreciated and valued in Georgian society. Friendship and respect for relatives or family friends has a big influence in society's development. High appreciation of personal contacts is one of the main obstacles in diminishing the level of corruption in Georgia. For example, if a Georgian is the CEO of a company and there is vacancy in that company, the CEO always tries to find somebody who he knows: a friend or relative. Frequently he will hire a less qualified person just because that person is his friend, or the son of his friend, or relative consistency etc. Sometimes people get lived through fraudulent means.
- The implicit vs explicit: People in Georgia rely heavily on tone of voice, gestures, postures, social status and social settings in interpreting words. It is very rare to receive a direct answer or response to a question.
- Male vs female: It cannot be said that females' rights are abused in Georgia or that they are in a worse position (in most activities) than males. This fact in general is caused by historical experiences. For example, the most powerful ruler in Georgia's history was a woman – King Tamara. Georgia has never been stronger during its existence as it was during the reign of King Tamara. Also the first person to preach Christianity in

Georgia was a woman. Until recently these two women were Georgia's favourite historical characters. Nowadays we have many female ministers, deputy ministers, CEOs, etc. Even the chairman of the Georgian parliament is a woman. From my working experience in several offices at least 30%–40% of the workforce were woman and they were always considered qualified and important employees. Their opinions were always appreciated.
- Education and age: The education system in Georgia is mostly influenced by the old communist system. Recently the government has taken active steps to harmonize this system with Western standards and some significant improvements are now in place (lowering the level of corruption, new generation of lecturers and professors who have fresh and forward-looking views).

Ghana

- Individual vs group: In Ghana the importance of an individual is to a large extent related to the group he or she is associated with and how much power he or she has.
- Formal vs informal: Although creating a relationship is very important we believe in formal authority.
- Vertical vs horizontal: It is a very bureaucratic and hierarchical system. Hence vertical society.
- Personal contact: Personal contact is not very important.
- Explicit vs implicit: Nonspoken means a lot and issues are mostly implicitly expressed. Therefore it is very important to read between the lines.
- Male vs female: It is a male-dominated culture where more often than not women are discriminated against, with fewer women in very top positions.
- Family values: Family values play a major role in our culture and sometimes people above a certain age who are not married are always viewed with suspicion.
- Education and age: Education and age really add value to an individual, the higher your educational level or age the more respect you may get from society.

Honduras

- Individual vs group: Honduras society is more group than individual oriented. People want to belong to a certain group, and are not comfortable doing things on their own. A person usually seeks to be part of a group or club, in which the members act and think very similarly.
- Formal vs informal: Interaction and behaviour are rather informal in some, but not all, business situations.
- Vertical vs horizontal society: Society is mainly horizontal. Communication with different hierarchies is not a problem. The difference between employees or people in certain positions is not an issue to communicate; they are respectful and even friendly.
- Personal contact: In Honduras, personal contact between two persons depends on the type and how close the relationship is. To greet someone for the first time, you usually just shake hands. If there is a little bit more trust, a kiss on the cheek is enough. For close friends and family members a light hug with a kiss on the cheek is usual.
- The implicit vs explicit: Nonverbal communication is very important in Honduras. As typical Latin Americans, Hondurans tend to use body language and are very sensitive

to it. Reading between the lines is important, since some things are not clearly spoken, just assumed.

- Male vs female: Many women occupy important positions in Honduran institutions, including the president of the Central Bank. But still many women stay at home to take care of the children, while the husband works.
- Family value: Family is very important in Honduras. It is highly valued at any age. People spend a great deal of time in family units and most single people live with their parents until married.
- Education and age: Honduras has a high illiteracy rate. Companies require employees with university studies, and for management positions they require Bachelors and Masters Degrees. Companies specify that the applicant for a job must be around 21 to 35 years old. Older than that, it is very difficult to get a job, even with a high education level.

Indonesia

- Individual vs group: In general, Indonesians prefer to gather in a group. But in bigger cities, especially for younger generations, independent living is evident.
- Formal vs informal: Indonesians dress differently for formal and informal occasions.
- Vertical vs horizontal society: Indonesians are very respectful to their elders and superiors.
- Personal contact: In general direct eye contact between a man and a woman could be considered impolite and make the woman feel unconformable. It could also be considered as a symbol of aggression. Direct eye contact with elders could be considered disrespectful.
- The implicit vs explicit: In Indonesia, the Javanese are the largest population and their culture conflicts with other Indonesian cultures. In Javanese culture (port of Indonesian culture), implicit expression is more important than explicit expression. You have to read between the lines what the counterparty wants to express.
- Male vs female: In old times, males were considered superior to females. Females should follow what males said and couldn't be leaders. But now, there are equal opportunities for both male and female. Indonesia has even had its first female president.
- Family value: Family value is very high in Indonesia. Family matters are widely accepted as excuses to be absent from work or school.
- Education and age: People with a high education gain more respect and Indonesian people often put their academic degrees with their names. Unfortunately this condition makes many Indonesian people try to 'buy' their diploma rather than to earn it. For government or public companies, seniority is often considered when promoting people. But in private companies ability is more important.

South Korea

- Individual vs group: In general, Koreans prefer doing things in groups but not always. Our children start their education at primary school and learn to socialize with others. Men have to have military service for more than two years. As a result, we can see group culture in almost every organization.
- Formal vs informal: Korean society has lots of informal meetings in high schools, universities and other local communities that run parallel to formal organizations. Sometimes, such 'gossip' may cause problems for society in general.

- Vertical vs horizontal society: Korean society has a strong Confucian influence, as well as a military culture. So, it must be said that our society is vertical.
- Personal contact: We prefer emotional relationships, including family, friends, colleagues of the same school or company, and so on. We are willing to eat dinner with our guests and want to invite them. Also, we like to be invited to dinner. There are lots of informal relationships in organizations and personal contact is usual.
- The implicit vs explicit: Korean people prefer not to be talkative. And many people communicate with gestures and expressions.
- Male vs female: Until now, our society can be said to be male dominated especially in organizations, and the family.
- Family value: We put huge value on family.
- Education and age: Koreans attach importance to education and try to enter higher education. In general, we believe that higher education guarantees higher social position and more money. Our society is vertical. Age is a kind of standard to estimate a person's position in informal meetings.

Republic of Macedonia

- Individual vs group: Macedonian society is more group than individual oriented. People seek to belong to a certain group, the 'we' effect especially among friends is strong. In business life, the successful ones are those who work in a team.
- Formal vs informal: Communication in companies between managers and subordinates is formal, but communication among colleagues is informal. In private life, communication between people is mainly informal, though exceptions do exist.
- Vertical vs horizontal society: Macedonian business society is mainly vertical. Employees show respect for their managers or owners of a company. However, exceptions do exist in which the society of a company is horizontal. In private life, most relationships are horizontal. People from different social layers are friends and communicate with each other.
- Personal contact: Personal contact in Macedonia is in general close, but depends on the type and how close the relationship between two persons or a group is. Traditionally, people greet each other with three kisses on their cheeks, especially among family members. However, this tradition is being broken by many young people who instead of the traditional kisses prefer to hug each other.
- The implicit vs explicit: Nonverbal communication is indeed important in Macedonia. Macedonians tend to use their body language, facial expressions and gestures. Reading between the lines is also important.
- Male vs female: Many women occupy important positions in Macedonian institutions and companies. However, still many women stay at home to take care of the children and the household while their husbands work.
- Family value: The family is very important in the Macedonian society. It is highly valued at any age and by all members. People spend a lot of time in family units and most singles live with their parents until married.
- Education and age: Macedonia has a high literacy rate. University degrees are indeed important to find a job. Many parents expect their children to have a university degree. Age is often considered to be an indicator for maturity and knowledge in personal and business life.

Malawi

- Individual vs group: Individualism plays a pivotal role in Malawian culture. Group work does exist but ultimately, personal achievements count more than group achievement. This kind of culture must have been influenced by the British as Malawi was its colony.
- Formal vs informal: Malawians approach issues in formal ways. Decisions have at times been delayed due to long hierarchies that have to be followed to reach a final decision. It is considered an insubordination if you skip the formal approaches.
- Vertical vs horizontal: Organization structures are mostly arranged in a vertical form. Flat structures are mushrooming these days.
- Personal contact: Personal contact is regarded as essential in business circles. You may at times be unable to strike a deal if you avoid personal contact.
- The implicit vs explicit: The country recognizes both spoken and nonspoken expressions. For instance, it is considered bad manners to be chewing bubble gum while you are being addressed by someone in formal set-ups.
- Male vs female: The country was full of male chauvinists until a few years ago. This was so because it was generally believed that women were supposed to be housewives, caring for children at home and doing the entire household chores. These days feminism is widely being accepted by many although a significant proportion still considers that a woman cannot be equal to a man.
- Family value: Family values are highly considered although the Western culture is slowly eating into these values. Malawi has extended families to live-togethers. Support among family members is popular. However, Western cultures are diluting these values by making a few families believe and support only their immediate families.
- Education and age: Education is a status symbol in Malawi. Most people have been transformed through education. They are able to get good jobs and be well paid after attaining education. The country is emphasizing education for its economic advancement. Aged people are respected in my country. It is considered impolite to ill treat the elderly, for example in public transport; you need to offer them a seat if they are standing.

Mexico

- Individual vs group: Mexican culture is group oriented, the most important group being the family, then friends, and then the affiliation groups and work groups. Although I don't believe that Mexicans just accept orders from bosses without complaining or making a comment if they seriously disagree with it. Some changes are taking place in this respect because of all the individualistic influence we are getting from many of the foreign companies that have moved into the country, there is still a long way before, if ever, the Mexican culture would become individualistic.
- Formal vs informal: Mexican culture is formal, not only in the way you would be required to be dressed for work, or for a special meeting or event, but also in the way you address the elderly and superiors in a work environment. In the case of your superiors you would address them by their career title and then their last name. We have rules and regulations established by the government but also by society. Those in society you must follow in order to fit because if you don't follow those rules then people won't invite you to places and you would not have many friends. The ones imposed by the government are related to crime, corruption and tax evasion punishment among others.

- Vertical vs horizontal: There are still a lot of bureaucratic companies and institutions which make the culture a more vertical than horizontal one. But it is not like in some Asian countries where if you are old and have been in an institution for many years then you can get promoted. Of course having been in a company for a long period would mean you know it better and maybe that would give you a promotion but also if you are new and young but have the necessary skills you can get top management jobs. Also true is that in many companies, because of your contacts, you would get promotion or a job.
- Personal contact: Mexican culture has a lot of personal contact; people kiss when greeting and if very good friends or family they also hug. In the case of arriving at a party even if you do not know the people you would greet with a kiss. In a working situation you would greet with a handshake those who have just been introduced to you or that you have a very formal business relationship with, but if the business relationship is more informal sometimes kissing also takes place. Also important is that when making deals Mexicans trust the word and handshake of the person that they are dealing with, more than just a signed piece of paper.
- The implicit vs explicit: Mexican culture has a lot of nonspoken communication. People expect you to read between the lines and also we have a lot of double sense phrases which mean something spicy. You can only understand these hints if you have been brought up in that culture.
- Male vs female: Mexico has a macho culture, where woman still have to fight for equal opportunities in working positions.
- Family value: Family value is very strong. Family is the centre of the life for most individuals and the first priority of most Mexicans. Families are most of the time together, except when the children have to go away for school or they leave home before they marry otherwise it is common that they stay. Family will stick together through tough situations not only within the unit but also with cousins, niece and nephews. They will find a way to help a member of the family that is in need.
- Education and age: Education is still highly valued for management positions but in many technical ones what matters is how much experience the person has handling certain tools. More and more companies require people at all positions to have at least a high school education but for top management positions for many even a master's degree is required. In the past elderly people were considered wise and they were respected for their wisdom, unfortunately this has been eroding. It is shameful to see how some people treat the elderly; although it is still not the majority, most still offer them a seat, or address them as madam or mister.

Nepal

- Individual vs group: Nepal has a very individualistic concept in every sector. Working in teams is acceptable but individualism dominates in the entire sector.
- Formal vs informal: Both concepts may work in Nepal.
- Vertical vs horizontal society: In Nepal, our society is dominated by a bureaucratic system. So there is a high vertical society rather than a horizontal one.
- Personal contact: Personal contacts are very high in Nepal.

- The implicit vs explicit: Nonspoken expressions are more used in Nepal. We are considered as low context which means signs or nonverbal communications are often in use and understood.
- Male vs female: A very male-dominated society exists in Nepal. Recently, however, more women are found in positions in organizations and professions, but still the society is mainly male dominated.
- Family value: Family values are considered very important in Nepal. Everyone is bound to follow family cultures, values and norms and society consists of the same values.
- Education and age: Education in recent days is considered important in Nepal. But still there is the problem of uneducated people in rural areas.

Palestine

- Individual vs group: Palestine is a mix of both but it depends on the situation. It seems to be more weighted to group since the well-being of the group is a social value.
- Formal vs informal: Somewhere in between, but weighted more in favour of formal. For example, in the public 'government' sector relationships are more formal than in the private sector.
- Vertical vs horizontal society: Vertical society with flexibility. Flexibility depends on the situation of the individual company and the sector. But we still have high level of bureaucracy mainly in government structure.
- Personal contact: Personal contact is valued so much in my society and it is appreciated that people use the phone or email. But for special conditions that we face such as closures and isolation of the cities, people are depending more on electronic communication.
- The implicit vs explicit: Both the spoken and the nonspoken are used in Palestine.
- Male vs female: Opportunities for females are considered as average. It depends on the field and the sector and also on which part of the country. There are possibilities for women to get leading positions but the way is not easy at all.
- Family value: Family value is much appreciated; we consider a very close tight culture with big families that support each other.
- Education and age: Education is very much valued; people in Palestine consider education as an asset. Due to our history and the situation of being occupied there is a chance that we will be evacuated at any time, so education is one of our personal valuables. Age is also very important in terms of seniority, and to respect elders is clear in society and social events. For the business and private sector, to be respected relies more on achievements and capabilities.

Rwanda

- Individual vs group: Group.
- Formal vs informal: Formal.
- Vertical vs horizontal society: Vertical.
- Personal contact: Personal contact is important.
- The implicit vs explicit: Nonspoken – implicit expression is high.
- Male vs female: Female.
- Family value: Family value is very important.
- Education and age: Education and age are valued highly.

Taiwan

- Individual vs group: In Taiwan, people tend to prefer team work rather than be individual. In my opinion, we do not want to be unique among our peers. We prefer to co-work with other people as a team since we have been taught that uniting is strength. On the other hand, the feeling of belonging and affiliation is important.
- Formal vs informal: Taiwanese culture has been influenced by many countries, western and eastern, and also our traditional background. Therefore, the society is between formal and informal. In general, Taiwanese are not like the Japanese who have to watch their manners and behaviour so strictly. Nevertheless, Taiwanese are not unlike most Latin people, being informal and easy. We have more room and freedom in some aspects. However, because of Taiwanese traditional thoughts, we still behave very politely and our behaviour and attitudes change according to the situation and the people we deal with.
- Vertical vs horizontal society: Taiwan is a hierarchical society thus far. The structure in an organization is usually not flat, but several levels vertically. We respect elders in our families and also managers in workplaces. It is not very easy to be friends with our bosses unless it is not in the office.
- Personal contact: As we like to be with a group, we have more frequent interaction with family, friends and colleagues. We do visit friends without invitation and confirmation in advance, and you would not be rejected. Taiwanese are very hospitable and we are willing to listen to other people and help them with their problems.
- The implicit vs explicit: For language usage, we tend to be implicit because we would avoid the possibility of offending other people. Also, we do not express our own feelings and thinking directly. Therefore, there may be different implications behind what we say.
- Male vs female: Although there are more and more women working at higher management level, there are still disadvantages for female managers to work equally with male colleagues. In my previous experiences, there are successful female managers in high positions in the company and their performances exceed their male peers. However, the proportion is very wide. Women would sacrifice their own career in order to take care of their families; therefore, they would not be able to occupy the same position in the work places.
- Family value: In Confucian philosophy, the family takes a very important place in our whole life. We consider the family is the pivot and it influences many decisions we make. We may consult with the family before making significant decisions. Moreover, the family may stop members from getting divorced, for example, because we believe that we should maintain completeness.
- Education and age: High education is currently very common in Taiwan; therefore, when people are applying for new jobs, companies are likely to require a degree as the first criterion. Most sound companies have an HR department to control the quality of newcomers. For example, the company I used to work for set the education criterion and even has a preference for specific universities. Age could be one concern when companies hire new employees. Therefore, many middle aged people do not change their jobs easily because they know it is very difficult to start a new job in a new environment. In sum, a degree and age could be the first consideration granting you an interview, besides your working experiences.

United States

- Individual vs group: In the US, people are more individualistic. It is important to be successful as an individual. However, we do enjoy teamwork; though we enjoy individual praise and achievement more.
- Formal vs informal: We are more informal. We address our seniors and superiors by their first name. We also do not pay much attention to status and freely talk to all levels within an organization.
- Vertical vs horizontal society: Our society is a horizontal society. Not much attention is paid to hierarchy. Some old corporations still have such structures but the trend is moving towards flat organizations.
- Personal contact: Personal contact is fairly low. You must know the person very well to hug or touch. Typical interaction is a handshake; anything more is sometimes politically incorrect.
- The spoken vs nonspoken: The US is a spoken society. We are very verbal and expressive. People typically tell it like it is.
- Male vs female: We are typically male dominated and aggressive. But the trend is moving to a more balanced society with more and more women in top management and CEO positions.
- Family value: We are not strong on family value. Divorce rates are high and individuals are seen to pursue individual interests rather than be close to the family. Moving away from the central family unit is common.
- Education and age: Education is a huge asset. MBAs and PhDs are very well respected. Age is not as much a factor. It does not set one apart from the other. Age does not imply seniority in a career. It is more personal experience, achievements and success rather than age that are respected.

Vietnam

- Individual vs group: People tend to work individually and do not usually discuss matters to reach agreements. Once discussed, an individual will try to persuade others to agree with his/her own opinions rather than to find the best solution because they may not want to 'lose'. The definition of teamwork has only recently been taken into consideration, but in fact in domestic companies, it has not worked as well as it should have.
- Formal vs informal: It is formal in Vietnam's companies: women usually wear shirts, but no décolleté garments. Men also wear shirts, but no T-shirts. Teachers are not usually close to students in classes. Different social attitudes and behaviours are clarified for different positions.
- Vertical vs horizontal society: Vietnam is a vertical society. Employees must report to upline managers, otherwise they may be considered to show contempt. We separate different generations in the family, different positions in organizations, and the 'lower' have to respect and follow the 'upper'.
- Personal contact: Personal contact is very important in Vietnam, not only in daily life, but also for a smooth working environment. In daily life, the Vietnamese have close relationships with friends and neighbours. People can come to others' houses without having to make appointments. In work, a good relationship is indeed a factor to gain

success more easily. Salesmen usually build up a network of relationship with clients; sometimes it may be as close as with friends.

- The implicit vs explicit: In Vietnam, implicit expression is popular. People do not tend to directly express their ideas or feelings. We try to avoid negative assessments; we also do not usually use extreme words, behaviours or attitudes. Nonspoken language should be learned and understood.
- Male vs female: In the family, women still have to do all the housework, child care, etc. However, in offices, women have become more and more powerful and many managers are women. In rural areas, gender still remains a problem. The situation has, however, been improving.
- Family value: Family value plays an important role in everybody's life. Sons and daughters still live with their parents until they get married. Regularly, the first son has the most responsibilities with his parents; he still lives with his parents even after his marriage. Three or four generations living under one roof is popular.
- Education and age: Everybody receives an education and the elites will be those who have received a high education abroad.

SUMMARY

International business with its cross-border nature will have to deal with the culture issue – an issue which is more apparent and more critical to emerging markets for all their diversity.

Institutional banking must be concerned with a wider array of culture relationship. Cultural element is important because it is usually easier to adapt to things that do not challenge your own culture than to do things that do. But cultural awareness can hardly be acquired only by reading or attending training courses. It can only be accumulated by experiences and exposure to the practice of doing business in emerging markets. And it needs in-depth insights into its essentials.

Culture issues can be examined in many ways and the way this book does so is:

Individual vs group
Formal vs informal
Vertical vs horizontal (society)
The importance of personal contact
Implicit vs explicit (repressions)
Male vs female, and other items such as value of education, family value, religion, face, name, title, etc.

4
The Major Emerging Markets – BRICT: Brazil, Russia, India, China and Turkey

4.1 BRAZIL

4.1.1 Macro Environment

The largest country in South America, Brazil has borders with almost all South American countries. The country is part of Mercosul (Mercosur in Spanish), a common market formed with Argentina, Paraguay and Uruguay that represents around 65% of South America's GNP.

A country with enormous resources including iron ore, oil, etc., Brazil also has a large population. Its size and level of development have enabled it to develop a depth and breadth in industrial structure well beyond most other developing countries. The economy has been stable for the last eight years with inflation under control. Although the growth rate was low in 2005 due to a restrictive monetary policy and low confidence, it is rebounding with both the industrial and agricultural sectors.

Brazil maintains rigid and strong exchange control on capital investments, imports, exports and remittance of payments for know-how or licenses royalties and interest. The economy is characterized by its dual structure: a sizeable modern sector involving a minority of the population, and a large economic sector characterized by low incomes, causal employment, low or zero capital investment and often traditional products. As a result, people are aware of the coexistence of wealth and poverty, which is also one of the explanations why corruption exists in all levels of society. The most recent corruption scandal, nicknamed the Mensalao (monthly payment), involves the Workers Party. The Workers Party allegedly handed out top jobs to the nominees of parties that supported its legislative programme. European- and American-style democracy is yet difficult to achieve.

On balance of international payments, the country depends on foreign investments to sustain its internal deficit. For foreign investors, labour relationship is an issue. Brazil has a culture of labour suits and the legalization governing management and labour relations is outdated. Its judiciary is said to be slow.

The country needs a significant trade surplus to generate sufficient foreign exchange to pay the interest charges on its large external debts. Diversification in the external trade is seen in terms of markets and products. Exports are encouraged by various kinds of export and tax incentives. But the volatility of the currency is considered a risk factor for foreign investors. Advantages of the domestic market have made it possible to develop a substantial industrial sector geared primarily to domestic demand. In the long run this is a stabilizing factor for the economy towards external vulnerability.

4.1.2 Banking System in Brazil

The structure of the Brazilian financial system has changed significantly since the mid-1990s and, more pronouncedly, during the past three years.

Among the most positive features is the Central Bank of Brazil's conscious approach to a gradual strengthening of the system, which included improvements in regulatory framework, supervision and transparency.

Since 1987, the Central Bank has intervened in about 80 smaller banking institutions plus other consortia and cooperatives. The intervention of Banco Santos in November 2004 was one of such cases. The bank was basically financed by short-term and concentrated institutional deposits. The regulator's intervention was due to growing pressure on the institution when the market became uneasy with the bank's aggressive expansion and questionable banking practices. Other favourable events include the privatization of state-owned banks, the entrance of foreign banks and the consolidation and restructuring of the settlement/payment system.

In the commercial banking system of Brazil, concentration for the purpose of consolidation in an increasingly competitive environment is obvious. Consolidation implies first of all that the number of banks in operation in Brazil is on the decrease. On the other hand, there is 'flight to quality' for deposits. There are around 2500 financial institutions in Brazil. Together, the 10 largest banks in Brazil account for 75% of the system's deposit/assets.[1] Concentration is dominated by two public sector banks and the leading private sector banks, most of which remain under local control. There is notably a transfer of resources from the small- and medium-sized banks to larger institutions.

In Brazil, the American and European banking systems coexist. The European model is characterized by banks active in diverse forms of financial intermediation. The American model puts more focus on specialization. This combination contributed to the appearance in Brazil of banks engaged in multiple activities operating in tandem with specialized institutions such as investment banks and credit, financing and investment companies.

The arrival of foreign banks is also a significant event in the banking sector. Beginning in 1994 the Brazilian government consented to the entry of foreign banks. In only two years, 1997 and 1998, the Central Bank authorized the opening of 678 new bank branches.

Large national and international banks have been expanding their retail operations either by organic expansion or by acquiring loan portfolios from smaller banks. This also stimulated intense mergers and acquisitions among small- and mid-sized institutions as they strive to remain competitive on the market. The objective for them is to reach a wider public. The arrival of foreign banks has been favourable to more competition and more availability of banking products and services with the introduction of modern technologies. The existence of foreign banks helps the banking system to improve the quality of infrastructure and services or products available for clients through competition among them.

This participation of foreign banks has remained stable with the closure of some international banks' subsidiaries. To survive the dynamics of the Brazilian banking market, banks must not only achieve economies of scale but also flexibility and efficiency.

The regulatory framework in Brazil consists of two main regulatory agencies: the National Monetary Council and the Central Bank which have a division of labour among them.

[1] See *Fitch Rating* (Sovereign) on the Federative Republic of Brazil, p. 9.

The National Monetary Council is in charge of maintaining control of disciplining credit and the providing of guarantees, regulating the setting-up, operation and control of financial institutions, protecting the liquidity and solvency of financial institutions and guiding the application of resources in order to promote the orderly development of the economy. The National Monetary Council comprises a technical commission for currency and credit, and the advisory commissions. Side by side with the National Monetary Council, the Central Bank is entrusted with executing the policies established by the former. The regulation is very clear concerning each type of activity and required reports to different authorities. The lack of ambiguity in operations is also a positive point in doing business.

In general, the banking system in Brazil is characterized by a strong representation around the country. This helps a good development of business activities. Nevertheless, there are some unfavourable topics to be dealt with in the medium term. Issues requiring attention involve the large presence of public sector banks, mandatory allocation of lending, effectiveness of the legal framework and economic risks.

The Central Bank of Brazil has been active in trying to prevent depreciation of the local currency, as this could pose a problem to its stated top priority – the control of inflation under the target regime. To this end, the Central Bank acted to reduce liquidity in the system by imposing an increase in reserve requirements. It is selling dollars in the market daily to offset the imbalance generated by the outflow of hard currency due to the maturing foreign debt.

Nevertheless, the strong implication of the government in the banking operation can be an important handicap, which does not help the banking system to maximize its profits and improve, because the interest rate fixation is not completely market driven. For a better development of the sector and the whole economy, the government is now in close technical follow-up with the IMF.

4.1.3 Cultural Code

- Individual vs group: Individual oriented.
- Formal vs informal: Informal.
- Vertical vs horizontal society: Vertical.
- Personal contact: Very important. Personal relationship with the person in charge is regarded as key to success.
- The implicit vs explicit: Nonspoken is more usual especially for sensitive issues.
- Male vs female: Brazil is a male-oriented society.
- Family value: Very much. Family business is seen as normal.
- Education and age: Elderly people are usually respected. Education has an impact on one's career development.

4.2 RUSSIA

4.2.1 Macro Environment

Russia, a federative republic, is the largest country in the world with a territory of 17 million square metres covering the continents of Europe and Asia with a population of 144.4 million.

The country has vast natural resources and a well-educated labour force. As known to many, the Russian Federation was established after the collapse of the Soviet Union in 1991. The post-Soviet Union period witnessed the efforts of reforms to transfer the centrally planned economy into a free market system. The transition has been a painful one because GDP declined substantially from 1990 to 1998, followed by the deterioration of living conditions for the public. But 1999 saw the turning point and the average GDP growth rate has been approximately 6.4% per year in real terms. Today the Russian economy is achieving at least macroeconomic and financial stability, and the country's debt problem has been alleviated.

The economic structure under the regime of Soviet Union was dominated by military and heavy industries, as a result of the Cold War mentality. Today, the economy, 75% of which is in the private hands, is developing with exports of oil, gas and other raw materials. Russia possesses roughly one-third of total natural gas reserves and is ranked number seven for oil production in the world. Production of gas and oil remains stable.

President Putin's administration, with the goal of doubling the GDP, intends to develop the country to a full market economy. A targeted 7% annual economic growth in 2005 till 2015 needs more reforms on the side of government, aimed at de-beaurcratization. The government, however, is still interested in having its influences in some areas such as oil, gas and defence. In the natural gas sector, Gazprom, with a monopoly on the production of oil, is owned by government with a 40% stake.

Apart from the export of raw materials, the economy is also growing with many new industries, such as retailing, communications services, automotive sales, etc. Production of consumer goods, which was largely ignored during the Soviet Union period, is now also gaining strong and rapid momentum for growth.

A point to watch is Russia's accession to the World Trade Organization. This accession, like that of China's, indicates the determination of the country's leadership to commit to global rules and regulations in business. But the opening may present difficulties for local industries at least in the short run. In order to attract more international capital inflow, the government continues to make progress in corporate governance and in creating an investor-friendly environment. In this respect, currency control, which has historically been a headache to many foreign investors operating in Russia, was studied and new regulations came into effect. This has substantially liberalized the currency regime despite some regulatory particulars that were added.

4.2.2 Banking System in Russia

The banking sector in Russia suffered a period of confidence crisis in 2004 and remains a key weakness for the Russian economy.

The regulator of the banking system, the Central Bank of the Russian Federation, was founded on 13 June 1990. Originally it was called State Bank of the RSFSR. The regulator obtained its current name on 20 December 1991. The banking system in Russia today is the product of this regulator. Some important events are worth mentioning since the establishment of the Central Bank.

In 1991–1992 a wide network of banks was established. Soon after this (1992–1995) the system of supervision of banks and currency regulation was established. Moreover, a GKO government securities market was established in the same period.

Today there are more than 1200 banks in Russia, which can be grouped into four major categories:

- Government- and Central Bank- backed banks with government and Central Bank as major shareholders.
- Banks that are mainly owned by commodity producers.
- Small banks with diversified ownership.
- Foreign owned credit institutions.

Several structural issues in the banking sector in Russia are noticed:

- Concentration: The banking system remains dominated by a few large state-owned banks and a large number of credit organizations located in the Moscow and Saint Petersburg regions.
- Illiquidity of small banks: A large number of small banks are still vulnerable to liquidity issues, especially when the Russian law allows all household time deposits to be withdrawn on demand. This indicates that insolvency may occur if there is massive withdrawal of deposits, as evidenced in the 1998 crisis. The introduction of a deposit insurance scheme in December 2003 and the Federal Law on Insurance of Personal Bank Deposits in the Russian Federation give public comfort for the protection of depositors but there are still 300 banks that were refused entry.
- Free competition of foreign banks: The banking system is still restrictive to foreign banks' participation, which will delay globalization of the Russian banking system and limit access of foreign capital and banking know-how. On the other hand, efforts will be needed in the fields of transparency of shareholder, adoption of international accounting standards, etc., to make the Russian banking sector attractive to foreign institutional investors.

To address these issues, there has been progress in the reform of the banking system including the establishment in 1999 of the Agency for Restructuring Credit Institutions, the adoption in 2003 of the international financial standards by the Bank of Russia, etc. But the foundations of the sector make it vulnerable to a future crisis. Moreover, there are structural factors such as (over) dependence on the oil and gas sector, and insufficient reform in the rest of the economy will pose greater risk to Russian development than the banking system itself.

4.2.3 Cultural Code

- Individual vs group: Unlike other Western countries, Russia has its collectivism vis-à-vis individualism. A strong communal spirit is still found in Russian business practices today. This is explained by Russia's severe climatic conditions which have meant cooperation and collaboration rather than competition. This sense of togetherness is one of the traits that distinguish Russians from many Westerners. The long history of Russia as mostly an agricultural country made it possible for peasants to work together.
- Formal vs informal: Russian society is both. Russians are very status conscious and believe in equality. Rules and regulations (such as laws and codes of conduct in companies) can be very strict and precise, but informal relations can quite often mean more.

- Vertical vs horizontal: Strictly vertical. Since the beginning of Russian history authorities were ever present in people's minds and this culture has somehow separated society as a whole. This didn't change too much in the Soviet Union, nor did it change dramatically after its collapse in 1991.
- Personal contact: Personal contact can be even more important than using signs or rules and regulations.
- Spoken vs nonspoken: Nonverbal expressions of a person can be important, but not as important as in Chinese culture, for example. Nonverbal expressions differ from person to person, so the spoken word is a better 'measure' of a person. Thus, words are very important, and a person in Russia should take care of what he or she says.
- Male vs female: Predominately male. Needless to say, a woman has never been president since Soviet Union was established. Although, there were numerous queens in the earlier centuries, some of those governed in reality, not formally.
- Family value: Very high (in normal families). To illustrate, any problem within a family is kept from the outside world for as long as possible.
- Education and age: Over several centuries, older people were treated with respect and education was highly valued. During the 'democratic' rule in the 1990s, after the collapse of the Soviet Union, things became really distorted, when older people were literally 'devoid' of their pensions, and it became possible to make a lot of money without any education. However, this period seems to be over.

4.3 INDIA

4.3.1 Macro Environment

India has very often been compared with China in terms of population, long history, supply of cheap labour, huge internal market, etc. Both countries are racing at breakneck speed and both seem to have a bright future ahead.

However, apart from the difference on the political horizon – with Indian democracy on the one hand and Chinese authoritarianism on the other – India has it own characteristics and way of development. For instance, India nurtured its own entrepreneur and held multinationals at arm's length.[2]

India's economy is a parallel economy with an expanding services industry on the one hand, and an agricultural sector with a major labour force on the other. The services sector has been most dynamic especially with IT, telecoms and business-process outsourcing. Incredible growth of outsourcing companies made it a fact that these service companies are performing legal and medical work for clients all over the world. In 2005, services including banks, construction and small-scale trading activities accounted for 51% of GDP.[3] This means that while the global media marvels at India's software engineers, the country is also home to a quarter of the world's undernourished.

Indian capital and talent are drawn to the IT sector which generates decent earnings and has not been stifled by government regulation. In the financial sector, India has an advantage in its banks and capital markets. The privately owned banks will have to do their credit risk control on their borrowers, as they have little state guarantee for their nonperforming loans.

[2] See the article from the *Far Eastern Economic Review*, March 2006: *'India's coming eclipse of China'* by Hugo Restall.

[3] *Global Business: India, Country Guide*, published by Deloitte Touche Tohmatsu.

In general, a free market approach to the capital market will give commercial orientation to the market in the long run.

The economy's dependence on agricultural has declined thanks to governments' liberalizing reforms efforts. Meanwhile, India's manufacturing sector is growing rapidly. The second quarter of 2005 recorded a growth of 10% for the manufacturing sector. This is significant as the growth of the manufacturing sector may have an impact on potential poverty alleviation – much of the labour force involved in the agricultural sector may shift to manufacturing and income levels may improve accordingly.

Yet challenges facing India are many: infrastructure improvements to attract more foreign investment, a social plan to reduce the gap between the rich and poor, a shortage of human resources in management and operations, etc. are only some of them.

4.3.2 Banking System in India

India's banking system is characterized by a large number of financial institutions and instruments and is relatively overcrowed, fragmented and dominated by state-owned banks. Public sector banks hold around 75% of the assets of the banking system while private and foreign banks hold the rest.

There are approximately 80 scheduled commercial banks, Indian and foreign; almost 200 regional rural banks; more than 350 central cooperative banks; 20 land development banks; and a number of primary agricultural credit societies. The commercial banking segment comprises 27 public sector banks in which the government has majority ownership, 40 private sector banks and 33 foreign banks.

The banking system was developed in the 1970s as an instrument of government policy to finance public spending and investment by big companies. Prior to the initiation of financial sector liberalization in 1992, the Indian financial system essentially catered to the needs of planned development, and the government sector had a predominant role in every sphere of economic activity. Only recently has the Indian government recognised that this system is entirely unsuited to the millions of small, informal businesses that make up the bulk of the Indian economy.

The banking system has three tiers – the scheduled commercial banks, the regional rural banks, which operate in rural areas not covered by the scheduled banks, and the cooperative and special purpose rural banks. In terms of business, the public sector banks, namely the State Bank of India and the nationalized banks, dominate the banking sector.

Indian banking has finally worked up to the competitive dynamics of the 'new' Indian market and is addressing the relevant issues to take on the challenges of globalization. Banks that employ IT solutions are perceived to be 'futuristic' and proactive players capable of meeting the multifarious requirements of the large customer base. Private banks have been fast on the uptake and are reorienting their strategies using the Internet as a medium.

Competition mainly from new private banks and foreign banks is intensifying. On the whole Indian banks are set to play an even more important role in the country's economy. At the recent BanCon 2005, the Finance Minister said that banks' contribution to national income (GDP) would have to increase from 25% to 50% in the coming years. This would only be possible by raising the size of the banks. The expected consolidation in India's banking system will help bring synergy and a stronger capital base. Other reforms include strengthening prudential norms and a forward-looking refinement of the supervisory function of financial institutions in accordance with Basel II.

4.3.3 Cultural Code

- Individual vs group: Group or collectivist.
- Formal vs informal: Informal.
- Vertical vs horizontal society: In the public sector it is vertical but in the private sector it is mostly horizontal.
- Personal contact: Very important.
- The implicit vs explicit: Mainly nonspoken with high context culture.
- Male vs female: Male-dominated society but there is no restriction as to appointment of women in senior positions including prime minister.
- Family value: Indians rate their family value highly.
- Education and age: Importance of education (rather than family background) is catching up.

4.4 CHINA

4.4.1 Macro Environment

The spectacular rise of China is a major development of this century. Foreign trade and foreign direct investment have been a strikingly successful part of China's economic reform and development. The economy has experienced substantial growth.

Indeed, export helps the economy so much that the country is called 'the factory of the world'. However, contrary to the image of exporting too much, the economy of China on the whole is a 'Robin Hood economy' – its trade surplus with the US and the EU matches its trade deficit with the rest of Asia. With China positioned between the developed and developing worlds, any changes may have conflicting impacts on the south and north, that is a positive impact on the north and a negative impact on the south.

For all the hope for China's potential, it is still a developing economy confronting formidable challenges. Abroad, it must cooperate in managing the impact of its rise. At home, it must handle at least the following issues:

- The need for a social safety net: The restructuring of the economy has laid off thousands of workers who will need retraining, or eventually a social safety net for survival. Without such a safety net, social stability is at stake.
- The fragile financial system: Despite various efforts from the government to rescue many fragile financial institutions, fundamental changes in management and mentality are yet to be introduced in the financial system which is still dominated by the banking sector. The lack of corporate governance and widespread corruption has added an element of risk to the financial system.
- The disparity for regions: The ever-widening disparity between regions and the gap between the poor and the rich in general can be a potential source of social conflict and social unrest.
- The efficiency of its economic growth in terms of raw material consumption: The large consumption of raw materials for economic growth is already a hot topic at home and abroad. Efficiency in terms of raw material consumption is the key for sustainable growth.

The development pattern of China is unique and will remain so. China will move on but will not follow a predetermined course or model, because much will depend on its future internal and external policy, political priority, the actions of other regional and global players such as the US, and more importantly, unforeseen events.

Accordingly, doing business in China is to navigate the country's huge bureaucracy and red tape. With the 'empirical nature' of China's reform and its 'trial and error' formula, doing business there is also to navigate the maze of ever-changing rules. It is true, however, that despite difficulties and political uncertainty, China is emerging as one of the major economic powers, which has no doubt surprised all.

4.4.2 Banking System in China

The banking system in China after the 1949 revolution used to be a typical planned economy – no clear separation between the government sector and the enterprises, credits were allocated according to plan targets rather than on a commercial basis. The People's Bank of China (PBOC) functioned both as a central bank and as the only commercial bank in China. Most foreign banks were deprived of their privileges and left China. Only four foreign banks remained in Shanghai.[4]

The reforming days in late 1970s first saw the separation of functions of commercial banks: first the Agricultural Bank, then Bank of China. In 1984 the Industrial and Commercial Bank of China was established to take over the commercial activities of the PBOC. In the following years, dozens of national and local commercial banks were established. The ownership of banks also varies from pure state owned to state-enterprise owned. In 1982 the first new branch of a foreign bank was set up in the Shenzhen Special Economic Zone.

However, the NPLs (non-performance loans) soon became a problem. Today the estimation from the OECD is that these NPLs are so serious that it would cost China 29% of its GDP.

There are many explanations for these huge NPLs – from risk management mentality to government intervention.

In a swift move to recapitalize the four major state banks, the government implemented asset management companies in the spring of 1999 to deal directly with NPL collection. Asset management companies were established to bring the NPLs to market and have them securitized.

In fact, realizing the seriousness of the NPLs, China has until recently made great efforts in reforming the ailing banking system. Since 1998, the central government has moved more than 2.1 trillion RMB (around 0.26 trillion in dollar terms) of bad debt from the banking system. NPLs then dropped from 16.61% in the first quarter of 2004 to just 8.61% by the end of 2005. At the end of 2003, the government recapitulated the Bank of China and China Construction Bank with a further 45 billion dollars accompanied by a write-off of the two banks' accumulated NPLs.

After the cleaning up, the major task facing Chinese banks is to enhance their operating efficiency before the domestic banking sector meets the full force of competition after the WTO. Mainland banks are opening to foreign strategic investors in order to acquire the banking know-how (risk management, product development, etc.) and international

[4] They were HSBC, the Chartered Bank, the Bank of East Asia and the Overseas-Chinese Bank.

experience from their foreign partners to help them remain competitive in a new and tough business environment.

China's capital market is underdeveloped – the ratio of stock market capitalization to GDP is 17.5%, lower than that of India (107.2%), Taiwan (141.5%) and the Philippines (180.3%).[5] This enabled the banking system in China to attract most of the savings in the country. This also gave time for the banking system to resolve the NPLs. But it is apparent that what has been done is not enough. This is because there are a number of operational weaknesses for the commercial banks of China.

In terms of credit risk, information of financials for the borrowers can be biased, incomplete and unreliable. There are many loopholes in the accounting system. Very few Chinese companies are covered by independent credit agencies such as Standard & Poor's and Moody's. Despite recent efforts to improve, account managers in the Chinese banks have rudimentary loan pricing and risk management skills. There may often be local political pressure to lend to what are still the large influential corporations in many regions. Ultimately changing the credit culture within the big and other state banks may be the greatest challenge if a second NPL waive is to be avoided. An entire generation of bankers is currently being trained, learning to extend credit based on financial criteria and not on social and political objectives.

At the macro level, there are other structural problems within the financial system. The fact that depositors in China had no choice but to keep their money in banks despite paltry returns has helped the ailing banking system to adjust. On the other hand, funds are now lying idle in the banking system damaging the reinvestment opportunities which the economy needs for sustainable development. Poor capital allocation by banks is amplified by the dominance of the banking sector in China's financial system.

4.4.3 Cultural Code

- Individual vs group: The Chinese are very much group oriented.
- Formal vs informal: Moderately formal.
- Vertical vs horizontal society: Vertical. To listen to the boss is regarded as a merit in many cases. To challenge the boss directly is unacceptable and is not recommended. Proper reporting is also a must to many bosses.
- Personal contact: In China doing business via personal contact is very often crucial. 'Wining and dining' is the usual way of communication for business. Personal contact is even an asset.
- The implicit vs explicit expression: Nonspoken. The Chinese try their best to avoid being offensive and use negative comments in a euphemistic way.
- Male vs female: Men and women are supposed to be equal in many ways including career development. Many women are now in senior positions in companies. However, many families still believe in sons representing the family rather than daughters.
- Family value: Family is the basic unit in Chinese society today although the trend is declining. In the business sector family business is still popular in many parts of China.
- Education and age: Well-educated people are respected, so are the elderly. However, economic development and growing money-worship lead to less respect for the elderly.

[5] 'Economic analysis', the Bank of East Asia Limited, April 2006. Original source was from Bloomberg.

4.5 TURKEY

4.5.1 Macro Environment

Reforms starting in 1980 have changed the Turkish economy significantly. Under the free market guidelines, the economy is more open with promotion for international trade, encouragement of foreign direct investment and liberalized exchange controls.

The government has taken a number of measures including a new economic and monetary programme to decrease inflation and devaluation, put public financing onto a sustainable path, decrease real interest rates and restore economic growth.

Historically, the agricultural sector has been Turkey's largest job provider and a major contributor to GNP. Turkey's wide range of climate and soil conditions provides a favourable environment for good agricultural products such as grain, tea, tobacco, cotton as well as fruits and vegetables. There are, however, significant changes in the composition of the GNP with decreasing share of the agricultural sector in Turkey's GNP. The contribution of industry, especially that of services, has been seen to increase steadily. With labour cost advantages, manufacturing represents an increasing share of Turkey's economy, although a major portion of Turkey's manufacturing is state operated.

The government is trying to reduce its role in the economy in several ways. To dismantle price control is one of them. Privatization has been promised for almost as long as low inflation. One success from the government side was in fiscal policy – government spending is now under control.

Turkey's strategic location makes it a natural energy bridge between major oil and gas producing areas of the Middle East and Caspina regions and customer markets in Europe.

One significant boost for Turkey's economy is its accession to the EU. After decades of trying, Turkey has at last got a starting date for entry to the EU. The membership, once obtained, will change Turkey in many ways and will change Europe as well.

4.5.2 Banking System in Turkey

Like the case of China, banks in Turkey are important as they occupy the majority of the financial sector. Total assets of the banking system account for 90% of total assets of the institutions in the financial sector.

Turkish banks in general have been operating in a considerably less risky atmosphere since 2002. Weak banks were eliminated and remaining banks were recapitalized and restructured.

Banks can be classified into deposit taking institutions, mainly commercial banks, and nondepository banks. Public as well as private sectors (including foreign banks) are involved in both parts. The so-called 'soft belly' of Turkish banking is its highly price-sensitive time deposits. Average maturity of time deposits in Turkey is just over one month and the Turkish deposit holders have been very price sensitive. In the event of domestic liquidity or irrational competition, deposit rates may not fall as fast as the asset yields.

Among financial instruments in the capital market, government securities are still dominating. A notable phenomenon is de-dollarization – the share of foreign exchange or foreign exchange dominated items is shrinking. Turkish banking assets are thus moving towards domestic local currency and away from foreign exchange as a result of reverse currency substitution.

In Turkey's banking sector the high credit card penetration ratio is impressive. This supports Turkish banks' margins significantly. This segment is likely to grow in line with the growth of GDP and continue to support profitability of the Turkish banks. In the meantime the NPLs in credit card consumer lending would climb.

As far as the regulatory structure for the financial system in Turkey is concerned, there is no single authority in charge of supervision of all the institutions. The authorities responsible for supervising and regulating the respective financial institutions are the Capital Markets Board of Turkey, Under-Secretariat of Treasury and the *Banking Supervision and Regulation Agency* (BSRA).

A single independent authority composed of a seven-member board, BSRA was established in 1999 under the banking law enacted by the National Assembly. It supervises and regulates Turkish banks to make sure that they conform to international criteria and EU directives. It has extensive powers to issue or cancel banking licences. In regulating and auditing Turkish banks, it adopts internationally accepted standards.

Potential accession to the EU boosts the confidence and attraction of foreign banks' involvement in the banking sector. Foreign banks' participation has risen substantially, starting with Garanti Bank's JV agreement with GE consumer finance and Isbank's decision to sell its Petrol Office and Izmir Demir Celik stakes, followed by different foreign counterparties such as GE Bank (USA), BNP Paribas (France) and Rabobank (the Netherlands), although the deal for the acquisition of Sekerbank by Rabobank was later cancelled. Fortisbank (Holland/Belgium), Bank Hapoalim (Israel), UniCredito Italiano (Italy) and HSBC and Citibank are all active in this game of participation. This will improve the capital structure and profitability outlook for Turkish banks.

On 3 October 2005 Turkey's negotiation with EU stimulated the harmonization and convergence of the banking law with EU directives, international principles and standards. Reporting, auditing and transparency are being improved. Regulations are likely to meet the international standards, notably EU directives.

4.5.3 Cultural Code

- Individual vs group: Individual and group orientations are in fact mixed.
- Formal vs informal: Moderately informal.
- Vertical vs horizontal society: Vertical.
- Personal contact: Very important.
- The implicit vs explicit: Spoken/nonspoken, with the young generation in the first and the over-50s in the second.
- Male vs female: Females can play a role. In 1993 Turkey elected its first female prime minister, Tansu Ciller. In business, too, some Turkish women stand out. One example is the Sabanci group. Guler Sabanci succeeded her uncle when he died in 2004. In the average Turkish home, much has remained unchanged since 1923.
- Family value: Very much.
- Education and age: Education is important as an entry ticket to high society, and without which it is difficult to climb up.

SUMMARY

Brazil is the largest country in Latin America with enormous natural resources. The country depends on foreign investment to finance its internal debt but efforts are being made to diversify its external trade. A huge internal market is a stabilizing factor to this Latin American country.

Efforts are also made to reinforce the country's banking system including supervision and consolidation. Pubic-owned banks are still the major players. A point to watch is Brazil's currency and its fluctuation.

The culture for Brazil is individual oriented and informal. Society is vertically organized and male oriented. Personal contact is regarded as important in business in Brazil.

Russia is the largest country in the world with vast natural resources and a well-educated labour force, both of which are regarded as potential for this country's development. Transition from the communist Soviet Union to a federative Russia has not been easy or smooth as GDP declined substantially till the end of last century.

The economic structure has shifted from military and heavy industries to other new industries, such as retailing, communications services, automotive sales, etc., with exports of oil, gas and other raw materials for hard currencies. Russia's accession to the World Trade Organization indicates the determination of the country leadership to commit to the opening up of the economy. But this may present difficulties for local industry at least for the short run.

The banking sector is a key weakness for the Russian economy with structural issues such as domination of a few large state-owned banks, vulnerable small private-owned banks and limitation of foreign banks' participation.

Russian culture is assumed to be a collectivism perhaps due to the legacy of the communist days and its agricultural history. Society is vertical and personal contacts are important. The male population enjoys priority and the family unit is critical.

India's economy is a parallel economy with a developing services industry on the one hand, and an agricultural sector with a major labour force on the other.

The services sector, including banks, construction and small-scale trading activities, accounted for 51% of GDP and has been most dynamic especially with IT, telecoms and business-process outsourcing. India is thus a rich and poor two-tier economy. The economy's dependence on agriculture has declined thanks to government's liberalizing reforms efforts. In the meantime, India's manufacturing sector is growing rapidly.

India's banking system has been undergoing reforms from government instrument to market-oriented operations to serve especially small- and medium-sized enterprises. Commercial banks, rural banks and rural special banks are many in India but state-owned banks dominate the system. Competition pressure from private and foreign banks pushes state-owned banks towards globalization. As a result, merger and acquisition among banks is expected in the coming years.

India's culture is group oriented with a high value on family and education. The society is typically hierarchy oriented. There is a large gap between men and women in India.

The success of the rapid growth for China is mainly explained by its active trading activities and huge foreign direct investment. China imports a great deal of raw materials from producing countries, and exports vast amounts to the developed and developing world. The wealth created by this rapid growth is not distributed evenly, which in itself creates social problems.

The banking system is typically dominated by state-owned or state-controlled banks with NPLs proving to be a problem and potential hidden risk for the country. Measures are being taken to list the banks at home and abroad, and to introduce foreign banks for management and banking know-how. Such competitive pressure is supposed to help the state-owned banks solve their historical problems. The Chinese capital market is still underdeveloped which may prove a hindrance for sustainable economic development.

Chinese culture is a collectivism, implicit, with a high value on family and education. The society is hierarchy oriented.

Traditionally an agricultural country, Turkey has seen significant changes in its composition of GNP, with increasing share of manufacturing and services. Under free market guidelines, the government is trying to reduce its role and the economy is opening up to international trade and international capital flow.

Banks are the major source of finance in Turkey and the capital market is dominated by government bonds. The soft belly of Turkish banking is its price-sensitive time deposits.

Turkish culture is a combination of group and individualism. Women may play a role but men enjoy priority as in many Muslim countries. Society is more vertical than horizontal.

5

Sovereign Rating and Country Risk

5.1 COUNTRY RISK: DEFINITION AND ITS IMPORTANCE

A relevant discussion for emerging markets is country default risk. With all the difficulties in emerging markets, to evaluate and measure the likelihood of country crisis is interesting to many parties. If ever such a country default risk can be measured, how it can be ranked vis-à-vis other countries is important to business.

Our earlier discussion shows that countries indeed can be ranked according to different criteria, that is size of the territory, population, GDP, GDP per capita, GDP growth rate, etc. Countries can also be ranked according to *country risk*, the likelihood of country crisis.

The concept of country risk is especially important. This is because the excitement of doing business in emerging markets goes hand in hand with the risk and uncertainty of these markets.

Country risk refers to the willingness and capacity for emerging market countries to fulfil their financial obligation. This is not only a task for banks but also for multinationals once they have cross-border operations. If they invest in foreign entities, they will face risks associated with their project, risks in dealing with foreign currencies and their funding risks. Any international activities that cross the political frontiers of sovereign national states give rise to a unique risk concept – country risk, which represents the potentially adverse impact of a country's environment on multinationals' cash flow.

To a multinational, this concept can be used to monitor countries where it is currently doing business. This *country risk analysis* will also help its international expansion. Risk analysis can help multinationals avoid doing business in countries with excessive risk.

Similarly, a bank must know its claims on all of its clients in a particular sector such as food, raw materials, transportation, etc. Likewise, the bank must know its claims on one specific country. This will help the bank to manage its credit portfolio.

The difference between measurement of a bank's exposure to risk associated with a specific company or industries and its exposure to country risk is that the latter deals with cross-border financial flows. Today, to identify, measure and mitigate the country risk for emerging markets is becoming a profession for the banking industry and academia as well.

Moreover, for banks the evaluation of the risks for emerging market countries is important because it is linked to provisions required by a central bank. This implies that besides the actual credit risk to an individual borrower it is necessary, especially in the long term, to put aside money to account for the estimated potential credit risk for that country. There is, therefore, in banking terms, a *country risk premium* in the price quoted to a cross-border lending.

Many people, including bankers and their clients, are puzzled when a bank charges its client this country risk premium. In trade finance, which will be discussed more in detail later, the confirmation of a *letter of credit* will involve such a country risk premium. Even if the letter of credit is issued by the bank's own branch, the confirmation fee should include the extra on the country risk. The reason for charging this country risk premium is straightforward – although the issuing branch will have the money to honour its obligation, as long as head office is in agreement, the country where the branch is located may block the payment. If Citibank in one emerging market country issues a letter of credit, Citibank New York will have no problem confirming the letter of credit of its own branch. But a country risk premium will be charged, and the government of the country where Citibank is located, theoretically at least, may block the outflow for one reason or another.

To many banks, country risk analysis is the starting point for their *country limit* – the maximum exposure allowed to that specific country. Cross-border lending always has a country risk registration. Country risk is also important on the commercial side as the price quoted to each borrower has a composition of affiliated country risk as explained earlier.

Literature on country risk is well established and enormous. But in institutional banking practice, country risk discussion and its calculation can still be complicated and sometimes controversial.

First, how is risk for a specific country defined.

It seems not so difficult to give an 'academic' definition of country risk – country risk is macro-economic underperformance for countries/economies due to policy errors, liquidity on the national level, political changes, etc.

To a bank, country risk is the exposure to a loss in cross-border lending caused by events in a particular country which are, at least to some extent, under the control of the government but definitely not under the control of a private enterprise or individual.[1]

Country risk is further described as the risk that

> A sovereign counterparty either isn't able or refuses to fulfil international financial obligations or imposes restrictions on residents to meet their international financial obligations.

Borrowers in the country concerned don't meet their obligations as a result of crises which either arise from events like war, political and social unrest and natural disasters, or from a shortcoming policy of the national authorities with respect to establishing macro-economic and/or financial stability.

In essence, country risk consists of both *transfer risk* and *sovereign performance risk*. Sovereign performance risk is the total financial strength of the country to honour its external debt. This is linked to the evolution of classic macro-economic indicators. Transfer risk refers to the liquidity issue due to a sharp change in the exchange rate and/or in the levels of international reserves of the country in the coming months. It involves the possibility that the borrower may not be able to convert domestic currency into foreign currency, or get permission to remit that amount to its foreign counterparty. Consequently, transfer risks are the ability of the government to fund its debts from available foreign currency.

A country can go through liquidity problems without impact on its solvability or it can have a sound liquidity situation but structural weaknesses that affect its longer-term solvability.

A relevant example can be a project that may successfully generate local cash flows, but without foreign exchange the government will not be able to service its foreign debt. Just imagine the possibility that although the project in an emerging market country is

[1] P.J. Nagy (1994) *Country Risk*, Euromoney Publications Limited, London.

generating good income in local currency, which is sufficient to meet financial obligations under contract, the government, however, does not have the hard currency available to allow the remittance for serving the debt. Such transfer risk is part of country risk.

Another example is the well-known debt crisis of the 1980s. During that period, there was so-called 'Resolution 63 loans' under rescheduling and moratorium. It did not matter how profitable a Brazilian bank was in local currency terms, the country did not have sufficient foreign exchange reserves to enable repayment on such loans to foreign creditors. In practice this risk can be analysed in exactly the same way as sovereign risk provided that a (non-) financial concern is involved.

Country risk as such is supposed to be reflected in sovereign credit rating (country risk rating). Many credit rating companies publish such a rating on a regular basis. Many banks also have their own rating system and use that for internal country limit guidance.

Country risk is not only measurable but can also be priced as it is reflected in the market price. In financial markets, this risk is reflected in the yield differentials for market price of sovereign bonds. For example, if we notice that Brazilian sovereign bonds are sold at 210 bps higher than comparable maturity US T-bonds, the difference is the market perception of the risk difference and the compensation for that risk, which is called the 'country risk premium'.

5.2 SOVEREIGN DEFAULT: HISTORY AND CONSEQUENCE

5.2.1 History

Cases of countries not being able to honour their obligation are not new or unusual. Crisis in the 1980s in Latin America, the Peso crisis in late 1994, crisis in Indonesia, South Korea and Thailand in 1997, crisis in Russia in 1998 are all recent country risk examples.

Tracing back further, we find more country risk cases: in the early 19th century, a number of Latin American countries defaulted on European loans they had taken to finance the building of canals. Latin American countries ran into repayment problems throughout the 19th century, especially Argentina, which sparked a global financial crisis in 1890. In 1917, the new Soviet government repudiated the foreign debts incurred by previous rulers. The communist economy was closed to the rest of the world. In the 1930s during the Great Depression, the world economy collapsed and most developing countries, having found themselves shut out of the industrial country export markets, defaulted on their external debts as a result. Even some industrialized countries, such as Nazi Germany, defaulted on their foreign obligations as well.

Sovereign default can be either *debt repudiation* or *debt rescheduling.*

Debt repudiation is an outright cancellation of all a borrower's current or future foreign debt and equity obligations. Some communist countries have followed this course since World War II.

Rescheduling is more common in sovereign default. Rescheduling refers to the announcement that a country declares a moratorium or delay on its current and future debts obligations.[2] It then starts a discussion with creditors for new terms and conditions of the debt obligation to ease the difficulty it is facing. The terms and conditions to be negotiated

[2] Anthony Saunders (2003) *Financial Institutions Management – A Modern Perspective*, p. 331. Irwin McGraw-Hill.

are linked to a new maturity date. Discount of the principal may also be included in the discussion for rescheduling.

It was noticed that since World War II there has been more debt rescheduling than debt repudiation.[3] This is because international loan rather than bond finance makes rescheduling more likely. Bondholders are usually geographically dispersed whereas lending parties of loans are relatively small in number. This fact makes rescheduling easier and less costly. It is understandable that to get thousands of bondholders to agree to changes in the contractual terms on a bond is not easy. On the other hand, default on international loans may cause problems for lending banks as their balance sheet will deteriorate and if the deterioration is so much their solvency can be a problem. This is a concern of regulators of the lending bank countries.

In recent years, the prevention of large bank failures has become a priority. This leads to the situation that lending banks' governments are interested in facilitating the rescheduling by providing support. Thus, government-backed rescue packages arranged either directly or indirectly via World Bank guarantees are ways of subsidizing large banks and/or reducing the incentives for emerging market countries to default on their loans. The *Brady Plan* is an example of government initiative for the solution of emerging market debts.

5.2.2 Consequence

Fundamentally, international lending is plagued by defective property rights. Sovereign countries are legally independent, that is they cannot be legally forced to repay if they do not wish to do so. The governments can refuse to repay on time without the creditors being able to sue them in court or seize their properties. There are ways to measure the ability to pay but not to change the willingness to repay.

In history, there have been records that show that countries were forced to repay their debt. In the latter half of the 19th century Egypt failed to repay English and French creditors, who in turn forced the Egyptians to repay by taking over tax revenues of the country. France and Britain were backed up by their military power. Similarly, Venezuela faced such a situation at the beginning of the 20th century. But, in general, the days when some countries can force other governments to repay are definitely over.

Nowadays if and when there are sovereign debt problems, governments will defend the default with good reasons, some of which may be well established such as civil war, natural disaster, etc. But there may also be obvious 'reasons' for nonpayment: wrong momentary policy, a recession, unfavourable terms of trade, etc. Very often you may see that governments that want to postpone or cancel the debt are not the same governments that did the earlier borrowing. However, whatever the reasons used here, legally governments have the obligation to repay.

It is interesting to note that in almost all such sovereign default cases, both the borrowing governments and the creditors are interested in finding some solution to cover the *de facto* default. The repayments are therefore to be 'rescheduled' and terms and conditions are to be negotiated to have at least part of the debt repaid. Such an attitude is understood on the ground that consequences of outright sovereign default are various, serious and long lasting.

---

[3] For a detailed illustration on this see note 2.

First, political default runs the risk of losing face in the international community. The country is being isolated from the international community by its default. Diplomatic pressure is expected and cessation of aid flows is likely. Foreign direct investment is hardly possible any more. Instead capital flight will be more motivated as mistrust created by a sovereign default will in turn have an impact on the domestic economy generally. The country will have problems raising funds in the international capital market at least in the short run.

Second, sovereign default will lead to legal conflict in many cases as the creditors may consider legal action whenever possible against individual debtors, even though to sue the sovereign government is hardly feasible. As a result, exported goods and offshore assets could be seized for the enforcement of the verdict from the court. The name of the country will be on the blacklist for many years.

Third, on the international trade finance side, the impact is immediate and far-reaching. When payment on foreign currency is blocked or hampered, letters of credit issued by banks in the defaulting country will not be accepted by foreign correspondents. Trade finance will be difficult to obtain at least in the short run. The alternative would be barter and cash, which are neither efficient nor convenient. The price for confirmation of letters of credit from the country will increase substantially if the country reopens. This kind of shame for a defaulting country will be unsettling, so most countries will try their best to prevent it from happening.

5.3 COUNTRY RISK RATING PRINCIPLES

With the growing importance of country risk in the business community including the banking society, several agencies are involved in performing this profession. Credit rating agencies such as Standard & Poor's are developing a professional mechanism/principles for country risk evaluation.

5.3.1 Standard & Poor's

Like other credit rating companies for country risk evaluation, Standard & Poor's uses global criteria to evaluate sovereign risk. The analysis is applied in five main areas – political environment, economic prospects, fiscal flexibility, monetary policy and external finances.[4]

Political risk is the risk of change in a government, which will affect, directly or indirectly, a country's ability or willingness to pay its debt. Here the risk of change can be specified as change in the political structure, change in the leadership of the ruling party or change in policies within the existing government. Examples of political risk can be uprising of the opposition (growing) discontent with economic or social policies, vigorous external anti-government activity, etc. Some common forms of political risk include:

- Attitude of government towards foreign companies: In some countries it may happen that foreign assets are confiscated either peacefully or by force with no compensation
- Blockage of funds transfers: There exists restriction on remitting funds to foreign countries.

[4] Interested readers can read documents from rating agencies such as 'Sovereign Credit Characteristics by Rating Category', published by Standard & Poor's, 19 November 2003.

- Currency inconvertibility: Many of the emerging markets' currencies are inconvertible. It is thus difficult for business, as the smooth conversion of local currency into hard currency cannot be expected.
- War: Some countries may have conflicts with neighbours or internally.
- Bureaucracy.
- Corruption: Corruption can increase the cost of conducting business or erode profits. It will also reduce the transparency of the business environment.

Economic prospects can be many such as:

- Structure of the economy
- Economic mismanagement
- Size and structure of internal and external debt
- Structure and prospects of exports
- Domestic and creditor confidence in the government, etc.

Some quantitative measurements that are very often used in the economic field are:

- Per capita GDP: The average gross domestic product per person in a country, a measurement of relative level of wealth of countries.
- The debt service ratio: Total overseas earnings from the export of goods and services divided by its interest plus principal on overseas borrowing.
- The current account deficit.
- Import cover: The number of weeks of import of goods and services that is to be funded from the existing level of reserves.
- The saving ratio: Savings for both public and private sectors as a proportion of GDP.

Monetary policy and external finances refer but are not limited to:

- Interest rate policy
- Currency policy
- Inflation/money supply
- Balance of payments situation
- Access to international capital market, etc.

As mentioned, sovereign risk is linked to the macro-economic performance of the country. Hence the following changes may have an impact on country risk evaluation:

- Major devaluation of currency
- Major recession of the economy
- Major shift in economic policy, for example reduction of trade barriers or change in energy pricing
- Civil unrest
- Discrimination against foreign companies, etc.

5.3.2 Euromoney

As one of the country risk-rating agencies, Euromoney ranks countries according to a set of variables plus a formal narrative country study:

- Economic data (25%)
- Political risk (25%)
- Debt indicators (10%)
- Access to bank finance (5%)
- Access to short-term finance (5%)
- Access to international bond and syndicated loan market (10%)
- Credit rating (10%)
- Debt in default or reschedules (10%)

Countries are thus evaluated and rated on the above-mentioned variables. Attempts are made to assign 'grades' to both quantitative and qualitative variables. According to its importance, each variable will be assigned a weight based on which summary scores are to be computed.

5.3.3 Institutional Investor

Institutional Investor now has its country risk index which is published twice a year. Their index is based on surveys of loan officers of major multinational banks. Officers working in global banks give their scores regarding the credit quality of given countries. At the very beginning the full score was 10. Since 1980 it has been based on 100. Here a score of 0 indicates certainty of sovereign default and 100 naturally represents no possibility of default. The Institutional Investor then weighs the scores received from the officers surveyed by the exposure of each bank to the country in question.

5.4 LIMITATIONS OF COUNTRY RISK RATING

The purpose of country risk assessment is to let financial institutions, including nonbank financial institutions, ensure that their country's interest and exposure as a whole is in line with their risk preferences and earning targets. It will also ensure that the country policy of the bank does not inherently restrict business activities in a highly competitive market.

Admittedly, rating professionals, both internal and external, are trying their best to give an indication of risk by rating countries 'rationally and scientifically'. Due to the methodological sophistication, country risk rating as such encompasses a variety of limitations. For one, selection of indicators, the grading of these indicators and the assignments of weights tend to be subjective, even though the systems can be operated without further judgement. Nonquantifiable information or intangible factors are often ignored. For another, as the same weights and parameters are used to grade country risk, some country-specific elements may be ignored completely.

As country risk rating is used as a reference for decision making on country exposure and its subsequent monitoring, decision errors may occur when the rating system predicts that a country will experience problems whereas in fact it does not, or the rating system predicts that a country will stay clear of problems whereas in fact it ends up in trouble. These will lead to (potential) losses of earnings or losses of business opportunities for banks.

In fact, it is hardly possible to rate countries 'rationally and scientifically'. Think about weather forecasting. Despite the advance technology, weather forecasting is still not that accurate. To rate countries may involve much more complicated variables. This reminds us of realizing the limitations of rating systems.

As a matter of fact, country risk evaluation needs to be understood across disciplines. One or two disciplines such as politics and economics will not be sufficient. It is perhaps understandable that we do not have many experts truly competent in more than one field. The wide economic, social, cultural and political differences among countries in which banks have exposed assets, together with often rapid shifts in these countries overtime, make country risk forecasting hardly possible. Excessive reliance on the rating system is sometimes even dangerous, as there are fundamental deficiencies in the rating system, which are noticed during day-to-day operation.

First, country risk rating tends to be out of date when it is published. There is always a time lag in data collecting, data analysing, rating, publication and testing. In fact once it is put into the system, it is already out of date.

Second, many country-specific factors are important but are ignored. For example, size of the country is hardly taken into consideration for rating. If Malta and Russia are ranked as the same level of country risk, the bank may allow more or less the same level of country limit. This is of course embarrassing. Big countries tend to have a big internal market to absorb crises. Some countries may seem to bear high risk due to standard criteria. But they remain clear of difficulties in crises due to their country-specific conditions. China and India, for example, were supposed to follow other Asian countries during the Asian crisis but this did not happen due to many reasons.

Another factor that is beyond the scope of country risk rating is culture. There is a growing awareness on the impact of culture on economic development. It is well accepted that noneconomic factors and forces do affect economic behaviour, that behavioural patterns do differ among countries and that they do matter for development. But culture implies immutability and it is usually beyond the policy maker's control. Moreover, against the context of globalization, the 'contamination' factor plays a growing role in the performance of countries. The rating system usually evaluates countries individually. But the performance of a country may change due to changes made by their neighbours.

5.5 COUNTRY RISK EVALUATION IN PRACTICE

5.5.1 Country Risk Credit Committee

Although to evaluate country risk objectively is emphasized in every bank, the guidelines and practice of country risk evaluation vary from bank to bank.

As discussed, the concept of country risk examines both the ability and the willingness of the country to (re) pay. Many rating agencies devise and implement a country risk assessment matrix and rating system. Individual banks may choose either to have their own country risk rating system or to buy such information for a fee, instead of expending the resources to devise such a system. Even for those banks that have devised their own country rating system – most of them are big and global players – they have always reference to external credit agency institutions, so-called ECAI.

Financial institutions facing country risk assessment and country limit exposure will have to consider two practical issues – one is how to make strategic decisions in regard to country risk assessment principles, the other is how to register and monitor the country risk. The second issue will be discussed in more detail in Part III.

As for strategic decisions on country exposure, the greatest potential problem is that banks tend to rely too much upon rating systems and therefore abuse them in country limit decisions.

Most financial institutions adjust their country limit according to the rating publication. This function is performed by their country risk review team – so-called country risk credit committee. To avoid under or overestimating country risk to hinder commercial motivations, such a credit committee usually involves more than credit officers – a bank economist, country expert (very often the professionals from institutional banking), representatives from the country and senior managers who are in charge of the country/business lines. These individuals have different functions and perspectives. The intention is to have a consensus on the country assessment and exposure setting. A good orchestra needs a good conductor. Consensus on country assessment also needs professional coordination.

5.5.2 Techniques for Country Risk Assessment

As country risk assessment is so important, there are in practice various techniques used for country risk assessment particularly for those banks that intend to have their own independent country risk rating. The following are some of those techniques:

- Checklist system: A checklist system plays a role when a list of questions and/or statistics is proposed to be answered or collected, in order to give a judgement for a country. Questions may include those linked to a country's balance of payments, trade policy, external debts and liquidity situation, etc. A checklist system needs people who have had business exposure and are knowledgeable about the situation of the country.
- Scoring system: The intention of a scoring system is to provide a rating based on individual and specific indicators. Basically a set of statistical indicators are chosen and scores are assigned to the value of each indicator. These scores can themselves be weighted and then summed to reach a total score. Thus the establishment of this scoring system needs very careful selection and assessment of specific indicators. The selection and assessment should, ideally, both ensure maximum degree of objectivity and be informative.
- Early warning system: The earning warning system is a cause/effect analysis which foresees some potential problem and prepares itself by identify warnings as soon as possible. This will enable the bank to take proper precautions to protect its position. The purpose is to develop a long-term overall understanding of the fundamentals of the country. The focus will be on a few variables for monitoring purposes. The early warning system does not, however, necessarily identify problems when they begin to occur. The design of such a system needs a veteran's view on the cause/effect analysis on some of the warning phenomenon. For the early warning system, sources of information can be various including sources from BIS, World Bank, OECD, well-known banks, countries' own balance of payments, etc.
- Scenario analysis: The scenario analysis is an assumption/outcome analysis which intends to investigate possible occurrences in a country due to different assumptions based on some parameters. This analysis will choose two parameters, both internal (political development, fiscal and monetary policies, etc.) and external (oil price, US interest rate, value of relevant currency, etc.). With these parameters in place, sensitivity analysis will help to shape some likely scenarios. This will give a policy indication to country risk decision makers.
- Country visit: Visiting a country is important in the assessment of country risk. Here institutional banking professionals usually play a role. In some banks a visit is joined by credit people whereas in other banks credit people are purposely excluded to maintain their neutral stance, at least in theory. A visit to a country will give fresh, direct sources

of information not covered by official publications. On the list of people to be visited are usually found counterparties in the institutional banking department, central bank officials, companies, regulatory agencies, media, competitors (if possible), diplomats and sometimes academicians such as university professors. Each category may have its own function in providing relevant information.

Counterparties in institutional banking will offer a systematic view of their country especially the banking sector. In most cases, if not all, their views tend to be rather optimistic but systematic. Central bank officials will provide information on policies and the direction of policies. Their view is usually on the strategic level. Contrary to counterparties in institutional banking, central bank officials sometimes give warnings and point out some policy pitfalls.

Regulatory agencies will function more or less the same with an emphasis on regulations, which are of relevance to country risk. Examples can be the foreign exchange policy, banking licence threshold policy, bank branch policy and policies on import and export. These concrete issues are important for assessing the openness of a country. The media will open the door to a country's social life and highlight recent developments in various fields.

To visit competitors may turn out to be difficult knowing the competitive relationship. Not surprisingly, competitors will give you comments with reservation. But if such a visit can be arranged it helps to give you an idea of the market perception of the country risk. Diplomats, that is your embassy in a country, will give you a critical and direct, if not independent, view on the country with focus on the political side. They will also give you a summary of activities from companies and banks of that country. This will enable you to check and assess if your country risk attitude is too aggressive or too conservative.

Professors are usually not visited by bankers because, in the eyes of bankers, they are living in ivory towers. However, some of the professors do have a systematic framework and sharp insights on their country because they can look at things without being biased by any commercial interest. Incidentally, some professors may play a role advising their government. Their views could be forward looking as well.

There is no standard list of people to be visited but the intention of such a visit is clear – to get as many as possible sources of information on the country even if the information is conflicting. In the author's opinion, how the visit should be organized depends on your carefully defined purpose and concrete target.

For example, the purpose of the visit can be to find the latest data on a country, check the reliability of the data, find an explanation for discrepancy of data, understand the uniqueness of the political situation of a country, or simply to gain a direct feeling of a country. A visit to a country, if well organized, can prove to be indispensable for a rational and scientific assessment of country risk. Be warned, however, not to generalize your impression from one visit, especially for big countries. New Delhi does not represent India. Shanghai does not represent China and São Paolo does not represent Brazil.

Ironically, in practice we will very often find that taxi drivers are the barometers of the state of their nation, and you can have a direct feeling from them for country risk. The reason is perhaps that taxi drivers are contacting people from all walks of life. The categories of the clients they serve vary greatly.

In the process of assessment of country risk the essential point is the ability of independent analysis to strip out what is actually the noise and look at what the core ingredients are. You have to have a feeling for what is really happening in a country and what you should watch for.

5.6 RECENT CASES OF COUNTRY CRISIS IN EMERGING MARKETS

Until recently, there have been many cases of sovereign risk – the government at some stage will be either unable or unwilling to pay, such as Mexico, Brazil and Argentina at the beginning of the 1980s and the Russian and Asian crises in the 1990s. We will discuss some of them here and sum up some of the useful insights from a country risk perspective.

5.6.1 The Russian Financial Crisis of August 1998

The Russian crisis in 1998 was a typical example of country risk as it was, by its nature, a systematic crisis, including foreign debt payments, foreign exchange crisis and banking crisis. The underlying origins of the Russian crisis of 1998 are to be found in the country's economic structure, institutional environment and political process.

Externally Russia depends heavily on exports of energy resources and other primary commodities which make up 80 % of merchandise exports, and the weakening of global demand especially in Asia after the Asian crisis had a negative impact on the Russian economy. This was accompanied by a drop in world oil prices.

Internally, fiscal problems also had a push impact. During the 1990s, Russia's weak government was unable to collect taxes. The country was riddled with corruption and organized crime.

In the four years preceding this crisis, Russia enjoyed substantial capital inflows and a rouble/dollar peg became possible in July 1995. In 1997 the government managed to stabilize the rouble and reduce inflation with the financial support of the IMF and the World Bank for debt restructuring. After a short-lived and meagre recovery in 1997, the economic situation started to deteriorate in early 1998.

During the restructuring period, the government had slowed inflation by substituting borrowing for seniority. The government's attempts not to collect taxes or to reduce spending were very successful, and the state debt soared. When stock prices collapsed, concerns immediately surfaced over the possibility of a general financial crisis in Russia.

In the past, foreign investors, being attracted by the high GKO (short-term Treasury bills) yields, purchased large amounts of futures on the USD/rouble exchange rate. Russian counterparties were thus exposed to rouble devaluation. When the concerns over Russia's international reserve position and the credibility of its peg commitment increased, the foreign inventors began to shift their investment to other countries. This made it increasingly difficult for the Russian government to pay back its GKO debt. In July the government-owned Sberbank (State Savings Bank) declined to roll over it holdings of maturing short-term Treasury bills. This was a remarkable indicator of the fragility of the situation. Despite Russia's failure to abide by earlier IMF stabilization conditionally, the IMF entered into a new agreement with the Russian government and provided billions to back up the rouble's exchange rate. In the middle of August 1998, the Russian government abandoned its exchange rate target and the currency devalued by more than 300% against the US dollar since its pre-August level. Repayment of principal under credits received from non-residents for terms over 180 days were suspended for a period of 90 days from 17 August 1998. Russian short-term non-coupon Treasury bills (GKOs) and variable federal state loans bonds (OFZs) with a maturity of up to 31 December 1999 were to be converted into new, longer-term securities. This was an effort to reduce Russia's short-term repayment burden. Trading in GKOs and OFZs was suspended until conversion.

Triggered by the rouble devaluation and the freezing of GKO operations, the financial system became fraught. As a result the payments on the public and private external debt had been temporarily frozen. With the sharp devaluation of the rouble, major banks faced liquidity problems as retail and corporate depositors withdrew their money from the banks. Widespread panic resulted in a bank run. Sberbank (State Savings Bank), during the crisis, could maintain the majority of its rouble-oriented customers (pensioners and the low middle class) but lost over 30% of its USD-denominated deposits which amounted to $596 million. This hampered the function of the financial market, so that turnovers and liquidity of the circulated financial papers dropped drastically.

On the banking sector, a significant number of banks, many of whom were among the top 20 banks, suffered heavy losses on both forward foreign exchange contracts and short-term rouble-denominated government bond (GKO) portfolios. For fear of the collapse of the financial system, the Russian government and the Central Bank initiated a rescue plan for the banking sector, which included intervening in the daily operations of some problem banks. In the meantime, capital injunction and restructuring programmes were proposed.

This crisis revealed the deep-rooted causes in the financial system of the Russian Federation, especially in the banking sector. There was a lack of discipline in the banking sector and lack of prudential supervision as well. Many banks had primarily been involved in speculating in financial markets instead of being financial intermediaries. The financial environment was such that some large Russian banks just bought and sold Russian Treasury bonds instead of lending to industry. As in most emerging markets, banks' financial information was incomplete, accounting standards were unreliable and nontransparent and the hiding of problem loans was possible and massive. Along with this, poor transparency, inside lending, cross-share holdings and corruption led to serious corporate governance abuses.

The task for the Russian authorities was then to restore the solvency and confidence of the public in the country's financial system, to avoid a domino effect bank run. The rescue plan achieved the reactive purpose but there was no follow-up to ensure fundamental and strategic changes in the system.

The lesson of the Russia crisis confirms that systematic and not just reactive restructuring has to be imposed when needed. A special agency for credit institution restructuring (ARKO) was founded and two laws were subsequently passed (the law of restructuring and the law on the bankruptcy of credit institutions).

5.6.2 The Financial Crisis in Argentina

Argentina is the last in the long list of crises in emerging markets: Mexico in 1995, Asia in 1997, Russia in 1998, Brazil in 1999 and Turkey in 2001.

In 1998 Argentina entered into a recession that led to some loan losses. There was deterioration in bank balance sheets, however. The dominant factor for crisis was the fiscal problems of the Argentine government, which led to severe weakening of banks' balance sheets.

Argentina was running substantial budget deficits that could not be financed by foreign borrowing. To solve its fiscal problems, the Argentine government coerced banks into absorbing large amounts of government debt. When investors lost confidence in the ability of the Argentine government to repay this debt, the price of debt plummeted, leaving big holes in commercial banks' balance sheets. This weakening in bank balance sheets helped lead to a contraction of economic activity.

During the crisis periods for Latin America, the IMF and the US organized financial packages to avoid the collapse of involved nations and banks as well as the domino effect to neighbouring countries.

In the Argentine case, there was a package of US dollars for rescue which amounted to $2200 million by the end of 2000. However, the IMF refused to disburse US$260 million for December 2001, and was at risk for another payment of US$1000 million in the first semester of 2002. This had put Argentina on the brink of insanity and ended up with a moratorium.

A few days after the refusal of the IMF, the US president suggested to them that the US would not support an Argentine rescue. The Bush administration seemed to consider that continuous rescues over recent years had promoted a moral hazard.

The IMF has had a high profile in the Argentine crisis. The main reason for the crisis seems to be the excessive indebtedness during the government of Carlos Menem.

5.6.3 The Financial Crisis in Mexico

By the end of the 1960s and the beginning of the 1970s, the Mexican economy was enjoying an image of growth and monetary and political stability. The first problem that emerged was the balance of payments problem, as its current account deficit was a dangerous 7% of GDP in 1994. This was due to the market opening reforms undertaken by President Salinas' administration accompanied by an increase of imports. Its limited foreign reserves thus dwindled. This posed problems for the dollar peg. Within half a year, the peso plunged by nearly 50%. The deterioration of balance of payments and depreciation of the currency caused government debt, largely dollar denominated, to swell enormously. This was followed by the exposure of a number of bad loans by recently privatized banks. Many banks went bust. Interest rate rocketed and many Mexicans, particularly in the new middle class, defaulted on loans. This disruption of the function of the banking system pushed the currency down further. A series of high profile crimes during the beginning of 1994 and the weakened image of Mexico being stable and safe among invertors led to the reduced inflow of capital. Contraction of the economy was unavoidable. In 1995 GDP shrank by 6.2%.

Under such circumstances, a crisis would usually develop fast both internally and externally. But Mexico is a member of *NAFTA* (the North American Free Trade Agreement), which had come into effect on 1 January 1994. Bill Clinton, then president of US, reasoned that Mexico, the third-largest trading partner, must be rescued due to its importance to American jobs and investment. A $40 billion standby loan was arranged. Mexico managed to grow by 5–6% during 1996, 1997 and 1998. The economy regained its 1994 level in dollar terms in early 2004.

5.6.4 Asian Crisis

The financial crises in East Asia in late 1997 were in fact a series of crises that were experienced by countries in the region.

Until 1997 East Asia was a very attractive region for foreign investors due to the relatively high margins for banks and high inflow of funds. The economies of Indonesia, Malaysia, South Korea, the Philippines, Thailand and Singapore were booming with an 8–12% growth rate in the late 1980s and early 1990s. This was the so-called 'Asian Miracle'.

The crisis started with currency problem in Thailand. Massive speculative currency attacks led to eventual currency floating which in turn devalued the currency by more than half at the beginning of 1998. Other countries tried to defend their currencies through rising interest rates but finally all of them dropped significantly with the exception of Hong Kong, which managed to protect its currency due to a unique currency board system and resolute actions of government authorities.

This series of crises in Asia can be best described by quoting the headlines from the magazines including *Far East Economic Review*:

- 'A new miracle needed': 25 December 1997, *Far East Economic Review*
- 'O happy crisis: the benefits of being burnt': 8 January 1998, *Far East Economic Review*
- 'The day the miracle came to an end': 12 January 1998, *Financial Times*
- 'Watch for social unrest': 22 January 1998, *Far East Economic Review*
- 'Is Asia emerging or submerging?': 27 January 1998, *NIAS Research Paper*
- 'Are Asia values finished?': 22 February 1998, *Far East Economic Review*
- 'Kill or cure?': 10 February 1998, the *Economist*
- 'A poor grade for the IMF': 15 January 1998, *Far East Economic Review*
- 'Sayings of Chairman Milton: Asia Miracle is real': 26 March 1998, *Far East Economic Review*
- 'Re-building Asia': 26 March 1998, *Far East Economic Review*

The Asian crisis itself indicates that the currency issue was essential. When loans were lent in dollars, debts automatically increased if the foreign exchange rate slid. The crisis situation varied from country to country though. In Thailand, too much money was chasing too few opportunities. In Indonesia, corruption, connected lending, a weak banking system accompanied by fast growth, a credit culture with few risk management measures were all explanations for the crisis. In Singapore and Hong Kong a pawnshop mentality, that is when collateral was given, money was lent, stimulated a lot of blind lending for speculative purposes. In some of these countries bankruptcy law was weak and collateral was not easily realized.

Looking back to the banking sector at that time, we will find that relationship lending (Chinese community) or connected lending prevailed, which ended up with lending to friends and relationships without checking the credit. Credit skill was lacking in South Korea, Indonesia, Thailand, etc. Inside-group lending was not exceptional in some of these countries: the fact that a Summa Bank shareholder borrowed more than 55% of the assets was a good example. In South Korea, the banking system was inherently inefficient with a great deal of government influence. There was moral obedience to the government and banks simply accepted instruction from the government to lend to government-linked projects. This caused solvency problems for many banks. In Indonesia, banking system liberalization led to too many banks.

The Asian crisis triggered the discussion of the role of IMF for such a crisis. At that time, the IMF's Chief Camdessus initiated a new architecture of which six pillars were:

- More effective surveillance of countries' economic policies, through fuller disclosure of relevant economic and financial data.
- Regional surveillance, with neighbouring countries getting together to encourage one another – or put pressure on one another – to pursue sound policies.
- Financial sector reform, including better prudential regulation and supervision.
- More effective structures for orderly debt workouts including better bankruptcy laws at the national level of associating the private sector with official efforts to help resolve sovereign debt problems.
- A properly sequenced and cautious capital account liberalization which would allow more countries to access international capital markets.
- A strengthening of the international financial institutions including their financial resources.

Whether IMF's role was crucially positive is still an open question. But no doubt several interesting lessons were learned via these country crises in Asia. These lessons are still of relevance to us.

First, investment, if any, should be directed to productive sectors – sectors that will generate future income. Investment in an overheated property market is always challenged as a proper investment.

Second, foreign exchange risk should be carefully estimated if not fully hedged. Long lasting currency peg and its illusion was a definite catalyst in the crisis. This is why many countries shifted away from peg to a floating foreign exchange regime.

Third, a stable financial system is crucial to countries especially to emerging markets. There should be a good balance between liberalization and regulation. For bank lending, strict credit policy is a must to avoid government-directed lending and related party lending. A healthy banking system will consist of a proper capital/assets ratio and capital strength.

Fourth, a sound supervision agency for regulation and discipline is deemed a must at all times.

5.6.5 Country Crisis: Signs and Signals

The above discussion of cases of country crisis can help in understanding country risk and will throw light on the *signs and signals* of potential country crisis.

Country crisis in emerging markets usually undergoes several stages:

> A deterioration of balance of payments > disruption of the functions of the financial system > sharp decrease of currency value > capital flight > currency crisis > worsening of the balance of payments > contraction of the economy > full fledged country crisis internally and externally.

Deterioration of country risk is often linked to macro-economic performance of the country which is reflected in the balance of payments of that country. Any imbalance of foreign exchange inflow and outflow may cause problems in balance of payments. This imbalance may come from export shortfall due to commodity price falls or a world recession, especially those that depend on a narrow range of export of commodities. It can also be the decrease of repatriation of overseas workers' remittance.

Such a balance of payments problem may also be a result of excessive imports due to an overvalued exchange rate (Chile in 1981), or price rises (heavy reliance on imported energy, for example Turkey in the mid-1970s). Excessive service payments for the national debt due to the interest rate will have an impact on foreign currency reserve. Slowdown or cession of capital inflow when foreign direct investment is discouraged, capital flight due to lack of confidence in the country (social unrest, etc.) are all well-known factors for influencing balance of payments.

Country risk can be directly relevant in assessing an individual bank's performance. It is linked to both the borrowing bank and the lending bank. When a country unexpectedly runs into difficulties for economic and/or political reasons, a bank with loans outstanding to these difficult countries faces a number of problems. The lending bank's position changes over time with the development of these difficulties.

- Deterioration of the position of the balance sheets for banks: The first problem is that existing loans look underpriced in relationship to the risk. The necessity or desire to raise provisions or loan losses will show up in the profit and loss account immediately. If the bank has a significant proportion of its loan portfolio in doubtful countries, this may have the effect of depressing a bank's price of stock. It may also affect a bank's strategy in that country.
- Late payments: When country risk is in a downward direction, payments due will be delayed. Very often the penalty interest rate comes into play which can be lucrative. On the other hand, such management time can be wasted and proper financial planning is difficult if substantial arrears build up and rescheduling becomes inevitable.
- Rescheduling: When a country is in a really difficult situation, rescheduling is a face-saving solution. But rescheduling does impose some important costs. First, there is the risk that the situation proves to be so difficult that eventually some of the concessional arrangements have to be made and banks have to take losses. Second, the overall return from the relationship may be less than before.
- Write-offs to moratorium, repudiation, renegotiations, etc.: When all is said and done, and a solution is still not possible, write-offs are the last action for the lending banks. Since 1981, particularly after 1987, UK and US banks began to make provisions to show that they are on top of the problem.

The ability to pay is an indication of country risk. Willingness to pay is, however, not so obvious to measure. If there is a tight supply of hard currency, the challenge to the government is a 'willingness to repay foreign debt'. The authorities of the country must evaluate the costs and benefits to the country of not meeting its financial obligations.

Given the devastating effects and the increased frequency of country crises recently in emerging market countries, it is interesting to find out what phenomena there are that could give signals for country risk changes. Here is a list of some of them:

Unable to pay:

- Major devaluation of the currency
- Economic recession

- Natural disaster
- Social disorder and unrest
- Changes in government (unfriendly)
- Discrimination against foreign companies
- Commodity prices reduction – export shortfalls
- Decrease of regular income
- Oversees workers' repatriation of funds
- Excessive imports
- Capital flight

Unwilling to pay:

- Extreme economic hardship
- Weak and/or corrupted government
- Extremely radical government – mentality change
- A major change in government – regime change

SUMMARY

Sovereign countries are ranked according to their country risk. Any cross-border activities give rise to this country risk concept. It represents the potentially adverse impact of a sovereign country's environment on multinationals' cash flow. Evaluation of this country risk is a profession. Many rating companies publish such ratings on a regular basis.

Country risk is macro-economic underperformance of countries/economies due to policy errors, liquidity on a national level, political changes, etc. It consists of both transfer risk and sovereign performance risk.

There are many cases in history where sovereign countries were not able to meet their obligations. Such sovereign default can be either outright cancellation of debt, which is called 'debt repudiation', or announcement of delay on its current and future debts, which is called 'debt rescheduling'. Recent country crises include those in Russia, Latin America and Asia.

There are signs and signals to watch for the underperformance of countries. Many of them have seen stages such as a deterioration of balance of payments > disruption of the functions of the financial system > sharp decrease of currency value > capital flight > currency crisis > worsening of the balance of payments > contraction of the economy > fully fledged country crisis internally and externally.

Sovereign default may have serious and long-lasting consequences. It is not only face-losing but also brings future difficulties in the international community.

Credit rating companies use different rating principles to rate sovereign risk. The criteria used measure the political, economic and financial situation of the country. There are, however, limitations to be noted. In practice, techniques like a checklist system, scoring system, early warning system, scenario analysis and direct country visit are used.

Part II

Institutional Banking

6
From Correspondent Banking to Institutional Banking: Past and Present

6.1 THE ORIGIN OF CORRESPONDENT BANKING

Although correspondent banking nowadays is mainly used for bank relations in an international environment, it is not necessarily cross-border.

In fact it originated from a domestic context.[1] The story goes that small, local banks in operation at that time needed a money centre or a clearing bank located in the country's principal financial centre to clear their funds through the nation's banking system. In the United States, for example, the need for a correspondent system evolved initially to help process cheques. As banking institutions became large and financial systems more centralized, there was less need for such domestic correspondent arrangements within an individual country's banking structure. Consequently, correspondent banking as a business developed internationally.

At the very beginning, correspondent banking was merely the networking among banks or the network of interbank relationships in which one bank sells services to other banks or to nonbank financial institutions. The bank that provides the services is called the 'correspondent bank'.[2]

This kind of correspondent banking became more significant with the growing need of banking clients for their international business, for example settlement of international trade finance at places where the home bank does not/cannot have branches to realize their request.

The original need for (international) correspondent banking thus started for the settlement of clearing items and effecting foreign currency payments. For this kind of settlement, a bank will have to have an account maintained in the foreign country (a 'nostro' account, or 'vostro' account in the eyes of the foreign correspondent bank). Whether or not two banks can be considered as 'correspondents' is, in most cases, the existence of a test-key arrangement plus an account relationship.

With the development of international trade, any bank issuing a *letter of credit* on behalf of its client (applicant) which imports goods from abroad will need a relationship bank located in the exporter's country to 'advise' that letter of credit to the exporter. This makes correspondent relationships a must.

In the field of trade finance, a correspondent bank infact can contribute more. By 'confirming' the letter of credit, the 'advising' bank will become a 'confirming bank' and thus will provide help to the exporter by taking over the payment risk from the issuing bank, usually located in a foreign country. If the 'confirming' bank further 'discounts' the letter of credit, the

[1] See Nigel Wilkins (1993) *The Correspondent Banking Handbook* Euromoney Publications PLC.

[2] The bank, which buys the services, is sometimes called the respondent bank or downstream correspondent. See Chapter 14 of *Bank Management* by Timonthy W. Koch.

advising bank can function as a paying bank thus providing liquidity to the exporter. This will be discussed later in more detail under 'trade finance'.

Nowadays, a correspondent bank is not only a (foreign) bank that may help your settlement of international trade, it is also a business partner whom you may either buy product from or sell your product to. A correspondent bank is therefore an institutional client and correspondent banking is therefore now called 'institutional banking'.

Before we move on, let's first of all have a look at the environment of banking industry under which correspondent banking is developing.

6.2 THE INFLUENCE FROM THE GENERAL DEVELOPMENT OF THE BANKING INDUSTRY

Without doubt, the banking industry today is facing consolidation. Merger and acquisition is becoming a trend.

With merger and acquisition, the birth of super global banks becomes a reality. It seems that the need for correspondent relationships with other banks was expected to decrease. The argument goes that banks, at least the global ones, can have branches and representative offices for their business expansion and supervision abroad, instead of having too many correspondents.

It is true that the branch and representative network can be the 'ambassador' of the head office to the countries in which banks are active. On behalf of head office, they are dealing with government, central bank and other government agencies. They facilitate (arrange) visits from head office. They are the home bank's 'eyes' and 'ears', watching the development of the market, visiting local clients and banks for follow-up (head office visits once or twice a year) and providing the latest market development to head office. They are also risk analysts and risk checkers for the head office and help solve commercial problems.

However, the branches and representative offices cannot totally replace the business of correspondent banking. Correspondent banking is still an important business with potential to develop. In fact, many banks are paying more attention to their correspondents instead of developing their own branches and representative offices. This can be explained by several factors.

First, by using branches and representative offices, banks intend to be close to their clients. But a physical presence near to their customers' offices will be rendered less necessary by the IT improvements taking place in communications. Banks are becoming more cost and efficiency conscious so as to maintain their competitiveness.

Second, under the consolidation of the banking industry, we shall see that cross-border services develop, globally, around a framework of *interdependent* partnerships based on *division of labour*, *service integration* and *joint product development*. Banks can choose either to be 'big' or to be 'specialized'. They also have remote clearing access from centralized processing sites and strongly defined bilateral and multilateral corporate alliances. Banks without the critical mass of technical expertise may choose to outsource at least some part of their activities to those banks better positioned in the field.

Outsourcing is also due to the fact that some services can either be too expensive to provide independently, or cannot be provided because of regulatory constraints.

Third, over the years, the concept of correspondent banking has developed further from its initial trade finance and settlement services. A much broader range of correspondent banking services has been offered. Nowadays many banks are marketing their products towards other financial institutions, which are regarded as the same as individual and corporate customers.

To large banks, which are perhaps in a position to offer all-round services, correspondent banking has potential in the sense that interbank transactions can generate extra earnings. If banks want to fully utilize their existing resources, physical and human, they should be interested in offering correspondent services to other banks. They need correspondent banks to buy their products to reach economies of scale. They may also buy products from their correspondents as an outsourcing partner.

Smaller banks have to offer a full range of services to their customers in order to survive. But the demand for special transactions is unpredictable and infrequent. It would be too costly to invest in the technology and human resources to enable the bank to offer all-round services. A Russian bank's branch in Amsterdam may not have the expertise to evaluate the country and bank risk for Taiwan, with which the trade flow is exactly 'sporadic'.

To take advantage of economies of scale, services must be provided in large volume. Even when priced at a mark-up over correspondents' costs, these services are cheaper than if provided independently. Thus small banks with a limited customer base can hardly justify large investment to provide infrequently used services. However, they must be able to provide these services to remain a full service bank, and it is cheaper to buy them on demand. They need correspondents to help them.

6.3 CORRESPONDENT BANKING TODAY: TOWARDS AN INSTITUTIONAL RELATIONSHIP

As a result, banks themselves today are becoming more and more institutional customers to each other. This implies that correspondent banks are not only offering to each other services that cannot be offered by themselves, but are also providing the opportunity for banks to consider if the available service in the bank should be outsourced.

Trade business, for example, is under a great deal of pressure globally. Bank clients look less at where the supplier of goods or services is located and more at the quality and price of the goods or services. Banks are thus constantly under pressure to improve the quality and to get costs under control. Many banks are thus looking globally for outsourcing partnerships.[3] Banks nowadays call their 'correspondent department' a department for 'financial institutions'. Such correspondent banking relationships will be of a commercial nature as they may offer substantial earnings for banks on commercial activities such as custody, account handling, international trade settlement, foreign exchange and treasury products, syndication loans, etc.

The role played by correspondent banking does not stop at that. As we will see later, this correspondent network will change the risk portfolio of the bank by trading assets – taking in extra risk or selling out existing portfolio via *risk participation*, syndication and forfaiting. It may also change the liquidity position by taking deposits from, or giving deposits to, other banks.

What, then, remains unchanged today for institutional banking?

What remains unchanged is the fact that 'institutional banking', or 'correspondent banking'

[3] Bank of New York (BNY) is said to have globally over 50 outsourcing partnerships, of which 12 or so are North American clients. See *Trade Finance* report 'Trade services: busy behind the scenes', a supplement to *Trade Finance*, March 2004.

as we used to call it, is still a kind of relationship banking. It succeeds in serving clients by reaching the places that branch networks cannot, or where branches do exist but cannot offer the same service.

Any bank with the ambition to provide a comprehensive service to its clients will definitely need a sizeable network of correspondents around the world. The institutional banking department plays a crucial role in efficient utilization of bank limits, trade services, assets trading and in supporting the acquisition of new counterparties for foreign exchange and money market operations. It also supports the bank's funding by attracting financing from other correspondent banks in the form of bilateral borrowings, pre-export financing, post-financing and syndicated loan facilities.

Such an institutional relationship can be realized either on a reciprocity basis or on a one-way basis, with the correspondent bank simply serving as the agent for the originating bank in handling some specific transactions. Naturally, towards a particular bank there is inevitably a delicate balance between 'cooperation' elements and 'competition' elements in this correspondent relationship, that is a correspondent bank can sometimes be a 'partner' and sometimes a 'competitor'. This will be the crucial ingredient of the relationship. Such a balance between the two will change over the years and varies considerably from one relationship bank to another.

SUMMARY

Correspondent banking originated from a domestic context. It started with the need to settle clearing items such as a cheque. With the development of international trade, correspondent banking became a must. Nowadays, correspondent banking is becoming relationship banking, with correspondents as institutional clients of the bank. More often, correspondent banking is called 'institutional banking'.

Consolidation among banks does not reduce the need for institutional banking. This is because globally banks are working around a framework of interdependent partnerships based on division of labour, service integration, joint product development and risk distribution. Banks are more and more becoming each others' customers. Institutional banking is thus a sales department to institutional clients, which may contribute earnings to the bank as a whole.

For such partnership banking, there is inevitably a delicate balance between the cooperation elements and the competition elements.

7
The Products of Institutional Banking

7.1 ACCOUNT SERVICE AND CASH MANAGEMENT

As a sales team to institutional clients, institutional banking professionals are supposed to be not only *country* and *bank specialists* but also banking *product generalists*.

The products of institutional banking that can be sold are many. For the convenience of discussion, the products of institutional banking are divided into several groups:

- Account services
- Trade finance
- Financial market and/or investment products
- Other services such as custody, data processing services, portfolio analysis and investment advice, loan participation and syndication

We will discuss them one by one but focus will be more on *account services* and *trade finance* which are common for emerging markets. Financial market products have special application in emerging markets. Those more often used in emerging markets such as *repos*, *NDFs*, and *IRS* will be discussed in detail.

7.1.1 Account Services

As was mentioned earlier, correspondent banking originated from the need for clearing among banks. Banks throughout the world play an important role in settling debts incurred in international trade or other activities. An importer wishing to pay a foreign exporter will ask his bank to make the payment in different ways but the result will finally be reflected in the accounts which banks have maintained with each other.

With the need for clearing, account services follow. Every international bank needs access to clearing facilities especially for the major currencies in the world such as the US dollar, Japanese yen, euro, etc. Attached to the global exchange of payment instruments are the sophisticated reporting systems sufficient to enable banks to monitor the volume of funds being cleared. Without such services, the dealers in the dealing rooms of each bank will be at a loss for their position.

Accounts can either be 'vostro' or 'nostro'. In Latin, 'vostro' means 'your' whereas 'nostro' means 'our'. A 'vostro account' is thus an account maintained in the bank in the names of other banks situated abroad, and a 'nostro account' is an account maintained in the name of the bank with banks situated abroad. Banks need account services with other banks abroad, particularly in countries that have major trading currencies such as the US dollar, Japanese yen, euro, etc.

Account services are often linked to remittance and trade payment settlement. The rapid growth of international trade provides banks with opportunities of trade service and account service. A fee charged on the clearing and the deposit (or overdraw charges on the account) offers earnings for the institutional banking business.

Account services range from cheque clearing to settlement of international trade. Here price or pricing is not so much an issue as the excellence of operation – speed, convenience and precise execution of the order from the correspondent. It is not unusual that in the daily work of institutional banking, correspondent bank complaints are received for mistakes on amount, currency or value date.

The development of IT in this field has reduced more and more the operational costs. It has also reduced the need to maintain many accounts. Hence quality of service is becoming the focus of competition in this field.

In banking practice, big banks that have a large distribution network and good IT supporting system are more motivated to promote account services. The demand for account services comes from smaller banks that have neither the ambition nor enough supporting capacity to offer extensive account services. Bigger banks, especially those global players, are fully aware of such a situation and have their charging scheme.

Sometimes account services may seem tedious but may generate different types of revenue from correspondents – investment income from the deposits on the account, fee income for the services and interest income for an overdraft or for a loan. The earnings for an account service are listed below and can be substantial if the bank uses a proper price policy and strategy:

- The service fee on the account (many banks have minimum charges)
- The interest earned on the remaining deposit balances (many banks have minimum balances policy)
- Earnings on the value date[1] (usually an account will be debited/credited one or two extra days)
- Spin-off business such as foreign exchange deals, etc.
- Earnings on remittances (money transfer), etc.

For the first offering of account services to your correspondent, who is usually very price sensitive, a good price policy can play an important role, as the correspondent has no idea yet of your quality of service – the quality of service has not yet been tested.

For account services, the institutional banking department must also watch the development of your competitors' price structure closely.

For retail banking business the price of maintaining an account can vary due to a number of reasons. One interesting study carried out by Mercer Oliver Wyman for the Italian Banking Association compared the average price of maintaining an account in various European countries: Italy €133, France €94, Spain €86, and Germany €68.[2]

Due to the fact that there is a heavy factor of labour cost to maintain an account, economies of scale is an important consideration in institutional banking. In order to make account services a profitable business, a bank has to have enough accounts to justify the costs of an

[1] Value date: the date, that indicates when the funds on the account are available for use or, conversely, when they are likely to be withdrawn.

[2] *'A survey of international banking'*, the *Economist*, 21 May 2005.

IT automated supporting system and the labour costs. It is becoming obvious that account services are offered on a commercial consideration with the exception that some banks' strategy is to have market share in account services.

This cost consciousness is becoming so important that many banks have account analysis – an analytical procedure for determining whether or not an account relationship is profitable. The so-called 80–20 rule (80% of client relationship offers 20% earnings, and 20% of client relationship offers 80% earnings to the bank) will result in a different fee/interest structure and a different service level. This is also the case for correspondent banking account services.

Banks to be served are encouraged to centralize their service demand vis-à-vis their counterparty in order to get price benefits. The concept of a global relationship manager is thus developed to serve, among others, such a purpose. A correspondent that uses account services, foreign exchange services, custody services, etc. will get a better fee charge from the global relationship manager, who oversees all the activities with this correspondent.

Another trend in account services since the 1990s is the *client compliance policy* in order to avoid money laundering.[3] In the field of account services, customer identification as a fundamental part of an *anti-money-laundering* system is provided in several documents including the Basle Committee Statement.[4]

For offering account services to institutional clients, each bank is supposed to have *due diligence* guidance. This kind of due diligence applies not only to account relationships but also to all other relationships, establishing or maintaining with its scope of clients either a test-key arrangement, the opening of an account, a money market line or a fully fledged correspondent. Due diligence is now part of a series of well-defined procedures and tests instead of simply a duty of care.

Due diligence is based on the evaluation of so-called counterparty risk factors. This risk-based approach will be applied to determine the amount of due diligence that is necessary for a particular correspondent, that is the level and scope of the due diligence required. Before due diligence starts, you have to determine how intensive it should be.

This due diligence approach is systematic and consists of several risk factor reviews. Any correspondent relationship must go through the procedure and meet the requirements of the test.

What elements are to be checked for the purpose of due diligence?

First, domicile – the *jurisdiction* where the correspondent is based, and, in the case of a subsidiary and affiliated entity, where its ultimate parent is headquartered must be considered. This is because certain jurisdictions are internationally recognized as having inadequate anti-money-laundering standards, insufficient regulatory supervision, or presenting greater risk for crime, corruption or terrorist financing.

The *competence/capacity of regulatory authority* of a correspondent bank is yet another important consideration. A correspondent bank that operates in, or is subjected to, a regulatory environment that is internationally recognized as adequate in the fight against money laundering mitigates the risk.

[3] In December 1988, the Basel Committee on Banking Regulations and Supervisory Practices adopted a Statement of Principles, which covered customer identifications, compliance with law and cooperation with law enforcement authorities for banks to implement. The 1988 Vienna Convention for the first time addresses the issue that money laundering should be criminalized at international level. The 2000 Palermo UN Convention further provided a legally binding instrument committing member states to taking a series of measures against transactional organized crime.

[4] Other documents are: the FATF Recommendations, EC directives, etc.

The corporate legal form and the transparency of ownership structure should also be of concern. Consideration should be given to the relationship between the counterparty and its ultimate parent. Situations involving branches, subsidiaries or affiliates and the parent of the correspondent must be considered.

In cases where the correspondent is an affiliate that is not substantively and effectively controlled by the parent, then both the parent and the correspondent must be reviewed. This will give an indication of who really runs the bank. The location and experience of management may raise additional concerns. Certain facts unique to the branch, subsidiary or affiliate may dictate that an enhanced due diligence be performed.

An interesting point in this due diligence procedure is the concept of *PEP* (politically exposed persons). In the checking of management of a correspondent, the involvement of politically exposed persons either in the management or in the ownership of a correspondent may increase the isk.

PEPs are individuals who have or have had positions of public trust such as government officials, senior executives of government corporations, politicians, important political party officials, and include their families and close associates. A careful evaluation of such PEPs and their influence will give insights into the risk.

Other related facts will include the *business scope* and *customer base* of this potential correspondent – the type of banking businesses the correspondent bank engages in, as well as the type of the markets it serves, may present certain risks. Involvement in business segments internationally recognized as creating particular vulnerability to money laundering, corruption or terrorist financing present additional concern. Also, a correspondent that derives a substantial part of its business income from higher risk customers may present greater risk. Higher risk customers are those that may be involved in activities or are connected to jurisdictions that are identified as being especially susceptible to money laundering.

Due diligence not only answers the question of 'yes' or 'no', but also 'how much' or 'how far'. Relationships with the bank – prior or current – should be reviewed not only to determine the degree of reliance that may be placed on the knowledge of the correspondent but also to identify those that have presented the bank with a less than satisfactory experience. This kind of track record checking will give input for the bank to consider if the account services should be offered, what kind of relationship should be developed, or is the relationship worth pursuing at all.

Hence, all potential correspondents shall be subject to the appropriate level of due diligence review based on a risk profile. The due diligence review enables the bank to meet its 'know your client' obligations and facilitates the account acceptance approval process.

In conducting due diligence on a correspondent, many elements must be identified, documented and incorporated as part of the correspondent file. An appropriate degree of diligence is achieved through compliance with approved procedures and tests which themselves are defined by standards of care. Such well-defined standards of care should include but are limited to items such as:

- Domicile, organization and history: The jurisdiction where the correspondent's ultimate parent is incorporated and/or headquartered and where the particular operating unit conducts its business, as well as the corporate legal form (subsidiary, joint ventures, affiliated, etc.).
- Client ownership and executive management: Ownership can be state or private. If the correspondent is publicly held, are the shares traded on an exchange in a jurisdiction with

an adequately recognized regulatory scheme? Any significant controlling interests are a concern in the due diligence. The identity of the beneficial owners must be established for nonpublic companies and for those public companies that are not widely held. The structure, experience and background of executive management must be documented as well as the existence of any PEP in the executive management or ownership structure.

- Business activities: These consist of types of products and services the correspondent is allowed under its licence from the regularity authorities, as well as the geographic markets it serves.
- Products or services to be offered to this correspondent and the business purpose for the relationship with this correspondent: This consists of the products and services to be offered to the correspondent. Service level and range should be defined, that is only test-key and passive relationship, or fully-fledged correspondent banking.
- Regulatory status and history: Who is the primary regulatory body responsible for overseeing or supervising the correspondent (central bank, monetary authority or other regulatory institution)? Also, check the available media report or any publicly available materials to ascertain whether the correspondent has been the subject of any criminal, civil or adverse regulatory action in the recent past, or been seriously involved in some big local scandal.
- Relationship with the bank: Any prior or current relationship with the bank should be noted and assessed. Identify the potential to create a conflict of interest when establishing a new relationship with an existing or prior correspondent.

In particular, the bank should also check the *anti-money laundering controls* – evaluate the nature of the correspondent's anti-money laundering controls and the extent to which they are globally applied.

Such due diligence is in fact a specialized task performed by a specialized department under institutional banking. Desk study is not sufficient and it may be appropriate to visit the correspondent at their premises prior to or within a reasonable period of time after establishing a relationship. A visit of this kind will give direct information about the background of the shareholders and the strategy and competence of the bank and its market mission. The pending questions (including the questions from financial analyses) can be properly answered.

As mentioned, in addition to the regular due diligence, correspondents that present greater risks must be subject to enhanced due diligence. Automatically, an enhanced due diligence will be required for any correspondent organized or operating in any jurisdiction mentioned in the so-called watch list.

7.1.2 Cash Management

The competitiveness of account services to correspondents is very much linked to the quality of cash management service of the bank. Account services are often offered together with cash management services.

- Cash management is a service offered by banks for a company's (or bank's) cash flow processing, cash pooling and the message serving on its current account. The purpose is to help improve the efficiency of its day-to-day cross-border cash transactions. It also aims to provide timely, accurate information for internal control.

Cash management is also directly or indirectly an income generating unit. The revenues of cash management include:

- Transaction fees for debt and credit
- Float and foreign exchange spread
- Partial interest spread
- Set-up fees
- Account management fees
- Capital and reserve costs borne by the customer
- Electronic banking reporting fees, etc.

Obviously, the quality of cash management depends on the infrastructure of the payment. In Europe there is growing pressure to create a Single European Payment Area (SEPA).[5] Access to cash management is important to the correspondent because it will function as a liquidity management transfer system such as TARGET.[6]

Liquidity management will reduce, control and manage exposures of the bank and centralize cash and information management to determine the global position of the correspondent. This will also enable the correspondent to utilize its funds optimally and reduce transaction fees, spread and margins. All these facilities and infrastructure are emphasized in any offer from/to a correspondent.

As a basic product for institutional banking, account services are very often extensively promoted by many big banks, especially those located in the clearing centre of major currencies.

The marketing of account/cash management services will contain some typical items:

- The market position of the offering bank
- Its clearing system
- Its intentional network, etc.

Typical offering letters from banks who are usually global players may start with its market position:

> Xxx Bank is ranked no. x Bank in North America and no. x in the world. Our large network of xxx branches serves xxx million customers worldwide. In xxx, xx% of all payment transactions involved xxx Bank. In xxx, xxx Bank covered around xx% of the flows processed through the American payment systems, while in xxx we covered more than xxx% of clearing flows.
>
> Xxx Bank is established in the centre of North America and has always been at the forefront of new techniques in payment systems. We are committed to a long-term strategy for dollar clearing and cash management services. We have a long tradition and large expertise in the field of clearing business, which allows us to provide you with a highly professional and flexible service.

[5] There were several EU directives (regulations) to regulate the payment in Europe, such as EU Cross-Boarder (Payment Directive 97/5 to speed up cross-border Eurp payment under 50 000). EU banks are requested to provide information and transparent pricing. EC regulation 2560/2001 requested EC banks with low-value transfers below 50 000 (from 2006) to be priced as domestic transfers. To facilitate this BIC and IBAN codes are needed.

[6] TARGET – **T**rans-European **A**utomated **R**eal Time **G**ross **S**ettlement **E**xpress **T**ransfer system.

Some banks also emphasize the well-developed, convenient *clearing system*:

Xxx Bank has access to a multitude of clearing systems:

1. founding member and second largest user of xxx clearing system
2. STEP1 Settlement Bank
3. direct participant to STEP2
4. a direct participant of a local automated clearing house which is handling over xxx billion dollars daily

We execute some xxx cross-border payments per day. Some xxx banks maintain xxx vostri accounts in our books.

In case xxx Bank acts as intermediary bank for payments towards other countries: xxx Bank does not withhold any commission from the proceeds.

Correspondent network and *e-banking* will be highlighted as well:

We have been investing heavily in the automation of international payments and have installed an automated repair tool which has proven to be able to correct a significant number of payment messages that were not correctly formatted.

We have installed an automated inquiry system for our Customer Support (centralized professional, multilingual helpdesk), 30 business days on-line data: information is available real time for consultation and/or correction. Consequently, we aim to resolve all 'in-bank' investigations within 24 hours.

We can offer reporting via the Internet, which gives you real-time (consultation) access to your accounts in our books 24 hours a day. Our debit authorization is an on-line process.

Our dollar operations centre is based in New York. All payments from, or in favour of, banks are processed centrally in our Foreign Payments Department. To ensure that your payments are processed as efficiently as possible, please send your instructions by authenticated SWIFT to xxx; your receipts will also be centralized in the same department.

Our systems are designed to minimize the throughput time of all payment orders and to offer a high quality cross-border payments service. Payments received before our cut-off time are guaranteed forwarded to the bank of the beneficiary with same day value.

7.2 TRADE FINANCE

7.2.1 Various Ways to Finance Trade

Trade finance services are important because banks' corporate clients export. For any company, to export is either a way to expand its business or to diversify its client portfolio. Even for those corporate clients that have a steady and healthy home market for their goods, a wider market can lead to lower unit costs. The expansion of sales might prompt improved automation and production techniques, which in turn will lead to goods being priced more competitively.

Broadly speaking, trade finance not only includes the financing of the movement of goods but also the financing of services. The financing of railway receivables or telephone receivables between Mexico and the US are good examples.

Naturally straight forward payment and settlement can service trade finance – to transfer money from one customer to another to settle the trade business between them. This is reflected in our 'account services' discussion above. There are also methods of settling debts incurred in international trade where correspondent banking can be involved. In such cases, a correspondent bank is an agent bank to which the principal bank communicates instructions for action.

There are various ways to finance international trade such as:

- Open account: This is an arrangement between a buyer and a seller for the buyer to settle his debts with the seller at a predetermined future date (mentioned in the contract signed by both parties), perhaps at the end of the month or, say, a fixed period after each shipment. The seller thus has absolute trust that the buyer can and will pay at the agreed time.
- Advance payments: The buyer pays the money in advance so that the seller has both the money and the goods. This is usually under the 'seller's market' condition where there is absolute trust by the buyer that the seller will deliver the goods the buyer has ordered.
- Documentary collection against acceptance (D/A): Under this kind of arrangement title documents (bills of lading, insurance documents and bills of exchange) after the acceptance will be released if the bank of the counterparty accepts the documents and promises to pay.
- Documentary collection against payment (D/P): Under this kind of arrangement title documents (bills of lading, insurance documents and bills of exchange) will be released if the bank of the counterparty pays the agreed amount.

Without going into details, we can well see that a foreign correspondent will be involved in one way or another in the above-mentioned trade finance. Nevertheless the most important product is *irrevocable documentary credit*.

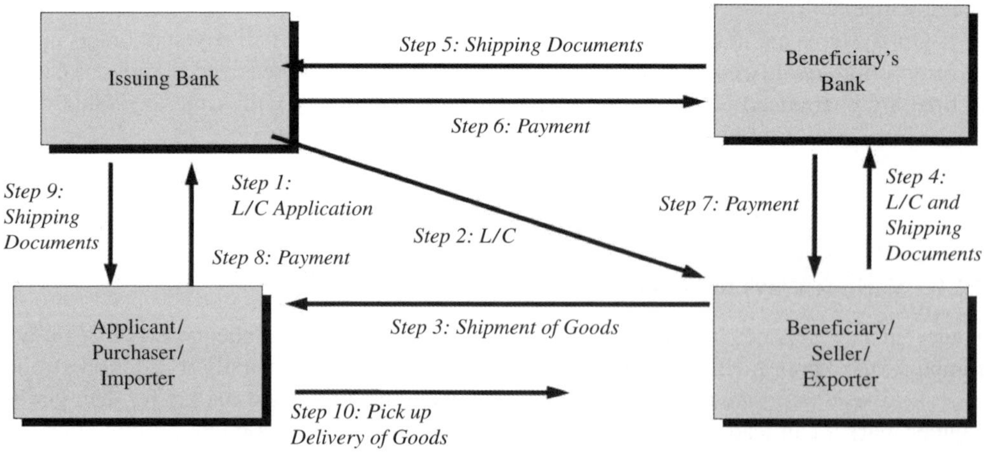

Figure 7.1 Basic description of a letter of credit

Payment for international trade is typically made by *irrevocable letter of credit*, meaning that once goods have been shipped, shipping and other commercial documents can be presented to the bank handling the L/C and payment should be made immediately, provided that the documents comply with the terms of credit.

In fact, letters of credit have played a long-standing role in the history of international trade. As early as the 15th century, Phoenician traders carried them to foreign ports in the form of clay tablets, stamped with the seals of prominent merchants. The letters of credit were then written on sheep skins and used by traders such as Marco Polo.

Today, around 15% of world trade with an estimated value of more than $1 trillion are transacted through the use of letters of credit.[7]

As described earlier in the letter of credit framework, a correspondent bank can be:

- An advising bank
- A confirming bank (by adding confirmation)
- A discounting bank (by paying the value of the L/C on a no recourse basis)
- A refinancing bank by allowing a longer period of payment from the issuing bank

Accordingly trade finance services offered by a correspondent bank can further be divided into more detailed categories such as:

- L/C confirmation (open): This is the most favourable type of credit to the exporter. Provided the L/C terms are met, the payment is guaranteed with the knowledge of the issuing bank by the confirming bank irrespective of the position of the issuing bank.
- L/C confirmation (open + refinance within L/C): On top of the confirmation of the L/C, to refinance within this L/C means that the confirming bank is asked to make finance available to the issuing bank and/or the applicant in relation to a letter of credit. The confirming bank thus allows some extended period for payment upon agreed interest charges. This kind of facility is set up when the applicant needs a deferred payment but the beneficiary cannot/does not want to offer it. The applicant and the beneficiary negotiate and settle the commercial contract which states that the exporter will be paid through an L/C. The L/C will be issued and payable at sight, but clearly indicates that sight payment has to be made to the exporter on the basis of bank-to-bank finance. In principle, the issuing bank has pre-contacted the confirming bank to negotiate documents at sight but offers a bank-to-bank refinancing.
- Discount of banker's acceptance: When a draft is accepted by a bank, it means the local bank of the corporate issuing the draft is co-accepting the risk. In case the issuer does not pay, the bank that accepted the draft can be called on to get the payment. The bill of exchange is drawn on a bank in the country of the beneficiary and it must be accepted before the time of discounting. After discounting from a correspondent bank, the beneficiary receives discount proceeds in full settlement.
- Discount of trade draft: Purchase of a trade draft can be with a bank aval. If a bank avalizes the trade draft, the avalizing bank has primary liability for payment at maturity although the bank is not a party prior to avalization. A correspondent can discount the trade draft with another bank's aval or avalize the draft themselves.

---

[7] See Donald Smith, 'ISBP: a winning formula?' *Trade & Forfaiting Review*, November 2002.

- Bank guarantee (trade related): A bank can guarantee a bill of exchange by issuing a payment guarantee to a trade debt. It is also called availizing the bill of exchange.
- Pre-finance of commodity export (delivery risk): This is to enable the beneficiary to obtain pre-shipment advances from a correspondent which acts as an advising and/or confirming bank, at the expenses of the beneficiary but under the responsibility of the issuing bank. It is for the applicant (buyer) to decide if he will authorize the issuing bank to allow this facility. The financing bank is not to police the loan.
- Import financing including stock finance: A bank can also finance imported stock to the buyer to give him time for further selling in the market.
- Trade finance advances (TFA commerce): Trade finance advances are short-term advances granted to selected banks especially those in emerging market countries. Such advances are limited to finance trade flows (e.g. agricultural business in Latin America).

  A point of notice is that the correspondent bank chosen should confirm that the local banking regulator authorizes such facilities as 'commercial debt' so that they will be qualified as such in case of debt rescheduling. This may give priority for payment in crisis.

  TFAs represent an interesting means to finance commercial trade. As a consequence, the relevant local authorities set up a general legal and control framework to protect and monitor such facilities. Under such facilities, either export credit lines or import credit lines received from foreign banks and granted to local customers will be under supervision as well.
- L/C refinancing (outside L/C): The advising/confirming bank is sometimes asked to make finance available to the issuing bank and/or the applicant in relation to an L/C. As a reimbursement and negotiation bank, the credit bank will claim the money at sight from the correspondent bank which offers to refinance. The issuing bank will be informed about the detailed amount to be received at the final date. Sometimes such an arrangement may be made without the beneficiary being aware as he will receive a sight payment L/C. This interbank financing or refinance between banks is very often used by those emerging market banks to which money market limits are not available or are available but insufficient.
- Forfaiting: *Forfaiting* was invented as a means whereby exporters could offer credit to their importers and then sell the debt receivables to a bank on nonrecourse terms. This is still a way for exporters to get cash immediately from a bank to which the exporters transfer the debt asset on a discounted and nonrecourse basis. In this way the payment risk is mitigated.

  Such deals can be either one-off or on an ongoing basis. The importer accepts the trade draft or signs promissory notes, which are guaranteed or avalized by a bank in the importer's country. The exporter then endorses the drafts or notes and hands them over to the discounting bank, which negotiates them without recourse to the exporter. The bank may either hold onto them until maturity or sell it further in the secondary markets.
- Factoring: *Factoring* is the assignment by a supplier and its customers (debtors) to a factor, in which the factor is to perform at least two of the following functions:

  1. Finance for the supplier including loans and advance payments.
  2. Maintenance of accounts (ledgers) relating to the receivables.
  3. Collection of receivables.
  4. Protection against default in payment by debtor.

Factoring deals with mainly non-negotiable instruments like bank receivables, whereas forfaiting mainly deals with negotiable instruments like bills of exchange, promissory notes and letters of credit.

- Export credit (with ECA plain vanilla or nonplain vanilla): To encourage exporters many countries have their export promotion agencies such as an import/export bank or export credit guarantee agencies. These agencies often offer an export guarantee to secure the payment from the buyers to facilitate the export. They may also offer an interest subsidiary for financing the bridge period of the export. This is a product offered by correspondent banking together with these agencies. The purpose is to promote the export of the country.
- Co-financing (commercial): To some countries, regional development banks may offer export insurance and other ways of financing with local banks. To cooperate with such regional banks a correspondent banking department provides information/access to such facilities from these development banks. This will be further discussed in country and bank risk solutions.
- Structure import/export finance, etc.: This refers to exports/imports to some emerging markets experiencing difficulty in paying in foreign currencies. Deals are structured and often import needs are continued with export capacities. A relevant case will be discussed in Part III.

In institutional banking, a well-known fact is that there are a good deal of L/C transactions where the ordering party (applicant) already indicates the issuing bank ('directly allocated business') and where under normal circumstances it is very difficult to change the bank. This does not mean that institutional banking is powerless, because the L/C flow will give the opportunity to make a proper follow-up ensuring that the next transaction may 'come your way'. Approaching applicants directly if allowed, or indirectly via the beneficiary, is an effective way to secure this part of business.

In trade finance, reciprocity is not yet fully developed and will be difficult to fully develop. In assessing profitability of a relationship, the mutual business made in the trade finance area depends more upon credit, pricing and service quality issues especially with banks from emerging markets.

Another arguable point in trade finance is that a bank should use its own branches more than correspondents, if and when possible.

Sometimes this argument does not work or is only wishful thinking, because usually a bank will not have an extensive network in another country. Furthermore bank branches in foreign countries are usually located in large cities. To deliver L/Cs to small cities or to remote areas of the country will not be that easy. The service quality is thus not comparable to that of a correspondent. Moreover, the applicant usually will nominate the bank they want to advise their L/C. This is one of the reasons why institutional banking is still a good business.

7.3 FINANCIAL MARKET AND/OR INVESTMENT BANK PRODUCTS

Interbank deals for financial markets are part of the aims of institutional banking. Financial market products cover the markets of foreign exchange, money markets, bonds, and equities and in some banks even commodities.

Products include foreign exchange deals, *fixed income products*, and products linked to stocks and bonds. It is noticed that financial market products such as straightforward money market transaction, repos, currency swaps, futures, options and other derivatives are either for risk management purposes (to change the risk portfolio) or for earning purposes (to generate income).

If we look into the product details for financial markets, we can find the following:

- Foreign exchange products
- Spot and forwards
- FX options/exotic options: binary (one touch, no touch and double no touch, etc.)
- Barrier (knock out, knock in, reverse knock in), average rate, etc.
- Deposits and straight loans
- Structured deposits
- Call accounts
- CP (commercial papers)/CD (certificate of deposits)
- Repo, cross-currency repo and tri-party repo
- T-bills (Treasury bills)
- Asset swaps
- FRNs (floating rate notes)

In the field of short-term derivatives, there are:

- Future rate agreements
- Interest rate options
- Interest rate swaps
- Bond options
- Credit derivatives, etc.

Some of these products, such as money market and foreign exchange deals, seem quite straightforward.

Indeed money market deals are simple interbank borrowing and lending, usually for liquidity purposes as the borrowing/lending is for short tenor. A money market deal is offered more on a reciprocity basis or purely as a relationship product because earnings on the money market are limited whereas the credit risk is highest (name lending, without any priority for protection). If the counterparty defaults, it is difficult to recover by any means. However, money market deals are unavoidable if the counterparty is active as a business partner and does other businesses such as foreign exchange business.

Generally speaking, these products are offered in different ways to banks in emerging markets from those in developed countries. The ways these products are offered depend on the risk and bank's attitude towards the risk. For example, *money market line* is a product to be offered to good names. Such a name-lending product is a package service offered to institutional clients. It is not unusual that a correspondent requests more money market limits which is not acceptable to the credit of the bank, whereas in other cases some big money market lines are available but the countryparty is cash rich.

Foreign exchange business is usually a must for remittance transactions. It is hard to imagine not to have a foreign exchange and money market relationship because a counterparty is actively using your bank as a major correspondent. Regularly one finds that the supply of money market and foreign exchange facilities is seen as the be-all and end-all. It is surely more mutually valuable to consider whether assistance can be obtained/provided. Products other than money market lines are offered to facilitate the needs of a correspondent.

- Repurchase agreement: *Repurchase agreement*, or 'repo' as it is called by dealers, is also an interbank product. A repurchase agreement (repo) is a sale of assets and a simultaneous agreement to repurchase those assets at a future date for the original value plus a return on the use of cash.

  Repos are short-term 'sales' of securities, with an agreed 'repurchase', providing the banks with temporary borrowings secured against the securities. The seller 'borrows' the value of the securities under the repurchase agreement and repays the funds a few days or weeks later by repurchasing the securities.

  All repos are driven by either the need to lend or borrow cash when money market is in short supply, or the need to borrow a specific security.

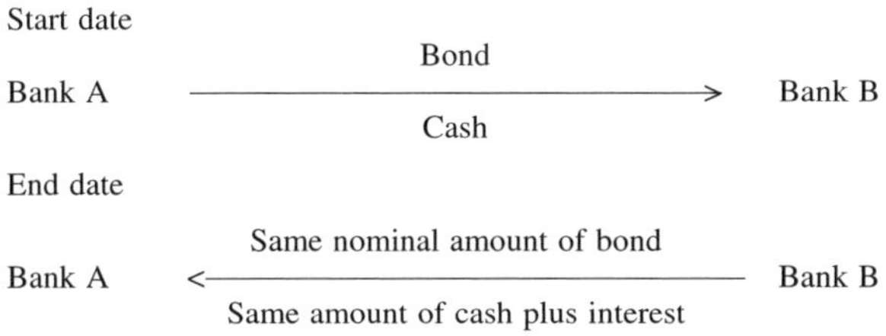

Figure 7.2 Flow of a REPO

- Interest rate swap (IRS): *Interest rate swap* is a derivative product. Under such an arrangement, the buyer acquires the payment obligation over a period of time and at an agreed fixed interest rate over a determined frequency of payments. This kind of arrangement is valid during operation of the principal, which alone serves as reference and cannot be changed. In return for this, the buyer will receive from the IRS seller a floating interest rate linked to a money market index over a period of time and at an agreed frequency of payments. At the point of agreement, the current value of all cash flows of the fixed branch is the same as the value corresponding to the estimated variable, starting from implicit rates. Consequently, the value of the IRS sold will be the difference between the current value of the future flows of the fixed branch and the current value of the future flows of the floating branch, which have been estimated from the implicit rates' starting point. When an IRS agreement is reached, this difference is equal to zero.

  Very often a correspondent may need a counterparty to sell this IRS agreement, either for the bank's own position or on behalf of the bank's clients. Of course due to bank risk and country risk restrictions, the credit committee in the bank may have limit on the tenor for the lifetime of IRS to limit the counterparty risk.
- Nondeliverable forward (NDF): As many emerging market countries have nonfreely convertible currencies, nondeliverable forward becomes a product especially for countries with those nonconvertible currencies or highly restricted currencies.

  The basic concept here involves a set of derivatives which cover notional currency transactions linked to foreign exchange forward swaps, cross currency swaps and coupon swaps. The typical arrangement for NDF is that these are contracts that involve no exchange of principal. The contract usually is fixed at a predetermined price. The most common settlement currency is US dollar. For the eastern European emerging markets, euro is sometimes used. The spot exchange rate is taken from an agreed source, at an agreed time and on an agreed future date.

The notional principal: (NP) USD 15 000 000
Trade date: 16 September 2005
Start date: 18 September 2005
Maturity: March 2006
Floating rate payer: xxx bank
Floating rate payment dates:
Floating rate: 6 month US$ libor
Day count basis: 360 semi-annual
Fixed rate payer: yyy bank
Fixed rate payment dates:
Day count basis: 360 semi-annual
Initial principal exchange: None
Final principal exchange: Party A to pay Party B an additional USD amount subject to the payoff formula:

$NP^*(1 - FXt/FXf)$
Where:
$NP =$ notional principal
FXt initial USD/euro cross rate is 1.244
$FXt =$ final UD/euro rate determined two business days prior to maturity date using Reuters pages
If the above payoff is positive Party A will pay to Party B such a specified amount at maturity
If the above payoff is negative Party B will pay to Party A such a specified amount at maturity
If the above payoff is zero no further exchange of cash flows will take place
Cancellation provision: not applicable

Figure 7.3 Sample of interest rate swap arrangement

7.4 OTHER PRODUCTS

Traditionally deposit taking and lending used to be major banking business. Nowadays all banks world wide do a lot more than the deposit taking and lending. They give financial advice, exchange foreign currency, deal insecurities and derivatives and manage investments on behalf of their clients. Consequently there are many other products marketed among institutional clients. We hereby discuss some of them, all of which need intensive interbank networking.

7.4.1 Custodian

Clients of the bank invest in stocks in the hope of achieving higher returns in the future. Before the date of actual selling, the stocks must be held in good hands to ensure proper settlement for the selling. This gives opportunity for custodian service which is an integral component of all active securities markets, both domestic and international.

A well-accepted custodian must settle the trading in securities promptly and without mistake. The settlement should also be correctly registered. During the period of investment, a custodian bank must also properly and correctly collect the payments of dividends for the investors.

A good custodian bank is usually the one with international reputation and extensive international network with investment bankers. To provide overall service on this needs good custodial service support and a good IT facility. Very often tax expertise will be needed as well for tax planning. This product will generate decent fee income for the bank and is therefore on the list of correspondent banking for most big banks that compete with each other.

A global custodian provides clients with multi-currency custody, settlement and reposting services. A custodian is also linked with *securities lending* business.

Securities lending transactions have grown substantially in recent years and their overall significance within the financial system has increased notably in the last decade. Securities lending facilitates investment and trading strategies that would not be possible without a liquid supply of securities available for borrowing, including 'fundamental short' strategies as well as market-neutral arbitrage strategy such as cash vs futures arbitrage, convertible bond arbitrage,[8] or dividend-related arbitrage.

A total package of custodian services includes:

- The safekeeping of securities
- The maintenance of a multi-currency securities account
- The settlement of securities trading
- The collection of interest, dividends and principals due for redemption on a due date
- The reporting of transactions completed and periodical delivery of hard copy statements
- Assistance with tax claims
- Handling and settlement of derivatives
- Cash project and cash management

7.4.2 Syndication

Syndication is another product which is intended for institutional clients. A syndicated loan is a substantial loan in which a group of banks work together to provide funds for one borrower.

Syndication is an important tool to enhance return on equity on the bank's portfolio as some of the existing exposure will be out of the book. It will also stimulate the bank's deal flow – to get rid of part of the existing exposure on the one hand and/or get involved in new deals from other financial institutions on the other.

In a broad sense, a syndication department's activities include:

- Sale of underwritten transactions to other financial institutions.
- Advice on structure, pricing, etc.
- Sale of loans from the existing loan portfolio to other financial institutions.

[8] Corporations issue convertible bonds with the option that the bonds can be converted into a predetermined number of shares at the discretion of the bondholder. An arbitrage opportunity occurs when there is a discrepancy in the price of the equity security and its convertible component. If the stock price increases up to the point at which the options are 'in the money' and the market value of the bond is lower than the current value of shares for which the bond can be exchanged, a positive spread can be obtained by buying the bond and converting it immediately. The bondholder can borrow and sell the securities to protect against a decline in stock prices.

As an increasingly important source of corporate finance, syndicated lending has reached over $1 trillion annually in the United States.[9]

There are many reasons for syndicated loans. For credit reasons, some banks may need other institutional clients' support to take over part of the existing portfolio. The credit department in the bank may put a limit on lending to restrict their risk exposure. In order to serve the clients – especially those important ones – banks may have to 'sell out' the risk portfolio. This happens quite often in big deals (shipping, aviation, energy, etc.) and/or for long-term commitment of projects.

The motivation for the inviting bank of syndication can also be commercial. By inviting other banks to participate in the deal gives opportunities to other banks, which may, at a later stage, return the favour when they have such needs.

The earnings from the syndication consist of two parts: the risk premium of the borrower under exposure and the arrangement/management fee. In practice this fee varies from party to party depending on the amount taken. A bank can choose a position as manager/senior manager/arranger/co-arranger depending on the specific responsibility and amount they take in the deal.

Procedure of Syndication

A typical syndication deal will have at least some of the following procedures:

- Advice on pricing/structure and sale possibilities
- Draft of proposal
- Internal credit approval for the potential own risk part
- Preparation of memorandum/package and despatch of invitations, answer questions banks may have
- Determine syndication strategy and arrange bankers' meetings
- Prepare list to banks and invitations to arrange banker meetings
- Handle confirmation and commitment and arrange closing ceremony
- Tombstone: announcement of the deal

Forms of Syndication

- Primary syndication: one or more trenches:
  arranger > participant
  arranger/underwriter > participant
- Secondary syndication:
  Transactions are sold after primary syndication into the 'open' market in London via LMA or on an 'undisclosed' basis (silent participation).

  Transactions often are offered with a considerable discount, expressed in % of the original amount ('par').

  US$500m Three-year revolving loan Noble Group

  6 September 2005 – *basis point* – Allocations have been finalised for the US$500m three-year revolving credit for Noble Group Ltd, sources said.

[9] Amir Sufi of Massachusetts Institute of Technology in his research paper: 'Information asymmetry and financing arrangement, evidence from syndicated loans', April 2005.

The deal was increased to US$500m from the original US$400m target.

Mandated lead arrangers ABN AMRO Bank, Banc of America Securities Asia, Fortis Bank, SG and Standard Chartered Bank HK held a combined total of US$155m to give a sell down of 69% on the increased size.

Eight banks joined at the sub-underwriting stage and were given the coordinating arranger title. Twenty-one more banks joined in general syndication.

Allocations are:

	US$ millions
Mandated lead arrangers	
ABN AMRO Bank	31
Banc of America Securities Asia	31
Fortis Bank	31
SG	31
Standard Chartered Bank HK	31
Coordinating arrangers	
Bank of Communications Hong Kong	23
Commerz East Asia	23
Commonwealth Bank of Australia	23
ING Bank	23
Maybank	23
Mizuho Corporate Bank	23
Royal Bank of Scotland	23
Wachovia Bank	20
Arrangers	
Lloyds TSB Bank	18
Australia & New Zealand	
Banking Group Hong Kong	12
Credit Agricole Suisse	12
Credit Suisse	12
OCBC Bank	12
Sumitomo Trust & Banking Singapore	12
UFJ Bank Hong Kong	12
Lead managers	
Banca di Roma Hong Kong	8
Bank of Taiwan Singapore	8
ICBC Asia	8
KBC Bank	8
Rabobank International Hong Kong	8
Managers	
Banca Intesa Hong Kong	4
Bank of East Asia Singapore	4
BBVA Hong Kong	4
Chang Hwa Commercial Bank Singapore	4
First Commercial Bank Singapore	4
HSH Nordbank Singapore	4
Natexis Banques Populaires Singapore	4
Cathay United Bank Hong Kong	3
Central Trust of China	
Offshore banking unit	3

Figure 7.4 Syndication loans statement[10]
Source: Reuters.

[10] Thanks to Reuters for permission to use this information.

7.4.3 Asset Management

Asset management refers to management of funds. Banks will structure funds for different themes and different risk return structures. The purpose of such asset management is to manage funds by professionals or experienced fund managers.

By using banks' knowledge, experience and research ability, this asset management is supposed to increase revenues in due course.

The final performance target is linked to the risk budget agreed with the client. Performance target implies risk targeting. Fund managers manage the risk budget actively. Both the level of risk and its allocation evolve over the time. They depend on the strength of the views and fund mangers and the trade-off between estimated return and the risk. Diversification is always emphasized in asset management.

Asset management as a product needs a distribution network. Hereby institutional banking as a relationship centre should help promote this kind of product. It is, however, not strange that the asset management business line has its own sales team and motivation system.

7.4.4 Bancassurance

Bancassurance is another example of a cross-relationship product used to promote business expansion cooperation among financial institutions.

A typical bancassurance arrangement involves a relatively vague *master agreement* between the insurer and the bank's head office, which envisages cooperation in various areas. Specific agency agreements still have to be negotiated at branch level because of the high degree of autonomy of bank branches.

For insurance companies, this is a cost-effective way to build distribution capacity, especially for new market entrants. It will also facilitate the penetration of new market segments. Insurance companies will benefit from the reliability of banks to sell its products.

For banks, this bancassurance will enable them to use current infrastructure to generate fee income. This stable stream can replace loss of income due to a narrowing interest margin. There is also a perceived need to move to a one-stop financial platform – banks are thus becoming a multiple products offering centre for the sake of convenience of their clients.

By doing this, it will help to achieve the target of increased retention of customers. This cross selling of insurance products through banking channels is looked at as a fee income product.

Banassurance has tremendous potential as it gives banks opportunities to better serve their clients and offer products that they may not have offered in the past – the bank can reach the customer in a direct or indirect way and build a strong relationship.

Bancassurance usually needs a strong retail bank network since it requires large and significant IT investment. It is profitable as indicated by a recent financial analysis of the banking and insurance sector – financial institutions offering both banking and insurance products outperform those that only offer one or the other by 20%. This clearly demonstrates the synergetic effect of offering both product lines.

Institutional banking can play a role for this kind of cooperation among banks by locating, evaluating, negotiating with such a potential partner and facilitating this relationship.

SUMMARY

The products of institutional banking can be divided into account services, trade finance, financial markets products and other products.

Account services are the basic services for institutional banking because a tested key arrangement and an account opened are often considered as 'correspondent relations'. Account services are linked to a banks' payment infrastructure and cash management capacity. Nowadays the 'know your client' policy requires that each bank perform due diligence for offering account services. Jurisdiction, competence of regulatory authority, shareholder structure, business scope, customer base, etc. should be checked and reviewed before an account relationship starts.

Trade finance is the 'bread and butter' business and is especially important to emerging markets. Payment is typically made by irrevocable letter of credit. Here more detailed ways of financing are involved such as confirming the L/C, discounting the L/C, forfaiting, factoring, etc.

Financial market products are linked to foreign exchange deals, purchase and sale of bonds, stocks or derivative products for risk and earning purposes. Special products linked to emerging markets are IRS, NDF, repos, etc.

Other products for institutional banking include syndication, asset management, custody and bancassurance. All these activities need interbank relationship and networking.

8 The Marketing Function of Institutional Banking

Effective marketing for institutional banking products entails more than just selling skills. It requires detailed knowledge of the market including cultural and historical background, the individual bank's strategy, management background, specific market position, etc. It also involves an understanding of the strategy and credit guideline in your own bank, in order to avoid the awkward situation where you are selling some products that your credit people may not approve to that particular correspondent.

It is well understood that different banks have different ways of marketing and even in the same bank the marketing process may change over time. The following is only a practical summary for reference.

8.1 MARKETING STRATEGY: MARKET SEGMENTATION

Correspondent banks can be your competitors as well as your partners. As such, a bank needs to have a clear strategy towards the services offered or risks assumed towards its institutional clients, since there could be corporate or retail clients inside the bank who are more important than your external institutional clients. Improper marketing for institutional banking is simply increasing the competition if the counterparty is a competitor rather than a partner.

A point emphasized before is that a more innovative approach may be to consider one's correspondent bank as a corporate with conventional needs in relation to areas such as funding, asset management and interest rate exposure which should be assessed as targets for products – without trespassing on their proprietary client base. That is why *correspondent banking* is more often called *institutional banking*. To target a multitude of potential institutional clients will nevertheless increase your costs. Segmentation of the market allows the banks to know to whom they should do their marketing. This will enable them to understand the potential better. Marketing strategy thus starts with the segmentation of your institutional clients.

In fact you may well segment your institutional relationships as one of the following:

- General correspondent: This refers to an institutional client with which a relationship is necessary, such as relationship with large top banks in other countries. The chance to use their service is large if ever your bank is interested in that particular country.

  It can also be a passive relationship that a foreign bank requested such a relationship using their own initiative. Many small and new banks always intend to establish a correspondent account for their international expansion. The products you can sell to these banks may well be limited by your credit guideline towards them.

A general relationship can also be with the central bank, stock brokers, security house, etc. Sometimes you may have a one-off deal with them. An institutional relationship usually starts with a general relationship, and then moves on to a close relationship.

- Close correspondent: This refers to an institutional client with which you have formed a long relationship and to which you have special and important needs, including those banks providing money market limits, clearing/account service, etc. to your bank. The relationship is thus active. Such a close relationship is based on mutual understanding and a satisfactory past record.
- Loyalty programme partners: This refers to an institutional client who is an active user of many of your products and services. Your strategy towards this client is to keep them for the future. You have to motivate them by offering special treatment (price, quality, rebate, etc.). This institutional client is supposed to provide more than average earnings and you have to put this client on to your watch list.
- Strategic alliance: This refers to an institutional client who is of strategic importance to you, such as a joint venture partner, branch network provider in the countries where you have no network, etc. It can also be a bank of your own group. Under these circumstances, relationship is very often one of commitment and you have to go 'the extra mile' to provide your service and support.

  Although the relationship is on a commitment basis, it is nowadays common that this commitment is also on a basis of mutual benefits.

Contrary to the belief that big banks are always your close partners, top banks are not necessarily always your marketing targets. They are too big and are very often approached by many foreign correspondents. It is difficult for them to pay attention to smaller players. If your bank is also a top player in your own country, you may indeed end up with communication in the global market with top banks in other countries. Hence market strategy depends on your own position in your home market and your needs towards foreign correspondents.

Marketing strategy also depends on the *life cycle* of a bank. A bank usually experiences development stages: establishment, consolidation, expansion and maturity/stability. In different stages the needs of a bank may differ greatly. The relationship with your correspondent changes over time as well. A general relationship may evolve into a strategic alliance relationship or the other way round.

Last but not the least, nowadays big banks are divided into different business lines which themselves function like independent banks. These business departments have their own preferred list of correspondents for their own marketing targets. Inside a bank the institutional banking department very often is only put under one business unit. This may sometimes result in uncoordinated marketing efforts or even duplication of efforts – an issue to be addressed for many banks in their marketing efforts.

8.2 MARKETING APPROACHES

A correspondent relationship relies on informal agreements secured by long-standing personal and institutional friendship. This kind of relationship will be developed by your marketing efforts. Different approaches are used for developing such a relationship.

8.2.1 Correspondence

It is neither necessary nor possible to visit each and every institutional client. To communicate with your prospects in writing, that is marketing by correspondence including e-mail, is therefore very common for institutional banking.

To market your bank is first to market yourself. Before you submit a business proposal to the potential institutional client, you have to introduce and sell yourself. If you are not qualified for this first step, you will never gain entrance to the prospect and therefore there will be no opportunity even to present a proposal.

In communicating with your correspondents for marketing purposes, it happens quite often (too often!) that a bank is too interested in what they are able to offer rather than what your institutional client really needs. To avoid this, a couple of questions should be raised before you start your correspondence:

- Is there any added value for you to your potential institutional client?
- Will he allow you to deliver the added value?
- Does he need this added value at this moment?
- How can you give confidence that you will deliver?

In fact, marketing to your institutional client is like marketing a car. A good car salesperson should emphasize the benefits to you of buying that car, rather than to promote the excellent characteristics of the car. So, you as a car salesperson have to talk about low energy consumption, high reliability compared with peers, better safety facilities, etc., instead of a long history of the car company, large network of branches, etc. A simple principle therefore is to say what they want to hear instead of insisting on what you want to say.

Around 2001 when the euro was to be issued, many European banks sent marketing letters to their correspondents and their account service sales people went all over the world trying to attract euro account opening. These banks did not realize that many countries outside Europe were/are using the dollar as a major currency. As a result of their marketing bombing, they did have some euro accounts opened. But many of them turned out to be idle or only occasionally used. This resulted in extra labour costs for maintenance and administrative inconvenience. Some banks did better in institutional banking. They succeeded in offering multi-currency (dollar/euro) accounts in Asia and the Middle East, where the dollar was/is still widely used. The correspondence to a specific client should therefore be tailor-made. One size does not fit all.

8.2.2 Regular Visit to Correspondent Banks

It's difficult to know an institution without meeting them face-to-face especially for a relationship which you define as a 'close' one. This is particularly important in Asian countries where no-seeing is no-believing. A regular visit to your institutional clients is therefore part of the task of the institutional banking department.

Regular visits are necessary as they will give you chance to check the financial information not available in the annual report. They will update your personal contact with the relevant personnel of your counterparty and give you a first-hand impression of the bank and the country. Some correspondent bankers even value the 'gossip' as a source of information, especially for the background of management, shareholder relationship, personality of some top management members, etc. These invisible things are essential for your marketing efforts but usually not available in the annual report. Of greatest importance is information on the management – who they are and what their backgrounds are. The competitive conditions they have to face and plans for future development can also be important as they are not supposed to be mentioned in the report. A tour round the premises can add value as well, so that outward impressions can be formed and compared with what you had in your mind before your visit.

A point often ignored is that the purpose of a proposed meeting is two-way traffic. While you are assessing your prospect, finding out what the prospect's needs are and whether you can help, the counterparty is also assessing you to determine whether you have the experiences and resources to help with problems.

The result or the quality of your visit is therefore very much linked to your preparation for the visit. To get the most out of a visit to an institutional client, you had better arrange and prepare it as early as possible.

The preparation for a bank visit usually includes:

- Reading background materials: Many of the background materials may provide you with information. Typically, an annual report and website of the relevant bank plus the report from professional rating agencies are good material to read. The *Financial Times* and the *Economist*, etc. also offer a great deal of analysed and detailed information for the country and perhaps for the bank you intend to visit. Very often there is too much available but you have to focus. For banks a Fitch IBCA report gives a summary of banks and their strengths and weaknesses.
- Arranging meetings: Some institutional bankers insist on meeting senior management of counterparties. The argument is that the level to be met will indicate how serious the counterparty is. But from time to time it has been noticed that for concrete deals you have to have face-to-face discussion with the relevant people. If your visit is for the purpose of information only, then senior staff may give you the strategic views and also the views from the management. In many banks, the institutional banking department is under either trade finance or the treasury division. You have to set your requested topics to them beforehand so that the counterparty will have a clear idea whom you really intend to meet and why.
- Briefed by colleagues before the visit: To talk to the colleagues with experience/exposure of both the country and the bank is a useful practice for an effective bank visit. Colleagues in the representative office are well informed of recent developments there. As always, each colleague you talk to may have his/her own opinion, which could be biased. Sometimes to be briefed by a well informed correspondent can be a good preparation because they have very often the same mission as you.
- Being active when you are there: Try to get a general feeling for the country when you are there. Read the materials available locally about the history, take in the stories in the local newspaper or simply look around at random. Of course, more intimate conversation and contact will give information on personal backgrounds including hobbies, education, even family situations, etc. – all this is only possible from such visits.

  To gauge day-to-day feelings of common people in the country is also possible. A taxi driver, for example, is the best 'country risk analyst'. I remember once I had a taxi driver in South Korea who used to be a very important person in a Korean bank. He gave me very good insights into the bank. He looked at the bank and the banking system in the country, using a so-called 'third eye' – a critical eye or an eye that will see more colours.

8.2.3 Senior Level Meetings

A senior level meeting is often seen as the key to fundamental success, especially when fundamental issues are pending for a decision. Senior level meetings are not held everyday. But these meetings may indeed promote mutual understanding, especially on the strategy side. Banks may invite correspondents for such a senior level visit. Many banks also have their management 'roadshow' worldwide.

IMF and regional development bank meetings (EBRD, ADB, etc.) can provide opportunities to realize such kinds of senior level meetings where important principles and plans (such as merger and acquisition, equity participation, etc.) can be discussed.

However, a senior level meeting cannot replace contact at an operational level. Problems that cannot be solved or a business development that is blocked is usually because one operational department is not willing to cooperate. Further, senior level meetings can usually be secured if a good long-term relationship already exists at an operational level.

Long-term relationships are built on trust and demonstrated performance. Such relationships require open lines of communication between multiple layers of the buying and selling organizations. Long-term relationships also require delivering on promise.

8.2.4 Work-together on Joint Projects

A good correspondent relationship can be reinforced by joint efforts on some projects, such as organizing seminars, share common topics (risk management in emerging markets, etc.), translating interesting books, jointly sponsoring social events, etc. By doing the project together, mutual understanding and trust can be established. The following is a preface written for the joint translation of a book:

> Xxx bank enjoys a long history of serving clients with business interests in China, having established its first office 100 years ago under the name of General Bank. The practice was re-established after the 1990s with offices in Shanghai, Guangzhou and Beijing.
>
> With 100 years of history of business in China, xxx bank is confident that the Chinese market will be an ever-lasting interesting theme for all businesses including finance services. Today, xxx Group, as a financial institution, is active in China for banking, asset management and insurance.
>
> xxx Group fully appreciates the privilege of having witnessed developments in China that are inconceivable at its beginning. In the meantime, xxx bank has also developed its in-depth knowledge of the market – plus the extensive, first-hand experience acquired in helping our European and Chinese clients.
>
> I personally have had the pleasure of visiting yyy bank in 2002 and now have the pleasure of cooperating in the translation of Ingo Walter's book *Global Banking*. Comprehensive discussion by Professor Ingo Walter and his colleague on global banking provides an excellent understanding of banking business. Our joint efforts with yyy bank on translation indicate again our interest and commitment to China. Many Chinese bankers will find the book essential reading for everyone interested in banking business.
>
> We are honoured to present the Chinese version of this interesting and valuable book. I would also like to thank all those – both in xxx bank and yyy bank – who have contributed to the translation.

8.3 MARKETING PRINCIPLES

8.3.1 Reciprocity

As business is 'to give and to take', 'reciprocity' as a principle is natural and fundamental for selling and buying institutional banking products.

Nevertheless, reciprocity however, is often used in a very narrow sense or, worse still, it is misused occasionally.

For one thing, it is sometimes very difficult to have a product-to-product and/or benefit-to-benefit match among correspondent banks. During some correspondent banking visits, the counterparty sometimes confronts its visitors with statistics of trade finance volume, indicating that they have channelled such and such volume of L/Cs to the bank, implicitly and explicitly requesing for business in return. In reality, however, we can hardly ignore the fact that a large portion of trade transactions can only be applicant/beneficiary originated – the ordering party (applicant) already indicates the issuing bank with little room for the issuing bank to play. Only a small percentage of L/C volume is at the disposal of the issuing bank. This means even if the issuing bank, out of their own goodwill, issues the L/C to its favoured bank, this favoured bank may end up with only an advising function. The beneficiary may ask the advising bank to channel the L/C to his house bank for negotiation and discounting.

'Reciprocity' in institutional banking may need a broader framework and more flexible arrangement. Very often compensation takes the form of demand of deposit balances – those 'due to' and 'due from' relationships. 'Reciprocity' can also take the form of training and money market (MM) line, especially for some small- or medium-sized banks.

8.3.2 Earnings Motivation: 'Profit Sharing'

To contribute earnings to the bank as a whole is at least part of the mission of institutional banking. As discussed, the institutional banking department intends to generate profits by its relationships with other correspondents. This is achieved by both buying and selling products. Sometimes the earnings from institutional banking will be realized in other departments of the bank and institutional banking has only a 'shadow booking'[1] instead of hard cash. But the earnings can also be 'hard cash' to the bank. For institutional banking, earnings from forfaiting trade receivables, advisory service, etc. are such examples of hard cash income.

Earnings motivation means implicit or explicit 'profit sharing' with your institutional clients. A 'rebate scheme' as an incentive has long been used in institutional banking. The

Dear Mr X

We refer to the pleasant meeting we had in your office a few weeks ago.

One of the very interesting topics we discussed was rebate on L/C business. We would like to concentrate our activities on the confirmation of L/Cs above USD 500 000 counter-value routed to our European branches, for which we are prepared to offer you on a 'case by case basis' part of the confirmation fee.

. . .

Figure 8.1 Rebate scheme

[1] Shadow booking is a banking term to refer to recorded earnings as a measurement of performance. As the name indicates, the recorded profits are only 'shadow' because the real hard cash is somewhere else.

We would like to invite you to pre-contact our Representative Office for each L/C exceeding a counter-value of USD xxx xxx, mentioning the following details:

- Currency and amount of the L/C
- Name of your branch, which will open the L/C
- Name and address of the applicant/importer
- Name and address of the beneficiary/exporter
- Validity of the L/C and payment terms (sight/deferred payment)
- Confirmation requests (without/may add/open)

Upon receipt of this information, our bank will contact the concerned exporter and pre-negotiate a confirmation fee with them. Based on the fee we could get from the exporter, we will offer your good bank part of this fee, after which your concerned branch may open the L/C to our counters with negotiation restricted to our bank's counters.

Once the L/C has been negotiated and repaid, our relevant L/C department will pay the pre-negotiated rebate fee to your bank, upon your special instructions (this fee can either be paid to the branch that opened the L/C or it can also be paid to the head office of your bank).

Please be aware that it is our bank's continuous aim to strengthen our excellent relationship with your bank and place both of us in a 'win–win' situation.

We reserve ourselves the right to stop this rebate scheme offer in future, however, with prior advice to you.

Looking forward to your comments/proposals,
We remain,

With very best regards,

Figure 8.1 (Continued)

idea is to share the profits generated from the flow of business in order to motivate the counterparty. Figure 8.1 is an example of a rebate proposal.

8.3.3 Complementary Relationship

Looking for a complementary relationship is also one of the principles of institutional banking. What kind of complementary relationship you are looking for depends on the characteristics a bank may have vis-à-vis its correspondent. Is the bank an investment bank or a commercial bank? Does the bank have expertise in one geographical area or in others, etc.

Banks may have different strategies, different focuses, different expertise and different coverage of their network. This provides for the need for cooperation with their correspondents.

Experience in institutional banking indicates that the more complementary two banks are the closer a correspondent relationship tends to be. The functions of institutional banking are then similar to those of branches or representative offices from your own bank:

- To find assets to generate a secure return for depositors' funds or proprietary assets.
- To dispose of assets where margins/interest rate exposures/hedges costs may make them no longer interesting.

When one bank considers a complementary relationship, the bank has to consider the layers of other banks. It is very common that banks are divided into 'tiers' according to their size. This concept of bank tier can give an indication of a complementary relationship.

Tier 1 banks are big banks which may offer all kind of services. These banks are sometimes called 'supplier banks'. They are banking supermarkets where most of the things you need will be available. The question is the quality and the price. A relationship with them is very often necessary particularly when your own bank is small.

Small banks look to larger correspondents to purchase a portion of their large loans that exceed the lending limit. In turn they would take participation from the same correspondent.

For big banks, the complementary correspondents can be some specialized banks where niche products are offered and where you may find targets for you're outsourcing efforts.

Although 'bank tier' can be an important indication for complementary relationships, it is too easy to conclude that small banks must look always to large banks. A complementary relationship may exist among the same tier banks due to different comparative advantages a bank may have.

The primary focus of institutional banking should be on operational products and the need both to service and be serviced as regards international payments, clearing, cash management and custody. These prime issues cause us to reflect on the ability of correspondent banks to support each other – with possible realignment of responsibilities being necessary. However, it may be valuable to consider the complementary prospectus for increased cooperation in nonoperational products. Such products may indicate areas of both balancing reciprocity as well as positive expansion of business areas – be it researching primary needs from one's client base, or improving one's technology to meet other correspondent bank's requirements.

Bancassurance is a good example of complementary nature among correspondents. As discussed, bancassurance is the use of a bank's distribution channels to sell insurance products. To the insurance company, to have an extensive network from an institutional client is a most effective way to build distribution capacity, especially for penetrating new market segments. For the banks, such a relationship will enable them to have fee income generated by using current existing infrastructure. Such a new source of income from selling insurance products is a stable stream that may replace loss of income due to a narrowing interest margin.

A complementary relationship will also help to achieve the

- reduction of capital requirement to achieve off-balance sheet treatment of debt raised by selling some of the portfolio which exceeded the existing limit, or room should be made for new, more interesting deals
- reduction of cost of funding by taking MM limit from correspondents
- diversification of funding services by helping its own clients to get access to funds and products not available without a correspondent
- reduction and diversification of the credit risk by syndicating in and out the risk portfolio

Correspondent banks may sometimes have further functions such as assisting other banks where they face restrictions on their operations imposed by the local regulatory authorities. Although there are obvious advantages of using local representatives their offices can support increasing marketing drive both for import and for export. There will also be a request for a proposal in the trade finance area where credit issues, quality of services (benchmarks), conditions, commitments, professionalism, etc. will be compared locally and where decisions on how to channel transactions one way or the other may be affected.

SUMMARY

Market segmentation is the starting point for marketing. Your market strategy depends on your segmentation of the target market. For this purpose, your institutional clients can be segmented into several categories such as: a correspondent for general purpose, a close correspondent, a loyalty programme partner or even a strategic alliance.

Big banks are not necessarily always your close partners as banks have their life cycle during which each bank may change its position vis-à-vis your marketing strategy.

Several approaches are used for the development of business with an institutional client. Correspondence are the major ones via letters or e-mails, spot visits, senior level meetings, working together on projects, etc.

Marketing for institutional clients follows some basic principles. Reciprocity is usually the fundamental one. But reciprocity should not be understood in a narrow sense. Rather, it is a broad framework based on 'give and take'. Creating earnings for your own banks and for the counterparty is naturally another essential point. A complementary relationship – to help each other – is also a principle which will enable the marketing effort to be more effective.

9

The Risk Management Function of Institutional Banking

The marketing function for institutional banking, is well understood. But the risk management function, which is one of the important functions for every bank, is often underestimated or simply ignored. This is because there is a credit department in every bank which is in charge of this function.

The major risk management function for institutional banking discussed here is linked to counterparty risks – the *bank default risk*, which is the credit risk of a bank, together with the default risk of the country where the bank is located. As country risk was covered in length in Part I, the present chapter will focus more on bank risk.

Bank credit risk concerns uncertainty about your correspondent bank's ability to service its debt on all its contractual obligations. The creditworthiness of a bank depends not only on factors such as economic conditions and industry trends, bank's financial strength, market value, equity value, asset value and capital structure, but also on reputation and management skills.

People may wonder, if there is a credit department in every bank, which is directly in charge of bank risk, where is room for institutional banking to function in the field of risk management?

Indeed, institutional banking's role for risk management is more on the advisory side, that is institutional banking is required to give positive/negative advice for the bank limit proposed, subject to the approval of credit. But such a role of risk management for institutional banking should not be underestimated.

A credit department usually works based on credit norms and rules, whereas an institutional banking department is supposed to give more vivid, up-to-date, direct, complementary information on evaluating a bank. Moreover, institutional banking is supposed to give input on the importance of the counterparty. Sometimes there is discrepancy on the evaluation between the institutional banking department and the credit department because institutional banking has more commercial motivation and interest. It can also be the case that information available to the credit is one-sided (only on the 'visible' side).

The added value of institutional banking to risk management therefore is that it offers a quite important source of information which can at least serve the role of cross-checking.

To have a correct and complete evaluation on your counterparty for either commercial or credit motivation will not guarantee the success of institutional banking business, but it will at least increase the chances of getting the foundations right. Thus bank evaluation is the job content of institutional banking.

9.1 BANK RISK EVALUATION

Bank risk analysis is not exclusively for institutional banking. It can be interesting to many parties such as government regulatory agencies, corporate treasurers and institutional investors. But it is important to institutional banking simply because the correspondents are institutional clients of a bank.

If we analyse a bank as a client, the general financial analysis for a corporate will apply. Bank risk analysis also starts with financial statements for a correspondent bank. This consists of balance sheet, income statement and statement of changes in shareholders' equity, cash flow statement and even the notes to the financial statement.

But analysis on banks differs from a traditional corporate analysis in that bank's financial statements, their mission target, social responsibility and impact, their internal structure and operation are different.

When a bank failure occurs, the sum of money in question can be astronomical for depositors and shareholders. In some cases, the contagious effects can be that the entire financial system and the economic stability of the country will be at stake – the repercussions can have knock-on effects throughout a country's banking system and economy as a whole. With the increasing globalization of financial institutions, major bank failures can even have cross-border effects.

On the other hand, the financial information for banks may be easier to access as all banks are requested by their supervisor (central bank) to release their financial information on a compulsory basis. The quality of the information, especially for those listed banks, is in general supposed to be better compared with the information of companies.

9.2 PRIVILEGES FOR BANKS: DEPOSIT INSURANCE

Banks are also different from companies in that they may have some privileges – they may be rescued if the government deems it necessary for the sake of stability of the financial system. They can also get access to the 'discount window' for borrowing money from their central bank when they face temporary cash shortages. The bank's deposits are often insured implicitly or explicitly in a pool arrangement by the government itself, in case the bank goes bust.

Given the fact that banks are usually under the supervision of their regulator – central bank – understanding the regulatory issues in that country is part of the comprehension of the financial health of the bank. For example, if the government of that country has a tight monetary money supply policy and demands for higher reserve requirement, the banking system may be squeezed of their profits, as they have to put more money aside as reserves.

To promote the stability of a banking system as well as to protect small depositors from losses due to bank failures, *deposit insurance* is introduced as one of the mechanisms employed by governments. This is a complementary element of an extensive financial safety net that includes banking law and regulations, central bank as last resort facilities and banking supervision.

The importance of such a deposit insurance system as one of the safety net players is demonstrated by the fact that around 70 countries in the world explicitly operate some type of deposit insurance system, not only in developed countries but also increasingly in the emerging market countries.

The deposit insurance system varies in the extent and the amount of the coverage that it will provide to depositors. In line with their objectives, the deposit insurance arrangements further specify the types of deposits guaranteed by the scheme. Countries aiming to protect their payment systems only limit the deposit insurance guarantee to deposits with commercial banks and to other depository institutions providing payment transactions. Some countries have adopted more than one deposit insurance system, typically one for commercial banks and one for other deposit taking institutions. Countries like Japan, France, Italy, Germany, Iceland and Norway have two systems.

There are different deposit insurance systems in different countries. We have chosen four countries, namely the US, Japan, Turkey and India.

- US: Deposit insurance system was established in 1934. It is under the Federal Reserve System and is officially administered and jointly funded. The government provided initial capital, bore losses of the S&Ls (saving and loans associations). Membership is compulsory for nationally chartered and for almost all state-chartered banks. The coverage limit has been \$100 000 since 1980.
- Japan: There are two separate deposit insurance systems in Japan – one for commercial and shin-kin banks, credit cooperatives and labour and credit associations, and the other for agricultural and fishery cooperatives. The first scheme covers demand and time deposit in domestic currency. As an amendment to the deposit insurance law in February 1998, the government allocated 17 trillion yen to a special account in the deposit insurance corporation. The fund can borrow from the central bank and the government can guarantee the deposit insurance corporation's debt.
- Turkey: Turkey Deposit Insurance Fund was established in 1983. It is officially administered and jointly funded. When the resources are insufficient the Fund may borrow from the central bank. Initially coverage was extended to deposits and Certificates of deposits (CDs) in Turkish currency and foreign currency denominated savings accounts for real persons in Turkey. In the wake of the crisis in 1994 all deposits have been brought under the coverage. The fund thus provides full coverage and for an indefinite period.
- India: The Deposit Insurance System in India was established in 1962 following two bank failures in 1961. Initially the system covered exclusively the commercial banks. In 1968 cooperative banks with a minimum size operating in states were included as well in the system. In 1975 coverage was extended to rural banks. The system is administered officially.

9.3 BANK EVALUATION FRAMEWORK

Deposit insurance, whatever it is, intends to protect the interest of depositors. However, banks with or without deposit insurance may go bankrupt anyway. To evaluate a bank, that is to judge the likelihood of its bankruptcy, is thus crucial in the banking industry.

First, a bank is a company. Like any other companies, a bank has a balance sheet as

$$\text{Assets (uses of funds)} = \text{liabilities} + \text{bank capital (sources of funds)}$$

An important fact about banks is that they operate by taking deposits from individuals, households or companies, on which they pay low interest or none at all. The assets are what a bank owns. Part of the assets a bank owns belongs to the depositors. They are also liabilities of the bank. Banks use the money to make longer-term loans to other individuals, households and companies, charging them higher interest rates.

In essence, banking as a profession is based on trust. But banks sometimes misuse depositors' money or they may make losses on their lending. Depositors do not usually have the inclination, interest, time or the capacity to really evaluate their banks whereas banks should be in a position to evaluate their clients.

When we analyse a bank's creditworthiness, at least the following elements come into the picture:

- The *size* of the bank, which is represented by its assets.
- The *equity* of the bank, which represents the bank's solidness.
- The *profits* of the bank, which represent the performance of the bank.
- *ROA* (ratio return on assets) and
- *ROE* (ratio return on equity ratio) both of which indicate the efficiency of the bank.
- *Net loans/total deposit* indicates the balance of the deposits and lending.
- *Capital adequacy ratio*: The indication of the cushion for absorbing nonperformance loans.
- *Shareholders analysis*: The indication of support in case of difficulties.

In bank risk evaluation, the *triangle relationship among profitability, liquidity and solvency* is important to have a balanced view of the bank. Put simply, the management of a bank is the trade-off among three targets: profitability, liquidity and solvency.

The fundamental objective of bank management is to maximize shareholders' wealth as in the case of all private companies. This will suggest that the bank managers simply invest in assets that generate the highest gross yields and in the meantime keep the costs down. For the purpose of profitability, a bank must either take on increased risk or lower operating costs.

Lower costs may seem a good and safe measure for increasing profits but cost efficiency has its limit and, understandably, a negative impact on a bank's development. You may hardly imagine that a bank can reduce the number of employees continuously with, however, the same earnings.

To take extra risk to boost earnings can also be a problem. Greater risk may increase income for the bank but the bank must prepare for compensating the loss by using its own capital. Greater risk may imply greater volatility of net income and loss in risk taking will erode the capital base and may have an impact on the bank's equity.

On the other hand, due to the nature of their business banks accept a liquidity risk by financing their long-term loans with short-term deposits. Therefore a liquidity crisis can arise when depositors decide to withdraw their deposits, thus triggering a bank run.

Without a proper institutional mechanism to correct this, this behaviour becomes a self-fulfilled prophecy, since it is rather rational under a crisis situation for depositors to liquidate their deposits. From a historical perceptive, liquidity crises were pervasive before central banks were established. Since then, this type of crisis has lost some importance because a central bank is functioning as a *lender of last resort*.

Nevertheless, liquidity problems, if not handled properly, can have an adverse impact on a bank's profitability and solvency. Under a bank-run period, the banks in trouble will have to liquidate their financial assets to make cash available to meet the needs of depositors. To liquidate the financial assets may mean that the *face value* of the financial asset will be

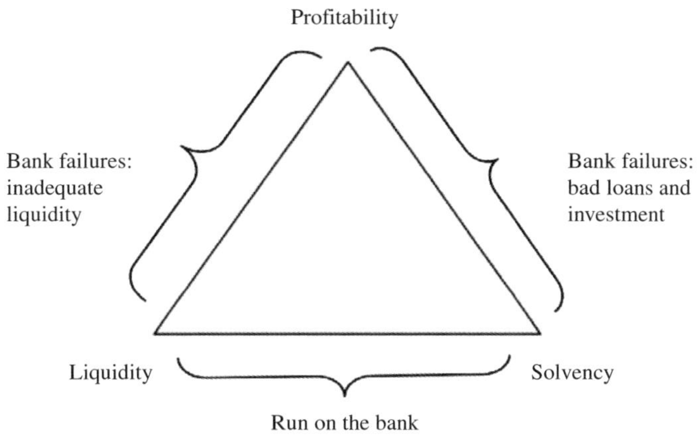

Figure 9.1 Triangle relationship of bank management

greatly reduced. In some extreme circumstances, liquidity problems may lead to the collapse of a bank, which is otherwise solvent. This is because the banks in trouble will have to accept reduction of the value of financial assets owned by the bank. This surely reduces the total wealth of the bank. When and if the reduction of assets value has reached a point where total own capital is eroded, the balance sheet will reach a status where liabilities of the bank are larger than the assets owned by the bank. The bank thus runs into insolvency.

Ratio analysis requires that you look for interactions. One ratio may give a clue that there is a problem and therefore that the clue must be followed by reviewing other ratios. Ratio analysis is a skill that can be acquired only with practice.

There are various models used for bank risk analysis purposes. The *CAMEL* model is often referred to. This rating framework for US banks can be of relevance for our bank risk analysis. The analytical framework, used by federal regulators to rate banks according to the Uniform Financial Institutions Rating systems, encompasses five general categories of performance.

CAMEL here represents:

C = capital adequacy
A = asset quality
M = management quality
E = earnings
L = liquidity

Under such a framework, a composite of one or two indicates a fundamentally sound bank. A rating of 3 indicates that the bank shows some underlying weakness that should be corrected. A rating of 4 or 5 indicates a problem bank with some near-term potential for failure.

Another rating system was introduced and promoted to avoid fraud and failure – the so-called *Crocodile system.*[1] This system intends to avoid potential fraud on the balance

[1] This system is described in detail in Howard Palmer's book *Bank Risk Analysis in Emerging Markets* by Euromoney Publications, 1998.

sheet especially when fraud is deliberate. It is thus more often used for analysing emerging market banks.

The Crocodile system represents some guidelines in identifying clues for fraud and cheating:

C = country of incorporation
R = reputation
O = organization structure
C = currency
O = operational structure
D = due diligence
I = international network of branches/subsidiaries
L = location of branch
E = earnings potential per deal

The Crocodile system places more weight on qualitative indicators such as reputation, organization structure, etc. It also pays attention to the 'twin risk' by giving weight to the country location, as indeed bank risk is often triggered by the economy as a whole.

For emerging market banks, the so-called *BASIC analysis* is worth mentioning.

BASIC analysis focuses on the following aspects:

Bonds = an indication of how strong the market perceives the banks to be
Auditing = central banks have a department to audit banks
Supervision = the competence of the regulator in supervising the banking system
Information = the reliability and transparency of information released
Credit rating = rated regularly by private credit rating agencies

Here corporate governance (auditing and information) and market valuation (bond price as a benchmark) add refreshing and dynamic value to the bank risk analysis. Market reaction to the Treasury bond of that country is an indication of the confidence of an investor towards that country. Confidence as such is not necessarily linked to one indicator. Rather it is a combination of rational analysis and market gossip. To introduce market reaction into risk analysis may have added value to the assessment of the risk. The ups and downs of the T-bond price may give clues to some underlying factors for the risk.

9.4 BANK RATING AND ITS LIMITATIONS

Professional rating companies such as Fiche IBCA, S&P and Moody's evaluate banks and rate them. But rating is not only the profession of rating companies. It is also the internal task of institutional banking in many banks.

For risk management purposes, many banks have their own internal rating and the use of rating is compulsory for bank's credit approval process, setting bank limits, capital adequacy and the calculation of price.

9.4.1 Bank Rating Methodology

Both *quantitative factors* and *qualitative factors* contribute to the rating of a bank. The quantitative drivers consist of the elements for bank risk analysis: profitability (net operating results/total assets, ROE, cost/income ratio), solvency (net worth strength/total assets), assets quality (NPL/gross loans, loan loss reserves/gross loans), size (total assets, liquid assets), etc.

The qualitative drivers consist of management quality, risk management (market risk, credit risk, NPL coverage by provisions) and quality of solvency.

Based on both qualitative and quantitative analysis, we then have the individual rating for a bank.

For overall creditworthiness of a bank, individual rating alone is not enough. This is because the support rating, either from the shareholder or from the monetary authorities of the country, should play a relevant role. Of course, the support effects come from both the ability and the willingness (to support).

On top of these individual bank ratings, we have to take into consideration country risk effect. The basic rule is that no bank may have a better rating than that of the country rating (sovereign rating).

9.4.2 Bank Rating Limitations

Bank rating does provide a systematic indication of bank default risk and therefore helps to assess and manage bank risk. Like country rating, it, however, has its limitations.

For one thing, bank rating is post-evaluation and the rating cannot immediately follow the most recent development. Rating is based on financials which are easily out of date – rating is always after the data are published. The analysis is thus automatically historical.

In fact, available data are a kind of snapshot but the financial situation is dynamic. Any rating model, however perfect it looks, cannot avoid the oversimplification issue. Bank risk is determined by hundreds of variables which are, understandably, not possible to represent in a single model, let alone variables excluded in the rating.

For another, rating can hardly (or perhaps intentionally should not) take into account the cultural and personal effects on the risk management. The rating model is very mechanistic, emphasizing the 'visible' rather than the 'invisible', 'quantitative' and 'qualitative'. It was not surprising that the Asian crisis was not forecasted. Credit rating can therefore only be used to recheck the risk rather than to set strict credit rules based only on credit rating.

Yet limitations on bank rating are not the most embarrassing things. What is embarrassing is that sometimes there is no rating available at all.

We know that bank rating needs to be recorded. In general, small, obscure, local banks are omitted from the list of ratings because ratings are only displayed for financial institutions that satisfy simplified criteria. Many new or small players are out of the scope of the rating agency. This will present difficulties for institutional banking as, without rating, the commercial need for a relationship will be blocked or delayed. It happens sometimes that an analysis is needed but there is lack of a rating record and the rating norms in this specific case are doubted.

There are other reasons for the absence of ratings. Ratings are not available if there are incomplete data; or if the financial institution is too young to have a significant performance record; or for banks that are either privately owned or closed to the public. Many of them are not good enough indeed, but not all of them. Some banks may not be of sufficient standard although some of them may provide important opportunities for business in the future.

In institutional banking, many unrated institutional clients can provide a business horizon simply because they are unknown to many parties. To many banks the unrated correspondents are often an unexplored part of a potential market where you may have your expansion of relationship. In banking practice, credit proposals are often declined because 'no rating is available'.

'No rating no limit' is indeed a common phenomenon in many banks. Sometimes you may ask yourself the question 'why don't they have a rating?' But if you visit these small banks and ask them to be rated, they often reply, very frankly, that since they do not plan to sell international bonds and that they know the rating to them will be poor, rating is of little interest to them.

Evaluating on banks must be possible without an official rating. Here we are faced the information gap to which an institutional banker can play a role. Some efforts in evaluating these banks will indeed be rewarding in the long run.

When we evaluate banks a fact we have to bear in mind is that banks, like companies, also have their life cycle – from small to big and from unimportant to important. If a bank can be contacted and an understanding developed at the early stage, this 'unknown' bank may have a long-term future. These banks are usually very serious since they have few 'friends' at the moment, as many other banks will pursue the same policy – 'no rating, no credit limit, no business'.

Experience indicates clearly that, once such a small bank attains a good rating, many banks will recognize the bank. For the purpose of relationship and risk analysis, we have to initiate practical ways to check the bank risk.

9.4.3 Evaluation of Banks: The Practice

Practical ways to evaluate a bank risk can be many but may include at least some of the following:

- Spot visit: A direct visit to the targeted but unrated correspondent is important as it will give you information including financials, management strategy, market position and market ambition of the bank.

  Apart from desk research of the macro banking environment, a detailed list of questions should be prepared for topics especially regarding the situation of that particular bank. An overview of their correspondents, uniqueness and comparative advantages, directors, supervisory members and even senior managers, shareholder background, motivation and commitment, development objectives and strategies, special risk focus, etc. should all be included.

  One obvious advantage of a direct visit is that you have a first-hand impression of the management. Although the impression could be biased the communication established may help to open future contact for further questions you may have. Moreover, this contact could be crucial in case you have problems to solve with this bank.
- Market checking: A spot visit alone is not enough to have a neutral evaluation because the targeted correspondent will usually present the best part of their bank. Market checking, especially the comments of their competitors, or one or two other relevant parties, is important to have an all-round opinion.

- Peer group comparison: To compare the financials of a small bank with that of a larger one is sometimes confusing and misleading. Peer group analysis compares one bank with other similar banks of the same size, target, etc. Sometimes a peer group analysis is relevant as the position of that correspondent can be clearer if put under the same group of banks in that country.
- Secondary market information: Despite all the above, you may still want to cross-check your evaluation in an objective way. One thing an institutional banker occasionally does is to sell the bank risk in the secondary market. For example, you are asked to confirm the L/C issued by an unrated bank – a bank that you intend to develop a relationship with. What you can do is to sell this deal in the secondary market, that is 'risk participation' – a topic which will be dealt with in Part III. This will put this 'unrated' correspondent's name in the market where many of other banks will show their interest, or at least their appetite towards this specific bank. It is usually called 'appetite checking'. This checking, although time consuming, will give an indication of whether the bank is acceptable or not, and how eager the risk is accepted in the market. Sometimes this process will also help you to learn skills from other banks on how they handle this kind of risk.

9.5 BANK FAILURES AND BANK CRISIS

9.5.1 Bank Crisis: The Concept

Banks may experience difficulties or even crises, or may even go bankrupt. Theoretically banking crises are conceptually defined as a period during which many banks became illiquid (short of immediate cash) or even insolvent (their liabilities are larger than their assets).

According to this definition, banking crises have both *liquidity* and *solvency* dimensions. In our early analysis on triangle relationship of bank management, it was noticed that a liquidity crisis will occur if a bank cannot honour its immediate contractual obligations to its creditors, even though its balance sheet net value is still positive.

A liquidity crisis means that the bank does not have the funds to meet the withdrawal of deposits at a given point of time, although over time it would be able to do so. This is the risk that without incurring unacceptable losses a bank may not be able to raise funds to meet obligations as they fall due. Illiquidity thus means the bank's inability to liquidate assets or to obtain funding to meet its liquidity needs.

Such a problem could be the result of market disruption or a liquidity squeeze whereby the bank may only be able to unwind specific exposures at significantly discounted values.

The essence of banking is the ability to provide payment – whether routinely from management of cash flows and access to money markets or, in times of pressure, from a cushion of liquid assets, or access to central bank facilities when contracts are due. The reduced value by selling at a significant discount will erode the equity base of the bank.

A solvency crisis, on the other hand, refers to a situation where the bank's liabilities exceed its assets in present value and the bank is effectively bankrupt.

A common phenomenon is that the failure of many emerging market banks is due to the fact that they emphasize too rapid loan growth which results in a liquidity problem first followed by insolvency. This is especially true when the banking environment suffers from some downturn, that is the economy is in recession or even crisis.

9.5.2 Bank Crisis: Signs and Signals

In practice, can we trace the warning signs and signals for potential bank failures? If yes, what are they? The following list of signs and signals is helpful for businesses in emerging markets:

- Delayed financials: When a bank's annual report is overdue or interim results are postponed, this may give an indication that the management is having problem with the internal auditors or external accounting firms or the latter has to check the figures further. In developed countries, banks very often pay attention to releasing their figures on time, or will give explanations for the delay.
- Inconsistent accounting practice: There are some 'tricks' that companies and banks, especially those in emerging markets, may play in manipulating their financial figures:

  - Adjusting the profits by means of connected transactions
  - Adjusting the profits by restructuring the assets
  - Adjusting the profits by means of interest investment
  - Adjusting the profits by means of time lag
  - Confusing the revenue expenditures and capital expenditures
  - Adjusting the profits by means of provision
  - Inappropriate pricing of inventories
  - Discretionary deferring of costs

  By using the above methods, a statement with a good appearance but fraudulent content is made public.
- Rapid growth in risk assets: The easiest way for banks to achieve assets growth is to compete for deposits with interest rate. When the interest rate for deposits is high, the bank is pushed for a higher return on lending. This may end up with risk assets. During a visit to an Asian bank, for example, which advertised 'Double your assets in 5 years!', the bank offered around 20% pa interest rate on the average. To maintain this obligation, the bank must keep above 20% lending interest otherwise the it would suffer negative income for deposits. Although the asset base of the bank will expand with deposits attracted such a game is dangerous.
- Deteriorating ratios: If key ratios like ROE, ROA and NPL are deteriorating, it is clear that the bank is in difficulties. To compare those ratios, we have to bear in mind the industry average. If the key ratios for all banks in that country are deteriorating, this also indicates that the environment in general is in difficulty.
- Rumours in money markets: Frequent and desperate borrowing (paying a price higher than the market rate, etc.) in the money market indicates that the bank has at least a liquidity problem or a problem of mismatch of maturity. Rumours in the money market may well indicate such a problem.
- Evidence of asset concentration: Banks, especially those in emerging markets, may tend to run after profitable industries such as IT, real estate, automobiles, etc. It is likely that the banks are attracted by short-term profits and concentrate their lending on one sector or region. This concentration may result in disaster if a bank lacks understanding of its diverse markets and/or does not have quality management for geographic diversification. *Asset concentration* may become a reason for bad loan problems.

A sound lending policy should stimulate portfolio diversification and find balance between maximum yield and minimum risk. In credit risk management, concentration limits usually refer to the maximum exposure to a single client, concerned group, and/or sector of economic activity (e.g. agriculture, textiles, etc.). On the other hand, the imposition of strict geographic limits can also create problems, particularly in the case of regions with narrow economies. In any case, a bank's business market should be clearly delineated and commensurate with its market knowledge and managerial and staff experience.

- Inside lending: In-house lending is more often for banks owned by a group/family. Inside lending is an overextension of credit to directors and large shareholders or to their interests, while compromising sound credit principles under pressure from related parties. Due to the influence of the shareholders or incompetence of a credit committee, lending to related parties becomes not only cheaper but also easier. Proposals linked to related parties will be ignored.
- Share price volatility: The share price of a bank is the market confidence towards the bank. If the share price becomes volatile, the investor's confidence becomes shaky. This will present management pressure to banks. Some banks will simply be unable to cope with the volatility.
- Deteriorating macro environment: A sound macro environment may give ease to banks even if they are having difficulties. When companies are in difficulties, the banks, which lend them money, may experience difficulties as well. Delays of payments, lack of ability to fulfil contractual obligations, etc. will be more likely to occur during recession period.

Bankruptcy for banks is an ongoing topic for academia and the banking community.[2] In real life bank failures can happen for various reasons. A number of bank failures are attributed to fraud. In other cases, failures arise from poorly diversified assets holdings and nonperformance loans within a concentrated industry. Credit risk analysis in the bank is deficient and the bank usually has too small capital to protect against the insolvency. Bank failures can also be the consequence of bad government policy.

9.5.3 Bank Analysis Format

In different banks there are different formats for bank limit application or bank credit proposal. But the purpose is to analyse their institutional clients in order to establish a credit limit and this in general consists of some of the following items:

- Purpose of bank analysis: The purpose of bank analysis is usually to establish a new credit limit or to increase the existing limit. But it can also be a one-off ad hoc approval for a pending incoming deal. Bank analysis for the purpose of acquisition/ equity participation should be done in other ways because it will include some investment bank items such

[2] There are mainly four approaches for assessing a bank crisis, such as asset, liability, capital account and government assistance approaches. The asset approach that focuses on the quality of asset and nonperforming loans (NPLs) ratio is often used as an indicator. The liability approach focuses on the liability side of banks' balance sheets. The essence of this approach is the incidence of bank runs. The capital account approach focuses on the capital account of the balance sheet, that is banks' capitals are exhausted and run into crisis. The government assistance approach identifies banking crises as at least one of the policies such as (i) large-scale nationalization of banks, (ii) deposit freezing, (iii) bank closure and (iv) bank recapitalization.

as earnings per share, market potential, shareholder structure, regulatory environment, etc. The counterparty will also present a share investment prospectus which, among other things, will have a special risk-reminder paragraph.

- Current/proposed limit to this bank: This part of the proposal will examine the existing limit and exposure. The currency used for the limit should be indicated. To many banks the US dollar is the currency but more and more banks, especially those in Europe, are using the euro as a standard currency for bank limit. Also short-term or long-term limit should be indicated as obviously the criteria and assessment approaches will be different.
- Sources of information: Sources of information include the range (direct or indirect) and comment on the quality.
- Economic/political factors: This is the macro analysis of the banking environment including country risk rating, ownership of the bank (private or state owned), regulation hierarchy, deposit insurance situation, and the role of central bank as a lender of last resort.
- Business and industry factors: This is the micro analysis of the bank's background including the areas of operation (wholesale or retail, etc.), assets concentration (lending portfolio, target client group, etc.), branch network and a kind of peer group comparison (rating in the peer, speciality of the business).
- Management: This part is a general presentation of the profiles of the management members, for example their career record, their educational background, etc. When possible, the performance of the management member such as decreasing NPLs, increasing ROEs, etc. is a point of interest. The strategic goal of the management, if available, should be included. This will give a clear direction of the future of the bank.
- Operation: Operational risk is recognized as an important part of risk management. Past experience with this relationship in the operation field is necessary. For emerging market banks, operational risk (rejecting documents under L/Cs, etc.) can be repeated. Such a record is therefore relevant for the present evaluation. If the relationship is newly established, checking with the market (other correspondents) which does have a relationship is important for this record of operation. Sometimes future plans for network expansion or IT improvement may also indicate the operational prospective.
- Financial: Financial analysis will be focused on three central points, that is solvency, liquidity and earnings. Naturally the financials should be presented in time series for a trend analysis. Some banks include access to equity markets (IPOs) – the bank's ability to acquire extra capital.
- Asset quality: Asset quality is an essential issue for the health of the bank. Asset quality covers the risk portfolio of the bank, short-term vs long-term exposure, diversification, foreign exchange rate sensitivity (foreign assets), interest rate sensitivity, etc.
- Summary: The summary usually consists of a *SWOT analysis* (strengths, weaknesses, opportunities and threats) which itself is a summary of the position of the bank.
- Recommendations: These are the concluding remarks on the amount of credit limit proposed and the nature of the credit (short or long term, committed or uncommitted, etc.).

SUMMARY

The risk management function of institutional banking is linked to country risk and bank risk. A bank's ability to pay depends on many factors including macro-economic conditions, banking industry trends, bank's own financial strength, market value, equity value, capital structure, market reputation and management skills.

The added value of institutional banking to risk management is that it offers quite an important source of information which can serve at least the role of cross-checking.

Banks are companies but bank risk analysis differs from corporate risk analysis. A bank's failure may trigger more social crises than that of a company. This is perhaps why many countries have a deposit insurance scheme. Usually, information on banks may also be easier to obtain.

The essence of management for a bank's insolvency risk is linked to the triangle relationship among its profitability, liquidity and solvency. Several models are used in bank analysis such as the CAMEL model, the Crocodile model and the BASIC analysis to check different aspects of a bank.

To rate a bank's likelihood for insolvency is performed by professional agencies. The input for rating consists of both quantitative and qualitative factors. Like rating for countries, bank rating has its limitations. Moreover many small and new banks do not have rating at all. This creates a problem for business development. Practical solutions can be a spot visit, market check, peer group comparison and secondary market check.

When a bank has a liquidity or solvency problem, bank crisis occurs. There are signs and signals to watch for in bank crisis: delayed financials, inconsistent accounting practice, rapid growth in risk assets, deteriorating ratios, asset concentration, in-house lending, rumour in the market, etc.

To evaluate a bank, there are different formats in different banks where targeted bank's financial information, market tendency, operation aspect, etc. should be examined.

10
Institutional Banking and Institutional Banking Department

10.1 THE INSTITUTIONAL BANKING DEPARTMENT

By name the institutional banking department is the department for interbank business. However, with the development of business lines within big banks, sometimes this task is decentralized to each business line. Institutional banking as a business can therefore be realized in different patterns and the institutional banking department itself may play different roles.

It is not uncommon in many banks that interbank relationship is handled separately by each business line and coordinated with one 'financial institutions department'. This is more often seen in big banks where cross-selling is promoted to avoid either missing selling opportunities or duplicating marketing efforts.

An institutional banking department can oversee all the commercial aspects of relations with institutional clients, as well as the risks therein, in order to encourage cross-selling and increase total revenues of the bank. It has overall and worldwide responsibility for relationships with institutional customers (banks, insurers, asset managers, brokers, etc.). In collaboration with other business lines, it is its objective to increase cross-selling and offer tailor-made solutions to its customers.

The organization of an institutional banking department varies from bank to bank. Several factors come into consideration such as:

- The internal and external needs
- Mission of the bank
- Hierarchy and organizational structure
- Expertise available in the bank

Moreover, it depends on the role the department is expected to play.

Several issues need to be addressed for organizing an institutional banking department. The following intends to offer a more detailed discussion of the relevant issues.

10.2 THE ROLES FOR THE INSTITUTIONAL BANKING DEPARTMENT: AN ACCOUNT MANAGER, A RISK MANAGER OR A RELATIONSHIP MANAGER

Institutional banking's role is threefold: the role of an account manager, the role of a risk manager and that of a relationship manager.

The first issue in institutional banking is whether the department should play an *account manager* role, a *risk manager* role, a *relationship manager* role, or all three.

An account manager role implies that the department is the centre of information linked to a specific correspondent bank. For example, if one of the colleagues in the bank wants to visit a bank in Latin America, he/she should contact the Latin America desk of the institutional banking department for background information, advice, etc. The account manager role is one of monitoring or maintenance of the account.

A risk manager role for an institutional banking department is different. With the special knowledge for the country and bank, the institutional banker is supposed to contribute to the management of counterparty risk in establishing lines, monitoring lines and in solving problems and crises, if any.

With direct and up-to-date knowledge on the counterparty, the institutional banking department plays an advisory role of credit risk as discussed. Sometimes there may be different opinions on risk evaluation of a specific bank and discussion should be encouraged between credit and the institutional banking department. The credit decision is basically taken by credit and the institutional banking department is supposed to give advice, which is crucial in some cases. This is because the institutional banking department has, in most cases, an overall view on the counterparty, whereas credit plays the role of safeguarding the bank's capital.

A standard way for this function to work is to involve the institutional banking department and give room for them to express their advice on each of the credit proposals, oral or written.

The knowledge, skill and contacts with foreign financial institutions should enable the institutional banking department to generate income for the bank as a whole by facilitating commercial relationship. The performance of the department can be evaluated by profit target – profits in 'hard cash' or in 'shadow booking'. This is the *commercial role* of institutional banking.

For a decade or so the concept of customer relationship management has developed rapidly. There are a number of definitions of customer relationship management, many of which are similar to each other.[1] The core concept is marketing and the business focus is more towards customers.

Financial institutions, like companies, are becoming customer-focused organizations. This will force banks to adapt their recruiting strategies and employee selection criteria to fit these requirements of the *customer-focused sales representatives*. For the institutional banking department, this is the *role of a relationship manager*.

The major point here is that the sales representatives are proactive in selling the whole product line to a single customer (or customer group) instead of, as in a product-focused organization, being a product specialist selling one product to many customers.

As a sales representative, the role of a relationship manager of institutional banking implies that the institutional banking department actively develops a relationship and does marketing, once a foreign bank is targeted as a commercial partner for one or more business lines. The relationship manager role also implies that any conflict or problem with a correspondent bank is supposed to be handled by, or at least consulted with, the institutional banking department. He/she must have teamwork skills, more breadth of experience, greater empathy for goals and more flexibility in being able to respond quickly to changing business conditions.

[1] Chye and Gerry (2002) defined customer relationship management as 'the process of predicting customer behaviour and selection actions to influence that behaviour to benefit the company'. Kincaid (2003) defined customer relationship management as the strategic use of information processes, technology and people to manage the customer's relationship with your company (marketing, sales, services and support) across the whole customer life cycle.

In day-to-day life, whether the institutional banking department can play one, two or three roles very often depends on the knowledge and/or skill built up by the institutional banking department and how it is organized within the structure of the whole bank.

Indeed, if the department is a real competence centre for knowledge, understanding and contact of banks and countries, it may play all three roles.

However, sometimes the role of an institutional banking department is reduced to an account manager function, registering bank and country risk exposure and doing other routine administrative work, such as opening an account, receiving visiting institutional banking colleagues from other banks, or attending receptions. Account managers visit banks with lengthy reports without delivering any commercial results. Such a scenario of 'cocktail banker' is what many banks are trying to steer away from.

Sometimes it is not the intention of the management of the institutional banking department to see its roles reduced to one of passive handling of incoming business. Rather, it is a result of human resource restriction or the guideline of the management.

The institutional banking department can do more. With the combination of these three roles for the bank as a whole, institutional banking, at its best, is often involved in the bank's overseas merger and acquisition policy. The department as a competence centre for banks and countries will evaluate targeted foreign banks for equity participation. The department will be involved in various stages for assessment, negotiation, participation and post-participation evaluation. The role is most distinguished at the assessment stage for mergers and acquisitions.

The assessment report of a targeted partner includes the definition of terms for equity participation, general introduction of the targeted bank, overview of the bank's business activities, issue pricing and dividend policy, competitive advantage, operations management system, background of the management team, development objectives and strategies, point of contact, and reference documents including permission from the regulator for this invitation of equity participation.

If a bank intends to invite international strategic partners, the institutional banking department will actively work together with investment banks, law firms and/or accounting firms if they ever have such a competence.

10.3 THE CENTRALIZED VS DECENTRALIZED PATTERN

Traditionally, institutional banking can either be under the trade finance department or under the financial market department or neither. There are always advantages and disadvantages for each of the structures.

Due to the risk nature of different products, institutional banking products are offered either to developed markets or to emerging markets or both. Even in the case that the same product is offered, the credit guideline could be different. Money market line offering is one of such examples. Money market line is not offered to 'difficult' countries. To some banks, there are restrictions attached to the money market offering (tenor, collateralized or not, etc.).

In general trade finance is more oriented to emerging markets whereas financial market products are more for developed countries. Institutional banking can thus be decentralized into the emerging market sector and non-emerging market sector.

An institutional banking department for overall relationship with foreign banks can give an overall picture of products selling and relationship development. However, it will be difficult to have competent personnel also have in-depth product knowledge for both emerging markets and developed markets. Under these circumstances the selling, if any, will thus be less effective.

What happens in reality is to have the institutional banking department as one department in small banks and two (trade finance plus global market products) in bigger banks.

The function of institutional banking can also be decentralized where head office is doing part of the job and a regional branch is doing some other part of the job. In terms of marketing, this pattern is preferred due to the principle of 'close to the clients'. The disadvantage is that each region will maximize their own benefits without releasing the global mission of the bank. Return on total country limit, as a result, may not reach its optimal level. Furthermore, credit risk management is in all banks almost always centralized. Hence the marketing function and risk management function may not match.

10.4 THE PERFORMANCE EVALUATION OF THE INSTITUTIONAL BANKING DEPARTMENT

Like other departments in the bank, the added value of the institutional banking department can be evaluated by various criteria. With the above-mentioned roles of institutional banking, the way of evaluation may also change according to the role(s) that the department is playing.

For most if not all banks a typical mission is to maximize shareholders' benefits. One of the most important criteria therefore is profits. But losses effectively prevented are also relevant in calculation despite being not easy to quantify. Hence the risk manager function is recognized by practice but it is not so easy to set up criteria for measurement.

The criteria for the function of an account manager are more biased toward workload, for example the number of accounts maintained. The earnings on these accounts can be calculated as well, although some income may appear on the other business lines such as foreign exchange earnings, custodian earnings, etc.

The relationship manager's function presents an obvious issue. It is probably neither possible nor necessary to the bank as a whole to sort out the precise earnings of the institutional banking department, which involves, theoretically at least, almost all departments and all products of the bank.

It is clear that measuring the performance of institutional banking is not an easy job, as the department is in fact a cross-business line department.

In many banks the concept of profit centre or nonprofit centre has been developed to measure the tangible value of each department. For institutional banking, there has been a long history of debate whether it is a profit centre or nonprofit centre. The discussion as such seems to be misleading because many of the contributions of the department are not calculated in the direct earnings for the department. Rather, the department, by utilizing its special skills, contacts and knowledge, helps contribute to the benefits of the bank, either in profits terms or in other terms.

Specifically, the criteria for measurement of the performance of institutional banking can be classified into several groups:

- Earnings on(cross-) selling: This is direct earning contribution, which may be indicated by higher business volume, higher product margins, higher business turnover, etc., such as money market earnings, L/C confirmation earnings, syndication and forfating earnings, etc.

- Products/service benefits: This refers to the contribution of ideas for new products, ideas of improvement of some tailor-made, existing products, and innovation of products suitable to a specific market, identifying some special needs of the counterparty.
- Market access benefits: This includes introduction of new customers to the bank and the support of existing clients. It also refers to the entrance to new markets, such as acquisition of new banks, etc.
- Problem-solving benefits: This refers to the added value of the institutional banking department for recovery of losses by negotiation with the counterparty, litigation, or the sale of bad debt to a buyer market. This will be discussed in Part III.

While precise measurement of performance of the institutional banking department is indeed complicated, to define the basic outline is, however, not so difficult under the framework of three different roles of the department. Many banks adopt a kind of 'shadow booking' system to measure the contribution of the department. Such a 'shadow booking' system will allow a record of earnings to be created (at least jointly) by the department but the real money is realized in other departments. The essential point is to ascertain not the exact but the broad orders of added value of the department.

10.5 HUMAN RESOURCE ISSUES FOR THE INSTITUTIONAL BANKING DEPARTMENT

The institutional banking department usually involves people with a general knowledge of products but a special knowledge of countries and banks. Institutional banking for emerging markets involves so-called 'local people' – people originally from these regions or who have lived there. These local people may help contribute to the understanding of the country and bank because of their ethical and cultural background.

Under some circumstances, the institutional banking department, when recruiting people, emphasizes that people working in the department preferably know the language of the region. This is to facilitate communication with counterparties. There is one interesting phenomenon, however – many institutional banking departments emphasize the importance of language rather than the awareness of culture.

For the sake of business development, some 'second generation' citizens may speak the language inherited from their parents, but may have little sense of the business development as they were born and grew up in a country to which their parents emigrated.

An interesting acronym is 'ABC' – America-born Chinese. These people are perhaps fluent in the language, but are not the same as those who have really lived in the area. Unless they are specially trained and exposed, their culture sensitivity is likely to be much less.

Institutional banking is a business of cross-border nature, and the department's job involves most of other departments in the bank. The success of institutional banking is related to the quality of its staff. Institutional banking therefore needs good staff who should have some or all of the following core competencies:

- Awareness of the strategy of the bank: This is because the institutional banking department is a window to the outside and should best describe the strategy of the bank. It should also serve the strategy of finding the right business and counterparties for the bank.

- Adaptability and sensitivity to different cultures: Given the cross-border nature of the business, culture sensitivity is of crucial importance for the department. To adapt to the culture of the counterparties is important as well.
- Ability to manage complexity and/or uncertainty: With the involvement of other departments and a large variety of products, the department must be flexible enough to accommodate the complexity. On the other hand, the department is handling international business and the environment for business can change suddenly. The ability to handle uncertainty is thus one of the required qualifications.
- Ability to work in international teams: As the department has a team from different national and cultural backgrounds, a team spirit for working with other people with various backgrounds is required for an efficient and pleasant working environment within the department.
- Language capability: To speak the language will facilitate communications with the counterparty.
- Broad knowledge of the products: The staff must have broad knowledge of the products so that they may help serve the needs of their institutional clients.
- The network in the relevant region: Staff have to know the people in the region they are serving. This will enable them to gain access to the region of their your targeted clients. The network will also add value to their risk management function.

In reality, not many are qualified in all areas, so that continuous training is a must. But the network itself cannot be achieved by training alone. This must be done by regular contact and face-to-face visits.

On top of all these, the institutional banking department as a relationship department is better able to maintain the stability of staff for the sake of the continuation of the relationship. On the other hand, it is not surprising that staff leave the department to pursue a more specialized business function elsewhere which can utilize the knowledge and network built up in the department. Under these circumstances, the institutional banking department becomes a kind of training school for country and bank specialists – a spin-off contribution of the department to the bank as a whole.

SUMMARY

Institutional banking business is done via the institutional banking department or via each business line with one coordinator in the bank. Whatever the structure, the intention is to promote cross-selling to institutional clients. The structure of the institutional banking department is linked to a bank's mission, internal and external needs, expertise available in the bank, etc.

The department can play several roles for the bank as a whole. Basically, it can play the roles of account manager, risk manager or a role for overall relationship with an institutional client. The recent tendency is to have the department as a customer-focused sales representative – a role of relationship manager. In reality, what role the department can play depends on the guideline of the management and the availability of human resources.

Some banks also organize their institutional banking department in a decentralized way. For example, trade finance and financial markets can each have their institutional banking function, or the function of institutional banking is performed partly by the head office and partly by the regional office. These arrangements may have advantages and disadvantages.

Although it is still controversial to say whether the institutional banking department is a profit centre or not, it is clear that the performance can be evaluated by visible earnings and invisible benefits such as access to new markets, recovery of losses, etc.

Institutional banking is a kind of business that needs special staff to run it. Qualifications for the institutional banking department are different and sometimes even unique. Language capabilities, teamwork in an international environment, awareness of cultural difference among colleagues and to external clients are all regarded as core competences for the department.

11 Institutional Banking: Fraud Prevention, Anti-money Laundering and Basel II

Institutional banking deals with interbank relationships and facilitates interbank cooperation. It therefore has been involved in some recent issues facing banking businesses, such as fraud prevention, anti-money laundering and the Basel II arrangement which is changing many aspects of the banking industry. This chapter intends to discuss these issues in relation to institutional banking.

11.1 FRAUD

11.1.1 Fraud in General

Fraud started when business started. As long as there have been commercial systems in place for businessmen, there have been people who have intended to misuse them. Fraud therefore is not new and is both for emerging markets and for developed markets.

There are various fraud cases reported for the developed countries in the media. Some of the recent ones are:

- Adelphia Communications inadequately disclosed €3.1 billion in loans and loan guarantees to the family of its founder.
- Enron used a variety of techniques, notably SPVs, to hide losses and inflate revenue.
- Kmart repeatedly underreported losses and overstatements of revenues.
- PNC Financial Services Group used off-balance sheet entities and insurance contracts to hide underperformance assets.
- Tyco International undisclosed loans to some of its top executives, including its former CEO, and paid some of their expenses.
- WorldCom lent $400 million in loans to its former chief executive.
- Computer Associates International used accounting gimmicks to inflate revenue and enrich top executives.
- CMS Energy admitted to overstating revenue in 2000 and 2001 using nonexisting energy trades.
- Dynegy admitted to overstating by creating sham energy trades. It used of an off-balance sheet entity which was also under investigation.
- Royal Dutch/Shell admitted to overstating crude oil reserves.
- Lucent Technologies told the SEC that in late 2000 it would reduce reported revenue by $679 million.
- Reliance Resources admitted inflating revenue by counting questionable energy trades.
- Xerox paid a $10 million fine for inflating revenue from 1997 to 2000 by including payments on existing contracts.

- AIG 2005 was charged with misstating operating results for over a decade using 'finite' insurance contracts with no transfer of risk.

According to a report in the *Economist*, the chief executive of Refco, one of America's largest futures brokers (and its biggest retail commodities broker), was arrested on 11 October 2005. Federal prosecutors charged Phillip Bennett with defrauding investors in the firm's initial public offering, which took place in August 2005, by hiding hundreds of millions of dollars in loans to another company that he controls. Mr Bennett may face 20 years in prison as well as hefty fines.[1] Grant Thornton was fooled by a forged letter from Bank of America attesting to a €4 billion cash deposit by Cayman subsidiary Bonlat. A decade of fraudulent activities led to bankruptcy and €14 billion in bank and bond debt.

Instead of discussing fraud in general, our focus here will be more on fraud in the banking business for institutional banking. This is because to avoid losses from fraud is one of the tasks of institutional banking.

11.1.2 Fraud of Forged Bank Papers

Fraud can take many forms. Broadly, it can be *fraud of forged bank papers* or *fraud in trade finance*.

In banking business, fraud of forged bank papers means fraudsters use fraudulent papers to withdraw, unlawfully, money from the bank.

Banks handle bank documents and money, both of which can be forged. *Fraudulent papers* refer to those bank documents such as stand-by letters of credit, bank guarantees, bank checks, etc., which are falsely said to have been issued by banks. These papers are bank documents that can be forged. Institutional bankers find themselves in the front line protecting their own banks or the funds of their correspondent banks.

An often used fraud is to present the forgery of printed cheques to the correspondent banks to claim money on vostro accounts. With e-banking in place, bank papers are used less and computer fraud is became the centre of attention and looks like remaining so in the future.[2]

For all these straightforward fraud cases, banks have their basic security system. But banks are by nature vulnerable to fraud and organized crime because the majority of the money in the bank belongs to the depositors. Most of the attempted frauds are therefore detected at an early stage. The *tested telex* or *SWIFT* system is used to secure safe and exclusive communications among banks. Under such circumstances, fraud can take place only when internal staff are involved.

Recently, an employee of a South African bank near Johannesburg received an 18-year prison term after pleading guilty to seven charges of fraud. It was alleged that over a period of two months, while still in the employment of the bank, he issued guarantees without authorization and transmitted these guarantees via telexes and SWIFT messages to six correspondents in the Caribbean, Europe and the United States. The guarantees confirmed that the bank was aware of the transaction and had reserved clean, cleared funds of noncriminal origin to guarantee payment against receipt of a certified bank invoice. The unauthorized guarantee stated that 'this confirmation, executed with full bank responsibility, shall remain

[1] *Economist*, 'Financial scandal: a broker battered', 21–25 October 2005.

[2] See the publications of ICC CYBERCRIME: Risks and Responses Special Report in 1999.

in full force and effect for a period of one year and one day from the date first written above unless expressed in writing'.

As a result, the South African bank suffered a potential loss of $541.5 million. Needled to say, no funds had ever been deposited in the bank. Prompt action by the South African authorities appeared to have limited damages to a minimum. This is not the only incident in which employees in banks have sent out unauthorized messages which have caused substantial financial damage to their employers.[3]

To prevent such frauds, many measures are being taken inside banks for internal control. For example, the authorized amount of signatures by categories, double signatures to fulfil 'the four eyes principle', are more than common in most commercial banks.

Banks are meeting regularly to exchange views on fraud prevention. Blacklists of names of fraudulent banks and countries are circulated among banks by the regulators or by correspondent banks. Sometimes international police may also be involved to help in this regard.

Questions remain, however: How far can institutional banking help in fraud prevention? Can it help to identify these forged documents? What are the characteristics of these fraudulent transactions that attract the attention of institutional bankers?

To identify these fraudulent transactions, we have to know the banking system, track record, etc. In institutional banking some of the phenomena indicating fraud potential are worth noting.

For example, *transactions in large amounts* are an incentive for fraudsters to organize fraud. They are usually bank-to-bank transactions with high profitability with the payment condition usually under bank authorization with no collateral and upfront fees. The ICC Financial Investigation Bureau once reported a case where a company based in China saved hundreds of thousands of dollars for being alert to a suspicious dealing. In the midst of a deal involving a $50 million loan, the Chinese enterprise was carefully reviewing the documents involved and found them to be suspicious. They forwarded the documents to London for expert analysis. The documents were riddled with terms and language common to operators of financial fraud, including the nonexistent London Short Form 3034. Obviously, in this case the amount of $50 million is one of the motivations for the fraudsters.[4]

The *timing of fraud* is also important. Such suspicious transactions may occur more likely at the moment when people are not on their guard, for example Christmas or New Year period. Fraudsters may therefore easily use the relaxed atmosphere to escape the attention of people on duty and get their deals through.

11.1.3 Fraud in Trade Finance

In trade finance, a documentary credit system is based on documents that can be forged. Under a letter of credit, for example, it is not rare for fraudulent documents to be presented by the seller to the bank. These documents comply with the terms of credit.

Under such circumstances, the confirming bank is supposed to pay on a nonrecourse basis and send the documents to the issuing bank to claim reimbursement. The buyer believes that the cargo as described in the bill of lading has been loaded on board the ship and is on its way to its destination. It is usually at that destination that the buyer discovers that the cargo has not been loaded on board. The seller who presented fraudulent documents may have disappeared when the entire details are discovered.

[3] ICC Crime Bureau has more such cases.
[4] See ICC website: www.icc-ccs.org/main/news.php

Sellers themselves may also suffer losses by fraud. The seller depends upon the fact that the buyer will not be able to collect the cargo from the ship owners unless he produces the original bill of lading. To get this bill of lading he (the buyer) would have to go to the bank and pay for it. But with the help of a few false stamps, this fraudulent bill of lading would pass the internal examination and goods may have been released without the buyer paying for them.

A fundamental weakness in banking is that, for all the documentary credits, banks rely heavily on documents being correct. But most of these documents have very little security features to prevent their forgery. Many of the important documents are merely simple documents, which are not so difficult to reproduce.

Fraud can also be a trading fraud where buyers defraud sellers or the other way round. In these cases banks play the role of financier and may suffer related loss if one party is their client: if their client goes bust, the bank facility to that client may be defaulted. A fraudulent seller may ship complete rubbish to the buyer, or ship goods of lesser quantity or quality, or ship absolutely nothing at all.

The institutional banking department may help to minimize such fraud risk by checking into the background of both the buyer and the seller.

The due diligence policy has already been discussed (account services). Such a policy will calculate these risks. Nowadays a bank will not discount an L/C to a company without a due diligence check. The bank's worst case senario mentality further helps it to cover the losses, theoretically at least, by access to collaterals, etc.

In practice, some of the following tips are helpful for identifying trade finance fraud:

- Unusual features of trading background such as goods offered at a lower price.
- Buyer and seller are one unit.
- Request of payment conditions not in accordance with customary line.
- Unusual pressure for a quick acceptance of offers.
- Walk-in client who is very generous in paying the banking fee.
- Required documents are paper documents such as warehouse receipts, warrants, etc. which present more difficulties to check and can easily be reproduced.

In general, large and reputable companies have less chance of being involved in such fraudulent deals as their reputation will be at stake.

Needless to say, an institutional banker will be alert to these fraud issues. On the other hand, it is unreasonable to expect institutional bankers who usually are not involved in banking document handling to be responsible for the fraud. Most often they are involved in resolving and preventing fraud. This requires sufficient knowledge and experience on the topic of fraud, at least at the macro level.

11.2 MONEY LAUNDERING AND TERRORISM FINANCING

Since the late 1990s, *anti-money laundering* has become part of the agenda of institutional banking.

Money laundering as a concept has been defined in many different ways in different documents. A simple definition is that it is a conduct for trading criminal money – money got through dubious means. The general understanding is that all activities aimed at disguising or concealing the nature or source of, or entitlement to, money or property derived from criminal activities are regarded as money laundering. Therefore money laundering refers to activities to disguise or conceal money or property that is intended to be used in committing or facilitating the commission of serious crime.

Money launderers tend to seek out areas in which there is a low risk due to ineffective anti-money laundering procedures. The goal is to get the illegal funds to the individual(s) who generated them. Launderers, therefore, prefer to move funds through areas with stable financial systems without being noticed.

There are many reports on money laundering investigation. The *Financial Times*[5] once reported that Israeli police had frozen $376 million in bank accounts in order to investigate around 80 separate incidents involving 200 customers of an Israeli bank. The year-long investigation was made public by the Israeli authorities. They had questioned 25 bank employees and one customer.

Organizations like OECD[6] have a blacklist for countries involved in money laundering. The United Nations also has a convention against transactional organized crime which many countries have signed.

Money laundering usually involves several countries, and is becoming a global issue. It is linked with corruption that involves many people in different capacities with the aim to make quick and easy money. It is linked to crimes as well.

Crimes that generate huge sums of money can be

- Illegal weapon sales
- Smuggling
- The activities of organized crime syndicates, such as drug trafficking and prostitution rings

There are other sources of illegal profits usually in emerging markets but also in the developed world. Embezzlement, insider trading for equity and bond markets, bribery of government officials and computer fraud schemes can produce huge profits and create the incentive to 'legitimize' the ill-gotten gains through money laundering.

The process of money laundering is critical to these criminals to disguise the source of the proceeds from crime, as it enables them to enjoy these profits without jeopardizing their sources. Hence money laundering is very important to organized crime in general and to corruption in particular.

Although organized crime of one form or another exists in many countries, it is mostly a serious problem in many emerging market countries where corruption prevails, the legal system is unstable and loopholes are many.

Specific forms of organized crime that have been linked to money laundering in emerging markets may include more than those mentioned above. Armed robbery, tax evasion or customs fraud, exchange control evasion, motor vehicle theft are all elements of organized crime for the purposes of money.

Money laundering aims to frustrate the enforcement of criminal law by creating the justification for controlling or possessing money or property derived from any form of criminal activity.

---

[5] See the report under the title *Israeli Money – Laundering Probe Widens* by Sharmila Devi in Jerusalem and Jimmy Burns in London.

[6] OECD: the Organization for Economic Cooperation and Development.

Money laundering is a worldwide activity because of several incentives:

- Laundering can make it difficult to detect the underlying criminal activity that generates the profits.
- Laundering can sustain the enjoyment of the profits from crime or their reinvestment in future criminal activities. With time, laundering enhances professionalism in both the structure and operation of criminal syndicates, with managers and the financially astute intent on making it to the top.
- Laundering facilitates the development of transnational networks and linkages with criminal environments of disparate origins.

Law enforcement authorities in many parts of the world have come to the conclusion that by combating money laundering activities they can disrupt the cycle used by criminal groups to derive benefits from illegal profits, and thereby weaken or even destroy their viability. The argument is that if the primary motivation behind syndicated crime is economic, and the economic gain is removed, the crime will cease.

Money laundering has existed for many years but has attracted attention more recently because it is now linked to the financing of terrorism. Many banks tackle the issue of money laundering in tandem with the financing of terrorism, which is now on the top of the institutional banking agenda.

Since 11 September 2001, the American administration put the 'war on terror' at the top of the president's priority list. Other governments followed to beef up their political rhetoric.

More than five years after 9/11 and under such pressure, banks all over the world are making efforts to choke off funding for terrorists. As money is the lifeblood of terrorist operations, to stop the payment of their money will, it is hoped, help to restrict terrorism activities.

In day-to-day activities, regularly checking customers' names and those of related parties involved in their transactions against the blacklist for UN embargoes and American sanctions may identify possible terrorist matches. Banks are scanning their customers' accounts more carefully for signs of suspicious account holders. Accounts have been frozen and foreign banks have been stopped from doing business in dollars. The recent case of ABN-AMRO is one example.

Admittedly, to identify terrorists' funds is complicated due to the increasingly fragmented nature of terrorist groups and the fact that terrorists have been changing their money flows. However, banks are mobilizing their resources in this area. Anti-money laundering is thus also part of the daily job description of institutional banking.

11.3 ANTI-MONEY LAUNDERING INITIATIVES

Nowadays people find that to open an account or transfer money can mean numerous identification checks. This is because initiatives are taken in banks worldwide and efforts are made to combat money laundering. Millions of prospective and current customers are facing tougher compliance standards.

One issue in the fight against money laundering is the establishment of relevant law. Money laundering is not a specific crime for one bank or in one country and efforts to counter money laundering are still hampered by the lack of effective laws or policies in some countries. Europe is no exception. On this issue, Belgian Anti-Money Laundering (AML) law's enacted in 1993, and modified in 1995, 1998 and 2002, comply with the European Union (EU) directives and are regularly adapted to the current situation.

Recent events have led each EU country to establish their related laws to ensure that the task is properly done. Compliance officers within banks are appointed to carry out day-to-day tasks to reinforce those regulations, which are being transposed in the Belgian law. The EU directives are largely based on the 40 *Financial Action Task Force* (FATF) recommendations.[7]

The Financial Action Task Force is an international body based in Paris. It has developed nine recommendations including regulations for wire transfer, remittance systems and nonprofit organizations. So far 151 countries have committed to implementing the recommendations.

However, the problem of money laundering in some countries seems to be difficult to address when government officials are involved. Between November 2001 and April 2002, for example, Kenyan police arraigned 77 people in various courts on corruption charges. Most of them were low-ranking officials from district treasuries, the immigration department and the Kenya Revenue Authority. However, no actions were taken against cabinet ministers or high-ranking government officials.

To prevent the inadequacies in legislation, most financial and commercial institutions have put internal or sectoral measures in place to detect money laundering. This has been possible largely because most of these institutions, such as banks, have global linkages and thus benefit from the macro policies of their parent institutions. The major multilateral banks all have internal systems developed by their main offices to be used by all their branches globally. The anti-money laundering legislation of the United Kingdom (UK) (Money Laundering Regulation, 1993) and European Union (EU) (section 2(2) of the European Money Laundering Directive) are examples of the legal framework established to fight against money laundering.

Other anti-money laundering initiatives developed by commercial banks and requested by most central banks include:

- Implement internal controls, policies and procedures
- Establish identification procedures
- Keep records for a period of at least five years
- Recognize suspicious and/or unusual transactions
- Educate and train relevant employees
- Appoint an anti-money laundering compliance officer

In some of the main countries involved in the transit of drugs, financial systems are highly vulnerable to money laundering, with inadequate and partial controls for anti-washing. The sales of real estate, businesses and commercial contraband are vehicles for money laundering. The repeated detection of substantial amounts of money that inexplicably enter and leave these countries indicates that money laundering is active there.

There are problems and loopholes, however. For example, in some countries[8] established laws only penalize the activities of money laundering in connection with illicit drug trafficking.

[7] Entities involved in such supervision in Belgium are the Belgian Banking and Finance Commission and the Belgian Financial Intelligence Processing Unit (BFIPU). The supervising authorities of any country where any bank maintains an operational presence also carry out their equivalent missions.

[8] Ecuador, for example, has established 'the Substance Law Psicotrópicas and Estupefacientes of 1990' (Law 108).

These activities include the illicit enrichment, conversion or transference of assets. In other countries individual laws are to be established to penalize the washing of the gains obtained by any crime. Besides to establish money laundering as an independent offence, many countries also need to provide a legal framework to establish a unit of financial intelligence. Regulations are emitted in agreement with established laws for such a unit of financial intelligence. These regulations require that the financial institutions maintain information from the national agency for drugs. Special units were created to collect relevant information to prevent money laundering from the sale of drugs. In the meantime regulations required that the financial institutions inform the national agency of suspicious transactions. The supervision authorities of banks, that is central banks or monetary authorities, will have the ability to sanction the institutions that do not cooperate. The banks must maintain registries of the financial transactions for six years. There are laws of due diligence or banking negligence that make it the responsibility of individual banks to assess if their institutions launder money. Under many circumstances banking directors can legally be responsible if money laundering from the proceeds of drugs happens in its institution.

An interesting point is that some existing laws create conflict regarding the fight against money laundering. For example, the law of bank secret requires that banks have no right to release internal information to external authorities but anti-money laundering should allow investigation.

Other problems that create conflict with a regime of anti-money laundering include the absence of regulations enabling financial institutions to exercise due diligence, the lack of information requirements on large amounts of money that enter or leave a country, and the weak regulation for the marginal players in the financial sector such as exchange houses.

In general, the issue of financing of terrorism has not been taken seriously enough in each and every country. It is not penalized at all in some countries. Nevertheless, more and more countries have ratified the *Convention of International Nations for the Suppression of Financing Terrorism.* Steps have been taken to prevent the use of gold and precious metals to wash the assets of terrorists.

For institutional banking, money laundering is the task of compliance. This compliance issue was partially discussed for due diligence of account services.

In dealing with correspondents with their accounts, systematic approaches were institutionalized inside the bank. These approaches include a *know your customer policy*, due diligence, account monitoring and supervision.

- 'Know your customer' policy: A know your customer (KYC) policy requires adequate identification of the customers, including financial intermediaries and beneficial owners at the inception of all client relationships with banks. Such information is maintained in the bank records and updated on a regular basis. Banks rely on the laws and regulations in force, which may prevent the opening of accounts to some companies or individuals. The anti-money laundering compliance structure of the bank vis-à-vis its correspondent, and the anti-money laundering compliance structure of each international branch of a global bank, must conform to the requirements of local national law.

  Knowledge of the activities, background and business of a client or counterparty is a prerequisite to entering into a relationship or transaction with such a party. To possess such knowledge is necessary to be able not only to fulfil duties of care to such a party, but also to perform obligations relative to the fight against money laundering, crime, terrorism or other illegal acts.

- Due diligence: Due diligence is the reasonable care and checking for accepting or dealing with a client. In this connection, banks are presumed to have conducted due diligence in accordance with policy in accepting and dealing with that client. This is not to be confused with account opening procedures. All material counterparties to a transaction should be investigated to ensure anti-money laundering regulations are met. In the event of suspicious activity, the case should be reported to the compliance officer inside the bank under the internal hierarchy. The collection of sufficient information at the beginning of an account relationship enables the bank to understand the intended purpose for which an account will be used and its expected level of activity. It also gives banks an indication of the approximate customer net worth and the likely nature of funds that would feed the account.
- Account monitoring: To check at the inception of an account relationship is important but a follow-up is more important. Banks have implemented account-monitoring procedures that review ongoing account activities, including wire transfers, which will make the detection of suspicious or unusual activities possible.
- Suspicious account activity: recognition and reporting: Banks are spending money to train their employees to recognize suspicious operations. Unusual amounts, currency, frequency of transfer or other suspicious activities must be reported to the appropriate compliance officer. He or she is responsible for determining whether a report should be filed with the appropriate authorities. All activities that indicate potential money laundering, terrorist financing or other financial crimes are reported to the appropriate authorities while related documents must be kept for five years or more.
- Embargo, control lists, blacklists, etc.: Banks also keep records, update blacklists and have a policy that complies with the embargo rules defined by the government and the relevant authorities. New account opening and movement of funds related to entities submitted to embargo or blacklists are subject to specific controls.
- Offshore banks: Relationships with offshore or shell banks are only authorized if their parent companies are reliable, with strong and recognized shareholders.

Anti-money laundering is becoming a must for banking. From an organizational aspect, within the EU the compliance officer or the money laundering officer for banking operations is established, who are responsible for implementing relevant procedures that are consistent with local laws. As far as the Netherlands is concerned, supervision through the *Meldpunt Ongebruikelijke Transacts* (MOT) is organized by the *Wet Identification Dienstverlening* (WID).

With the progress of anti-money laundering measures, it is noticed that in the labour market the demand for compliance officers has increased substantially in recent years. As a result the compliance staffing and services industries are booming. Compliance officers' salaries have increased. Related software vendors touting scanning programs are making quick money.

A new problem facing the banking industry is the expenses. All these compliance requirements and anti-money laundering initiatives cost a great deal of money. Extra money will need to be allocated for training inside banks because an anti-money laundering training programme will have to be provided to the employees on a systematic basis. These programmes are adapted to the operational activity of each business group and unit, especially the back offices.

The precise amount for compliance and anti-money laundering is not so easy to estimate. According to a KPMG survey of 200 banks, those interviewed increased investments on anti-money laundering activities by an average of 61% in 2002, 2003, and 2004.[9] In addition, tens of millions of pounds are spent each year in London alone on data storage and retrieval to satisfy a requirement that banks' client and transaction data be kept for five to seven years. Similar rules exist in America, Singapore and other European countries. The fight against money laundering and terrorism financing is thus neither easy nor cheap.

11.4 BASEL II AND ITS IMPLICATIONS TO INSTITUTIONAL BANKING

Discussing institutional banking without mentioning the Basel II framework is impossible.

Published in June 2004 by the Basel Committee after nearly six years of work, the New Basel Capital Framework (commonly referred to as Basel II) has been designed to enable financial institutions across the globe to determine their capital requirements more accurately and to improve their risk management capacities. This new Basel framework for banks' prudential risk management, negotiated by the Basel Committee of rich country bank regulators, is due to come into force in January 2007.

The new capital structure is based on three self-control pillars:

$$\text{Bank's capital ratio (minimum 8\%)} = \frac{\text{Total capital}}{\text{Credit risk + market risk + operational risk}}$$

The Basel II framework is a result of several business lines including financial institutions. To its credit, the Basel Committee created the new accord after lengthy deliberations that included extensive input from financial institutions, industry associations, consultants, technology vendors and other regulatory bodies worldwide.

For the flexibility of implementation of this framework, the Basel II implementation deadline varies quite significantly and expands on the national jurisdiction. The US and Australia, for example, have committed to the end of 2007. Other countries such as those in Asia have chosen either a more aggressive time plan (end of 2006) or postponed the implementations to 2008 or 2010.

The countries that are lagging a bit behind favour a more gradual and phased implementation. By phased implementation we refer to the three pillar stages.

- Pillar I Minimum capital requirements: Here minimum capital requirements refer to both credit risk and operational risk. The first pillar is purely quantitative, assigning risk weightings to different types and maturities of assets, according to the credit rating of the counterparty, relying on more sophisticated banks to calculate their own capital allocation.
- Pillar II Supervisory review process: The next pillar depends on an assessment of the bank's management and performance by its supervisor, whose skill and competence could make a huge difference to how much extra capital the bank might be asked to allocate.
- Pillar III Market discipline and disclosure of risk information: This pillar concerns disclosure and market discipline. Again, the ethics and disclosure standards of the local financial market will play a role.

[9] The *Economist* special report, 'Financing terrorism', 22 October 2005, p. 74.

Worldwide, banks are facing multi-dimensional challenges when implementing their Basel II projects, which will definitely require the strengthening of existing internal processing.

Another challenge is to achieve regulatory compliance by meeting the Basel II requirements in the three pillar accord: that is the capital calculation approaches, the supervisory review process that emphasizes features like validation stress testing or economic capital and the external disclosure of risk information.

To institutional banking and the correspondent business, there are many implications.

First, in the near future compliance with Basel II will become part of the evaluation of bank risk. Basel II intends to let banks build a more sophisticated risk management analysis, employ advanced capital allocation models and adopt a risk-adjusted performance measurement framework. If a bank makes use of all of Basel II's risk analysis tools, it can incorporate risk costs properly. Obviously those banks that are Basel II compliant will certainly be in a better position in correspondent banking. Credit limit to a correspondent will be very much restricted to these criteria.

Second, Basel II implementation will last for couple of years. Those who have done their job well in advance may help those who are lagging behind. According to one Ernst & Young survey done in December 2004, the majority of banks surveyed (245 participants from 12 Asian countries) indicated that they are either in the early implementation stages of their overall Basel II compliance programme or have not yet started. Some of the institutions cannot estimate their overall Basel II implementation costs. Cooperation in Basel II implementation can be an interesting and new topic in the field of institutional banking. The subject of Basel II itself is an opportunity for institutional banking business.

SUMMARY

Recently, institutional banking has been involved in several important issues such as fraud prevention, anti-money laundering and Basel II arrangements.

Fraud has existed for a long time in business for both developed and developing countries. In the banking business, fraud can either be fraud of forged bank papers or fraud in trade finance.

It is known that banks are handling papers that can be forged. Forged banking papers include stand-by letters of credit, bank guarantees and bank cheque. Of course money itself can be forged.

There is no standard formula to prevent fraud in banking but papers for transactions in large amounts are more likely to be forged. Fraudsters also tend to find weak points to get their deals done.

Fraud cases in trade finance take many forms. Documents required under letter of credit can be forged by the seller so that the buyer will not get the goods they need despite the fact that they have already paid. The seller may also suffer if title documents such as bills of lading were released without payment to the banks. Direct trading fraud cases are also not uncommon.

Money laundering nowadays is linked to terrorism financing, thus attracting a lot of attention in banks. Activities aimed at disguising or concealing the nature or the sources of money derived from criminal activities are regarded as money laundering. Laws are being established and initiatives are taken to fight against money laundering. Banks are now under more strict compliance request from their regulators. A 'know your customers' policy is widely applied in the banking sector.

Basel II intends to enable financial institutions worldwide to determine their capital requirement vis-à-vis the risk management capacities. A new capital structure is based on credit risk, market risk and operational risk.

Banks are implementing Basel II rules according to their own timetable and strategic principles. This capital structure arrangement will have an impact on banks' price policy, risk policy and performance evaluation.

Part III

Institutional Banking for Emerging Markets: Product Marketing, Risk Management, Risk Mitigation and Problem Solving

12
Characteristics of Institutional Banking for Emerging Markets

No doubt the subject of institutional banking covers both developed markets and emerging markets. However, when the topic of emerging markets and that of institutional banking come together, a simple question will arise: does institutional banking have any unique functions and characteristics for emerging markets?

The answer is 'yes'. In fact there are many. For one thing, problem solving is, understandably, more intensive and more crucial in emerging markets than in developed countries, given the irregularity of the market and nontransparency of the financial/legal system. For another, a good relationship – day-to-day personal communication – usually provides better chances for product marketing and risk management in emerging markets. Moreover, products are usually tailor-made to cater for the needs of the markets. One successful lesson for one case in one country cannot necessarily be repeated in another.

In the meantime, many special financial skills are more often used in emerging markets, notably those for commodity finance, project finance, micro finance, etc. This is because emerging markets are very much involved in raw materials export (commodity finance), long-term infrastructure development (project finance) and poverty reduction (micro finance).

Furthermore, development banks like World Bank, EBRD, ADB and other regional development banks, all of which have development as their mission, are more active in emerging markets. IMF, as another international organization, even plays crucial roles in some emerging market countries especially when a country is in crisis. Institutional banking for emerging markets will have to deal with these regional and global development banks. The subject of institutional banking for emerging markets will not be complete without a discussion of the activities of these development banks. All these lead to our interest in the characteristics of institutional banking for emerging markets.

12.1 HETEROGENEOUSNESS

The coverage of emerging markets ranges from large countries like China and India to tiny economies like Singapore and Hong Kong. Hence emerging markets are by definition heterogeneous in their macro-environmental, cultural and historical backgrounds, political system, etc. The heterogeneousness is also due to the fact some of the 'young emerging economies' have been growing up in more ways than one.

This heterogeneousness is best seen on maps coloured by the degree of risks. Many banks have maps of the world on which countries were painted according to their risk rating. The heterogeneous nature is vividly reflected if categories of countries are painted in different colours. The emerging market part is more 'colourful' (i.e. with many colours) than the mature market part.

This fact indicates that institutional banking for emerging markets will have to accommodate this heterogeneousness. Marketing approaches and risk management attitude should also vary accordingly, especially from one period to another.

It is already noticed that in the different stages of development for the emerging market economies, the products available to a particular country will change, as well as the acceptability of the risk. This implies *vertical* (partner relationship) and *horizontal diversification* (products) for institutional banking, that is institutional banking business should be diversified in terms of partnership, moving from top to lower categories of counterparties, and products moving from few to more in accordance with the development level of the counterparty. Some banks have a principle of dealing with the top five or ten correspondents with fixed categories of products. This may limit their business opportunity.

Due to the heterogeneous nature of institutional banking for emerging markets, the task of institutional banking is more country specific than product specific. Many banks thus organize the institutional banking according to geographical divisions.

As mentioned earlier, a typical arrangement to accommodate this heterogeneous nature of emerging markets is that the institutional banking department is divided into an Asia desk, a Latin America desk, a Middle East desk and an East Europe desk. In many banks, emerging market countries are further divided into several groups (country group one, country group two, etc.) according to the risk and various categories of products offered and promoted to each of them.

For the purpose of risk management, trade finance is offered to most of the emerging markets. For this part of institutional banking, the link with the trade finance is closer. A natural structure is that institutional banking works side by side with the trade finance department, either under the trade finance department or parallel with it. Even under trade finance, there are variety of products to be offered to a variety of countries. The products range from bank guarantee to confirmation of L/Cs, from banker's acceptance to open confirmation towards a letter of credit.

12.2 VOLATILITY

Emerging markets are typically volatile in many fields as discussed in Part I. This volatile nature covers their stock market, their commodity market, their monetary policy, their exchange regime and the incentives arrangements for foreign direct investment.

This volatility nature has been most evident for the stock markets in emerging markets. Various researches have examined the stock market volatility for different countries over time sometimes using econometric models. Results seem to indicate this changing nature of risk and return trade-off in different markets.[1]

As volatility is apparent in most activities, changes are more likely to occur in emerging markets. Changes that do occur are quicker and more unpredictable. This implies that overall strategy for institutional banking should always take the worst case scenario into consideration, with emergency measures standing by.

[1] See paper by Ninon Kohers, Gerald Kohers and Theodor Kohers presented at 2005 Financial Management Association National Meeting in Chicago, Illinois, *Emerging Stock Market Volatility: Common Trends over Time.*

The volatile nature of the emerging markets has an impact on institutional banking activities. For emerging markets, banks are more active for and more interested in short-term self-liquidating activities. This will position the bank in the most flexible setups to adjust its exposure according to the development of the risk.

Due to the volatility of the market, experienced risk management skills turn out to be crucial in this part of business. Valuable assets in institutional banking for emerging markets are those people who understand the volatility, and those who are prepared for the volatility. Instead of getting panicked and surprised, they will become alert when a crisis comes, but see business opportunities for their bank to explore. In their eyes, a crisis may enable them to penetrate into the part of institutional banking business usually not accessible to them before.

12.3 NATURE OF RELATIONSHIP

Duc to low transparency of operation, government meddling and ever-changing regulatory environment in emerging markets, it is not surprising that personal relationship plays a more important role in business there in terms of risk management/problem solving and marketing of products and services.

We know that the web of relationship is important everywhere. A fact all businessmen are aware of is that how well one is connected is fundamental. The success factor is therefore not only what you know but also who you know. But this is particularly true and important in emerging markets.

In the developed world, bankers also prize connections. But there the system of ‘give and take’ pervades all business relationships at all levels, not just among a few chosen friends. In business, the emotional basis is implied or required – you know him/her and very often like him/her. In the emerging markets, however, the relationships are often a few chosen ones and the question is simply do you have the access to the person or not?

There is no denying that a relationship can have its darker side. But the absence of a strong rule of law and a recognized merit system, plus the nepotism in government agencies, all combine to create a vacuum in which power becomes personal. Family background and social ties may be more important than professional attainment. In emerging markets, we sometimes have to live with the fact that a relationship is the key to business success.

Of course, ‘relationship’ is not simply tapping into a network. It is also an obligation to return favours. This implies constant attention to cultivate relationships and careful maintaining of good channels of communication. This is why some banks select people not only for their professional background but also for their social profile.

The importance of relationship, however, should not be exaggerated to the extent that only relationship counts. It is true that in the end it is often the product or the deal that counts. But the weight of relationship cannot be ignored for business in emerging markets. On the other hand, relationship is a long-term commitment and accumulation. Institutional banking is by nature a relationship business. A professional, competent and well-connected team in the institutional banking department, preferably speaking the local language, should be *the* asset of institutional banking. Regular routine visits to follow up local development are part of the job of institutional banking.

12.4 EXOTIC SOLUTIONS

Exotic solutions echoes the heterogeneous nature of emerging markets, as emerging markets have their diversity and considerable country variation. There is no standard menu for questions and answers. Institutional banking professionals have to deliver exotic solutions for institutional clients in emerging markets.

A close scrutiny of emerging market countries reveals that there are many unique situations to be addressed. *Dollarization*, for example, is a special phenomenon for emerging markets.

Dollarization occurs when inhabitants of a country use foreign currency in parallel with or instead of domestic currency.[2] Dollarization can occur unofficially without formal legal approval by the countries' governments, and officially when the government decides to use foreign currency alone as an official payment instrument. In a dollarized economy, economic players consider that to keep their deposits in national currencies is dangerous and accordingly keep their deposits in some hard currency, mostly in dollars. Gradually, this leads to switching from the use of national currency to the use of foreign currency.

Due to the lack of transparency and commitment to the exchange rate target, some countries especially those in Latin America, the near east and eastern Europe have no choice but to adopt the US dollar as a country's currency. Dollarization has been advocated as a monetary policy strategy for some emerging market countries.

Given the nonconvertibility of many national currencies for emerging markets, the national currency issue serves as another example. A well-known fact is that most of the currencies of these countries are nonconvertible. Foreign exchange business therefore needs exotic solutions. *Nondelivery forward* is common as an exotic solution to hedge currency risks in emerging market countries.

Financing trade is also different. We will discuss later the various detailed product requests in trade finance from emerging market banks. In letter of credit business, *silent confirmation* is the only way of financing trade for countries like Iran, China and Vietnam. It is the task of institutional bankers to design tailor-made solutions such as silent confirmation plus letter of assignment to secure the bank's position in the whole transaction.

On the whole, in dealing with emerging market correspondents, there are exceptions. For some of the banking systems for emerging markets, there is not an obvious central bank and the functions of central bank are played by different government agencies. Palestine is such an example where there is no central bank in the banking system.

Islamic banking is yet another example. In fact Islamic banking is a unique emerging market phenomenon. In Muslim communities, the growth of worldwide financial networks and of the reputation of Muslims for trustworthiness has fostered expansion of Islamic banking. More than 35 Islamic banks have sprung up across the 29 member states of the Islamic Organization Conference. Here deposit and lending must be done in accordance with Shariah principles (Islamic laws and regulations based on the Holy Quran and the Sunnah, i.e. the preaching of the Prophet Muhammad). Successful correspondent banks are those that can act as a bridge between Islamic banking, which provides Shariah compliant services to its depositors, and clients. Such a bank may gain access to funds of Islamic depositors by offering them a tentative interest rate on their deposits which may fluctuate depending on the profit or loss the bank has sustained in a financial year. Most of the high profile transactions including M&A, which have been done in the Middle East region over the past

[2] See www.wikipedia.org

couple years, have some component of Islamic finance. This trend is expected to continue. Exotic solutions must thus be provided vis-à-vis Islamic banking, that is some form of Islamic finance capacity must be established, such as a fully fledged dedicated subsidiary having an Islamic finance unit of varying size. Those who do not have such a capacity must try to rapidly build it or give it serious consideration.

In some other emerging markets, *micro finance* is a hot topic. Micro finance is a way of providing finance to the poor in emerging markets. Institutional banking needs expertise and knowledge in this field to serve the needs of this part of finance.

Especially for emerging markets, institutional banking business requests a bank to hold its position to provide innovative and consumer-sensitive services and technology solutions in its operation.

12.5 CULTURE SENSITIVITY

A true analysis of institutional banking for emerging markets would have to consider the culture aspect. When in Rome, do as the Romans do. When dealing with Romans, think of the way Romans think. In fact any business will have to consider this element as it is critical to understanding other cultures when doing business.

In the business context, culture is about do's and don'ts. This can be compared with driving a car.

Each country has its own rules, norms and regulations for driving. Each country has its own infrastructure as well. You have to make adjustments when driving in another country.

In the UK, vehicles are driven on the left. Adjustments are also made when negotiating junctions and roundabouts, for example. In Kuwait, there is a minimum rather than a maximum speed limit so adjustment is needed here too!

The same is true for business in emerging markets. You have to be sensitive and adjust your marketing and risk management efforts because the norms and rules are different with many loopholes, and infrastructure in most cases is just being built.

The unique nature of emerging markets makes culture sensitivity one of the most important success factors. Institutional banking for emerging markets is thus different from institutional banking for mature markets. The selection of staff may have different considerations.

In institutional banking for mature markets, whether the relationship/account manager is male of female, is not that important as for emerging markets. Male staff will be preferred as a relationship manager dealing with Muslim countries, or dealing with countries in the Middle East in general. Similarly, people who have previous exposure to emerging markets, be it on a business level or personal level, can help.

The subject of culture is so essential for emerging markets that we will come back to it later in the following chapters.

SUMMARY

Institutional banking for emerging markets presents some characteristics. First, institutional banking will have to accommodate the heterogeneous nature of emerging markets. Institutional banking business should be diversified in terms of partnership (moving from top to lower categories) and products (from few to more) according to the situation of your correspondent. To accommodate this heterogeneousness, the institutional banking department should be organized according to the geographical or cultural background of its correspondents.

Volatility of emerging markets further requests flexibility of a department's strategy with a worst case scenario mentality but emergency measures standing by. Experienced risk management skills will be especially important.

With low transparency of operation, government meddling and ever-changing regulatory environment, personal relationship emerges as more crucial for businesses. The success factor is not only what you know but also who you know. How well you are connected is fundamental.

Due to their diversity, considerable country variation and unique characteristics, emerging markets require institutional banking to deliver exotic solutions to business. Specific phenomenon such as dollarization and specific business practice such as Islamic banking are good examples for the argument for an exotic solution.

Last but not least, sensitivity to culture difference is an important characteristic for institutional banking business. Institutional bankers should be familiar with the do's and don'ts in emerging market countries and understand the underlying cultural norms. Being sensitive to these culture differences means being sensitive to the opportunities for business.

13
Specialized Finance for Emerging Markets

For institutional banking in emerging markets, to accommodate characteristics unique to emerging markets is not enough. Skills and knowledge unique to the market situation will also be required. This is because in financing emerging markets counterparties, some special forms and techniques of financing prevail. Institutional banking business will come cross these kinds of 'specialized finance'.

As we will find out later, financing in emerging markets is not only a question of *who* but also one of *how*. Activities of institutional banking will be linked to some forms of specialized finance for profit purposes or for risk considerations. Thus to be familiar with these special finance skills is necessary for institutional banking professionals.

Admittedly, some of these special forms of financing may also exist in developed countries. Project finance, for example, is used in Eurotunnel transactions. These forms nevertheless are more often used in emerging market countries. This is due to the fact that traditional balance sheet financing, that is financing based on the borrower's financial strength, often presents difficulties. Moreover, there is a lack of hard currency in emerging market countries and repayment must be linked to hard currency income in the future. Banks will have to focus on the future cash flow of the borrower to secure their position. The art of lending to emerging markets – and the fun of it as well – has become both risk chain analysis and risk chain management.

Emerging market countries mostly export raw materials to earn hard currencies (*commodity finance*), they usually have an underdeveloped infrastructure (*project finance*), and access to finance is not so easy for these economies (*micro finance*). In this chapter we will give a brief discussion on commodity finance, project finance and micro finance. Each topic deserves its own book.

13.1 PROJECT FINANCE

13.1.1 Scope

Project finance refers to financing individual large-scale industrial or infrastructure projects. Finance is usually provided for the medium/long term.

Typically project finance involves funding a company specifically set up for the project which is yet to be released but which is not eligible for payment guarantees from the government. This company is used as a *special purpose vehicle* (SPV), with a structure in which the repayment of the debt is secured by the cash flow generated by the project itself. This occurs without, or with limited, recourse to the project sponsors (shareholders of the SPV).

Historically, project finance is supposed to be largely an American invention.[1] It was used to finance oil companies during the 1930s, particularly in Oklahoma and Texas. The story goes that few big oil companies at that time could have financial resources to search for oil. Their balance sheets were usually too weak for large-scale borrowing. All they had was oil underground and some equipment. As pointed out, the traditional way of secured lending with a strong balance sheet was precluded, or lending with collateral 'assets' seemed hardly possible. Lending based on future revenue flow was thus an attractive way for the borrower and the lender. Given the demand of large-scale oil and gas development, 'project finance' emerged as an important means of finance accepted internationally.

Since the early 1990s project finance has known substantial growth and has been frequently used to finance:

- Utilities (power generation and distribution) projects
- Telecom networks
- Oil and gas plants
- Bridges and toll roads
- Water sanitation projects
- Petrochemicals
- Nonferrous mining and metallurgy, etc.

The rationale of project finance in general is linked to several factors:

- Short of budgetary capacity
- Short of professional management, especially for emerging market countries
- Short of hard currency

13.1.2 Characteristics

Project finance, by nature, is a kind of finance linked to a project, be it a power station, bridge, railway, etc. This is different from normal corporate finance. Under corporate finance, corporate is the focus. Lending to the corporate is evaluated by current cash flow, capital reserves on its balance sheet or other forms of collateral, such as guarantee of another company which has enough financial strength.

Project finance, however, emphasizes the completion of the project as a prerequisite. The assets of the project company secure the lending. But the loan is based on the *future receipts* of the project. The evaluation is based on the feasibility as well as the income-generating capacity of the project.

For corporate finance, the borrower has all the liability (of repayment) whereas project finance is usually based on a nonrecourse or limited recourse basis. Under project finance, the lender takes all the risks such as repayment risk (the cash flow ability of the project), transfer risk (the foreign exchange control of the borrower), foreign exchange rate risk (the fluctuation of the exchange rate between the currency borrowed and the currency in which project generates income), technical risk, operation risk, etc. The essential security to the lender is the project's future cash flow. Under corporate finance, the loan is repaid by total cash flow of the borrower whereas under project finance the lender usually gets repayment

[1] Roy C. Smith and Ingo Walter (2003) *Global Banking*. Oxford University Press.

from the project's own cash flow. As more risks are involved and recourse is limited, the risk premium is usually higher. But some risks must be distributed by insurance (such as country risk, etc.), export promotion agencies, etc. The nature of liability contingent and the period of liability are limited.

13.1.3 Products/Product Structure

There are three basic parties in project finance:

- *Project sponsor*: the party who puts up initial equity.
- *Lender(s)*: the party (parties) who provide loan finance.
- *Borrower*: the project.

There are other parties which have special names in project finance:

- *Primary risk takers*: the party who provides 'guarantees' in case specific risks occur.
- *Residual risks takers*: the lenders.

For large infrastructure financing, *BOT* makes an appearance. BOT means the 'build, operate and transfer' model of infrastructure projects. In most cases the government is involved for a concession and private capital is encouraged to participate and develop the project. After the operation of the project for a certain period of time, the project will be transferred to the government.

As project finance serves special sectors, a typical procedure will imply the following steps:

- Project consultation (project structuring, modelling, legal and technical consultation, etc.).
- Finance arranging, including co-financing with multilateral institutions such as the World Bank, IFC and regional development banks (ADB, EBRD and IDB, etc.).
- Underwriting/participating in the finance.

13.1.4 International Network

As project finance has co-financing with multilateral institutions, international development banks are very often involved including:

- International Finance Corporation (IFC)
- European Investment Bank (EIB)
- Inter-America Development Bank (IDB)
- Asian Development Bank (ADB)
- European Bank for Reconstruction and Development (EBRD)

13.1.5 Risk Management

For banks, the procedure for project finance is project risk analysis, risk distribution and risk reallocation.

Project risks are attributed to the specific participants. This major risk allocation among the parties involved is defined in legal documentation.

Each project has its unique set of risks. Project finance risks include: completion risk, operating risk, supply risk, market risk, credit risk, currency risk, syndication risk, funding risk, legal risk, force majeure, environment risk and political risk.

These risks may arise during different phases of a project, or may be linked to various activities and interconnections between the different authorities and institutions. As such, they have an impact on a project for its financial situation in general and its cash flow in particular.

Risk analysis for project finance indicates that project finance risk can be put into two categories:

- *Pre-completion risks* including financial risk, political risk and project completion risk.
- *Post-completion risks* including cash flow risk and political risk.

Some of the risks in project finance are risks common to other forms of finance such as credit risk, foreign exchange risk, etc. These risks are supposed to be examined in the general frame work of risk mitigation. But some other risks are unique for project finance which need special mitigation techniques.

For risk management purposes, we have to follow the life cycle of a project and examine each risk in more detail.

Completion Risk

Whether the project will be completed or not is a major concern in project finance. Without the completion of the project, future cash flow is zero. This risk arises during the construction phase of the project and represents the greatest risk as the project itself consumes huge amount of funds without generating any revenues at all if not completed.

The contributing factors to noncompletion of the project include, among others:

- Technological feasibility
- Project management organization
- Engineering company and main suppliers' standing and business reputation
- Physical environment
- Project overspend, etc.

Normally, the project is considered completed after relevant technical and financial tests. This procedure will ensure the readiness of the project for commencement of its operating phase, and thus the ability to generate income sufficient for repaying its debt obligations.

Sometimes delays may occur. Why are projects not completed according to the plan? Beenhakker[2] elaborated on several major risk scenarios or events:

- Shortfalls in expected capacity, output or efficiency (power plants, aluminium smelters)

This will result in the inability of the facility to generate sufficient income to meet its financial obligations.

---

[2] H.L. Beenhakker (1997) *Risk Management in Project Finance and Implementation*, Quorum Books, p. 3.

- Shortfalls in the expected raw material supply

This will lead to lower than expected capacity which eventually leads to less revenue available to service the debt.

- Cost overruns

Cost overruns may occur due to unexpected increase in labour cost, construction materials, equipment, supplies and extra construction of utilities required for the project, force majeure such as earthquakes, wars, floods, fires, strikes, etc.

To mitigate these risks several tools are to be used:

- Contractual undertakings and associated guarantees

Under the construction contract, the contractor is responsible for the timely completion of the project at the fixed price and at the agreed level of technical performance. If the contractor fails to fulfil its obligation, it must compensate the project company through a liquidated damages (LD) provision.

- Contingency funds

These funds are usually incorporated into the construction budget ranging from 5 to 15% of the total construction budget. Sometimes contingency funds can be arranged via contingent lines of subordinate debt provided by third-party contractors, stand-by L/Cs and various sponsor guarantees.

- Private insurance

Private insurance allows protecting the project from construction risks, which are not covered by any of the other participants. To finance the project, the lending bank would require the project sponsor or construction contractor to have the following insurance:

- Construction all-risk insurance
- Adjunct liability coverage
- Advance loss of profits insurance
- Delay in start-up insurance

Lenders usually require completion guarantees from project sponsors who unconditionally guarantee that performance will be as expected in terms of time, quantity, quality, etc. Under such a guarantee, the sponsor should cover any and all cost overruns. Typical tools under such a guarantee scheme are performance bonds, guarantees (including stand-by L/C), etc.

Engineering consultants must assess the technical aspect of the project for completion. A performance check via the track record of the same company sponsoring similar projects is quite important.

Operation Risk

Once the construction of the project has been completed, the project will enter into the operation period. The project must operate efficiently and properly to achieve the projected output and generate the revenue. Post-completion risk analysis includes, among others, commercial viability of the project such as labour and raw material supply, environmental risk, economic and financial environment, political and legal environment, etc.

The major risks appearing during this stage are: changes in operating costs (unplanned pollution penalty, etc.), price of the output, cost and availability of the input (price increases of energy or other materials), operating efficiency of the facility (downtime, technological obsolescence), experience of the operational management, etc.

Operating risk may also include inability to meet output targets or quality specifications.

There are a number of instruments that might effectively mitigate the above-mentioned risks such as contractual arrangements which distribute the operational risk to some relevant parties, contingency reserves which may absorb the unplanned increase of costs or decrease of the revenues, technology guarantees which may maintain the operating efficiency of the facility and management and training agreements which may ensure the performance of the operational management.

Market Risk

If the project is completed according to the plan and operates properly, the remaining issue is the sale of the product generated from the project – the market risk.

Market risk is linked to future demand for the product or service supplied by the given project. As lenders rely mostly on the project revenue derived from the off-taker, to serve the debt financing, the risk in volatility in the project's earnings is of great concern.

A market risk occurs when the price of the project's output falls, market share reduces due to competition or other factors, demand for the project output decreases which leads to output excess, or quality of the output is deteriorating.

Mitigation measures can include derivative instruments in the market such as futures, forwards, options and swaps. Measures also include a special hedging programme, quality control programme or forward purchase agreement with a buy-back clause.

Political Risk

Political risk exists not only in developing countries but also in developed countries. As the projects financed by banks have a long-term nature, political risk assessment and mitigation are important. This has been discussed in Part I.

13.2 COMMODITY FINANCE

13.2.1 Scope

Commodity finance involves the extending of credit to finance the purchase and sale of raw, semi-refined or semi-processed material of an animal, vegetable or mineral nature.

Traditionally credits were extended to commodity trading firms which act as middlemen between producers and processors. They are frequently privately owned and internationally oriented. Financially, they are characterized by extensive use of bank credit, high leverage, large volume and low profit margin. As the trader's margins are small but turnover is rapid, the liquidation of assets is expected to provide fully for serving debt.

Recently, many of the commodity traders have become more integrated into the supply chain of commodities, that is either commodity producers do their own exporting themselves or traders invest in fixed assets in the distribution, to secure the cheap and stable source of commodities. Traders and commodity producers even invest in port terminals, processing plants, etc. Commodity traders are thus becoming commodity dealers.

Commodities are typically traded on *commodity exchanges*. A 'commodity contract' can be classified as:

- Agro-products including tropical commodities: Grain, oil seeds (corn, wheat, soybean), food and fibre (cocoa, coffee, sugar, orange juice) and rubber, spice, cotton, nut, vanilla bean.
- Livestock and meat: Cattle, leather, fishmeal, feed-meal, etc.
- Base metals: Copper, copper cathodes, steel, alumina, aluminium, lead, zinc, iron ore, coke and coal.
- Precious metals: Gold, silver, platinum.
- Energy products: Natural gas, heating oil, unleaded gasoline, crude oil, liquid chemicals, LPG, etc.

As a benchmark for investment in the commodity markets and a measurement of commodity market performance, the *Goldman Sachs Commodity Index* (GSCI) is a broad index of commodity price performance, calculated primarily on a world-weighted basis and comprises the principal commodities that are the subject of active, liquid futures markets, containing 49% energy products, 9% industrial/base metals, 3% precious metals, 28% agricultural products and 12% livestock products.

In the last five years, active markets have developed for electricity products, that is, electricity futures for delivery at specific locations, for example California/Oregon border, etc. Following the deregulation of electricity prices, these markets have mushroomed. More recently, OTC markets and exchanges have introduced weather derivatives.

Commodity markets allow participants to exchange risk. Farmers, for example, can sell their crops at a fixed price on a future date, insuring themselves against variations in crop prices. Likewise, consumers can buy crops at a fixed price for future delivery.

13.2.2 Characteristics

The characteristics of commodity finance are related to the fundamentals of commodities. Commodities differ from financial assets in several ways.

First, they may be expensive or even impossible to store. Metal can be stored but the cost of warehousing is high. Solar energy cannot be easily stored at all; neither can electricity. Second, commodities may generate a flow of benefits that are not directly measurable. For example, a company that manufactures copper pipes benefits from an inventory of copper which is used up in its production process. This is the so-called *convenience yield* for the holder of the commodity.

In general, commodity finance is trade finance – financing flows of goods, only the flow is linked to commodities. Commodity finance is, however, unique in the sense that it is very large in its total size compared with general trade finance, and that the size of an individual deal can also be large. A rough estimation of export of primary commodities accounts for one-quarter of total world trade volume. Most commodity finance comes from emerging countries in Africa, Asia and Latin America. Contracts for commodities can easily be worth more than a million.

Moreover, commodity trade as a whole has more transparency than the trade of textiles, machinery, etc. The price of many commodities is transparent as they are listed in the commodity exchange. Very often the major players are also well known in business circles. Commodity finance is a specialized finance that requires banks to have equally specialized knowledge.

The following are characteristics of commodity trade:

- Large turnover
- Often low profit margin
- Fast asset conversion: self-liquidating
- Emerging market linked

As the margins on profitable deals are smaller compared to the size, if one deal goes wrong it can wipe out the profits of many successful ones. This fact of low profit margin pushes the commodity traders into considerating the deal as a package – the price of the commodity, the shipping and forwarding cost, and the warehousing cost together will decide the total profits of the deal. This explains why commodity traders are now entering into the supply chain for building ports and investing in processing plant.

The nature of commodity finance makes it difficult for trading companies to get credit based on their own balance sheets. The fixed assets of trading companies are usually far too small compared to the turnover of the deals they are involved in.

Trading companies usually have small equity bases and they work on very small margins. They make profits through the large volumes they transact. Moreover, many of the producers, processors, traders, exporters and importers are from emerging markets where credit is not easily available or accessible.

Finance via banks plays an important role in facilitating commodity trade flow. In many cases, banking finance is essential. By smartly using various banking facilities, trading companies can leverage their deals with their limited equity. By cleverly using collateral control and title to the goods under transaction, banks can finance the trade (not the trader) with limited and mitigated risk.

In commodity finance, credit is extended to firms in the forms of short-term loans to finance:

- Import and export
- Domestic sales or trades
- Cash and carry transactions
- Consignment sales

At times, commodity finance can be quite lucrative, especially when the bank can properly mitigate its risk and have good control of collateral. By taking risks associated with top quality customers, such as the multinational oil, grain and steel companies, commodity banks may have handsome spreads.

13.2.3 Products/Product Structure

Letter of Credit Linked Finance

Back-to-back finance: One of the most significant ways of easing price risk in commodity lending is the establishment of a back-to-back trade. Under this scenario, a trader will effectively buy and sell the commodity at the same time. As there is always a time lag, a position would be created for this brief moment.

The bank issues a letter of credit on behalf of the client (trader or intermediary) who has an L/C issued by another bank of the buyer. The buyer's L/C is used as collateral. The back-to-back credit offers rather more latitude for issuing a countercredit in favour of the supplier of the goods on the basis of credit that has been received. It is in fact an ordinary documentary arrangement, under which the documents are needed to be able to dispose of the original documentary credit (the master L/C may be presented). This is obviously a new credit granted by the bank issuing the countercredit.

Therefore prior to issuing the back-to-back credit, the bank must carefully check the status of the intermediary who applies for this back-to-back facility for the following:

- Is he considered reputable?
- Does he have a good record in his field?
- Is he familiar with the type of deal for which he has requested a back-to-back credit?
- Is he used to dealing with the products in question?

Front-to-back finance: Front-to-back is similar to back-to-back but the issuing bank issues the L/C before the bank receives any L/C to its counter. The idea is to provide finance to the importer (trader) in the form of letter of credit. This credit L/C facility is based on trading background and relevant documents. The facility is secured by trade flow and is more flexible than back-to-back.

Stand-by credit/guarantee: Among credits, stand-by credit occupies a special position. Its origin is in the United States, where commercial banks are not allowed to give guarantees. In order to be able to provide such a service, the guarantee has been moulded into the form of a credit: the 'stand-by' credit. This credit facility is in fact a bank guarantee to give the seller comfort. Therefore stand-by L/Cs or straightforward guarantees are used to secure payment in commodity finance.

Structured Commodity Finance

Our earlier discussion indicated clearly that there is usually little sense in looking for recourse finance to commodity traders whose own equity could easily wipe them out. Finance to commodity traders or commodity producers, if any, would have to be structured along asset-based lines. Like project finance, the procedure of structured finance is to analyse, distribute and reallocate the risks.

The classic structure for commodity finance thus continues to be based on a combination of taking security over the physical commodities in the form of a local law pledge or similar security interest. This is more often used for soft (agricultural) commodities.

Under structured commodity finance the receivables arising under the export contracts for the commodities are assigned to establish a collection account in a suitable offshore location into which purchasers of the commodities are directed to pay the assigned export receivables.

Various credit enhancement devices can complement the traditional core structure. Examples of credit enhancement include guarantees (payment or performance guarantee provided by a financial institution or other third party which will give payment or deliver security), insurance cover and, in the case of export contracts on a floating price basis, commodity price hedges.

By using a structure of this kind, lenders can reduce a number of risks inherent in commodity finance. Credit risk on the borrower may be mitigated by recourse to the off-taker(s) via assignment of export receivables, while currency/transfer/devaluation risk may be alleviated by receivables paid into an offshore collection account.

Stock Finance

Stock finance can be divided into bonded warehouse finance and non-bonded warehouse finance.

Bonded warehouses: Finance for a bonded warehouse refers to financing cargo stored in bonded warehouses against a pledge of warehouse receipts issued by warehouse operators/collateral managers internationally known such as C. Steinweg and Cornelder. Goods in bonded warehouses are stored under customs supervision and may only be removed under certain conditions. This may improve the bank's control over the goods. Moreover, re-export of imported goods stored in a bonded warehouse can be effected without custom clearance.

Non-bonded warehouses (including Port Authorities): The majority of nonbonded stock financing covers export-ready cargos of metals (such as zinc, lead and aluminium) at the loading port. Such nonbonded warehouses are operated by state-owned or private companies. Such companies will actually offer nothing else than the lease of warehouse space. If the banks intend to finance such warehouse stocks, the collateral management role is the key. Usually this role is to be entrusted in internationally known warehouses such as C. Steinweg and Cornelder. But more often nowadays, Port Authority-owned companies or reliable logistics companies with good records are becoming involved in performing this collateral management role.

For agricultural commodities, independent inspectors such as SGS are also involved in the collateral management for nonbonded warehouse financing.

Advance ratio and tenor depend on the financial situation of the borrower as well as the market value of the collateral.

Other Commodity Finance Products

Other commodity finance products are:

- Pre-crop financing
- Purchase of raw materials for processing
- Processing with recourse to emerging market producer
- Pre-export under FOB/DAF delivery terms
- Limited recourse finance for traders
- Pre-crop/processing with full recourse to OECD party

- Storage in emerging market ports with perfect title or full recourse to OECD party
- Pre-export with full recourse to OECD party
- Storage and distribution in OECD markets

13.2.4 International Network

International Chamber of Commerce

The International Chamber of Commerce is an important organization in trade finance. They set rules and regulations in this field. Uniform Customs and Practice for documentary credits (UCP) is a set of rules and regulations developed in response to practical requirements. They are rarely covered by law.

Banks' trade experts have been aware from the very beginning of international trade that it is impossible to master all the trading practices applied throughout the world. Instead, banking associations in various countries have been trying to code these practices. Under the direction of the International Chamber of Commerce in Paris a text was drawn up jointly by various banks and ratified in 1933. This was the birth of *Uniform Customs and Practice for Documentary Credits* (UCP500). Understandably, the manual as such has since been revised on several occasions, the last being in March 1993.

Commodity Exchanges

There are different specialized commodity exchanges: *LIFFE* (London International Financial Futures and Options Exchange) for coffee, *MATIF* (Marché à Terme d'Instruments Financiers) for agro commodities, *LME* (London Metals Exchange) for metals, *IPE* (International Petroleum Exchange) for petroleum and NYBOT, NYMEX, CBOT, etc.

13.2.5 Risk Management

Several key issues are important to commodity finance in risk management. Banks in the business of financing commodities must assure themselves of the *credit quality* of the ultimate buyers, the *quality* of collateral in hand, the *diversification* of commodity firm's exposure to the buyers and volume of business.

In general, commodity finance can be on a secured and unsecured basis. Unsecured loans are balance sheet finance – financially sound, high quality borrowers, and those large and most creditworthy companies. They have large capitalization and substantial cash flows. As such, they are often multinational by nature, banking with a couple of banks and borrowing at extremely thin spreads.

On the other hand, secured lending occurs when the bank's normal criteria for unsecured credit cannot be met due to

- Inherent volatility
- Thin capitalization of the borrower
- Esoteric industry risks

Secured lending is made possible if the bank can have possession of negotiable title documents, which represent commodities themselves. Title documents can be negotiable licensed warehouse receipts, LME warrants, negotiable bills of lading, etc. Secured lending is possible if the lender is secured by a pool of assets such as inventory and accounts receivable.

All secured borrowers will be on a transitional, collateral pool. It is often the case that the bank's normal criteria for the extension of unsecured credit are not met. As discussed above, in commodity finance, reference can be made for banks to refuse to accept the inherent volatility, thin capitalization, and esoteric industry risks. The banks use these for refusing to lend unsecured.

Security, if properly used, is a device employed to make a loan possible where otherwise it would have been impossible or unlikely. The credit objectives have been summarized by three main items: *protection*, *seniority* and *control*. Proper follow-up on this is necessary for risk management purposes.

- Protection: The net realized value of specific collateral should be sufficient to cover the bank's exposure, recognizing that the face value of the collateral may well have shrunk or will shrink during liquidation.
- Seniority: Priority of being paid over other lenders.
- Control: A detailed understanding of a customer's trade cycle is necessary to reconcile the tenor of each advance. Upon the borrower's sale of the goods and subsequent receipt of the funds, the bank's advance should be repaid, or collateral subtracted from the overall pool.

13.3 MICRO FINANCE

13.3.1 Scope

'Micro finance' refers to the provision of financial services to low income clients, including the self-employed. Financial services provided by micro financial institutions include small savings and credit.

Micro finance has evolved as an economic development approach intended to benefit the low income population. It has emerged as one of the most sustainable and effective tools for enabling the economically underprivileged to gain access to institutional financial services. In many countries, a large part of micro finance activity is confined to credit.

Although financial services provided by micro financial institutions generally include small savings and credit, some micro finance organizations also provide insurance and payments services.

In addition to financial intermediation, many micro finances provide social intermediation confidence, and training in financial literacy and management capabilities among members of a group. Thus the definition of micro finance often includes both *financial intermediation* and *social intermediation*. Micro finance is not simply banking: it is a development tool.

The need for such a development tool is based on the estimation that there are 500 million economically active poor people in the world operating micro enterprises and small businesses. Most of them do not have access to adequate financial services. To meet this substantial demand for financial services by low income micro entrepreneurs, micro finance practitioners and donors alike have to adopt a long-term perspective.

The history of micro finance shows that it arose as a way to finance the poor farmers in the 1980s in response to public doubts and general research findings about state delivery of subsidized credit to poor farmers.

Beginning in the mid-1980s, the subsidized, targeted credit modes supported by many donors were under steady criticism. This was partially due to the fact that most subsidized loan lending programmes accumulated large losses and required frequent fresh capital injection in order to continue their operation. In the 1970s government agencies were the predominant methods of providing subsidized credit to those with no previous access to credit facilities – people who had low income and who had been forced to pay unusual interest rates or were subject to rent seeking behaviour. The belief at that time, especially for governments and international donors, was that the poor required cheap credit and saw this as a way of promoting agricultural production by small landholders. Such a cooperative idea can be traced back to 1864 with the so-called Raiffeisen model developed in Germany. The focus of these concepts of the cooperative financial institutions was mostly on saving mobilization in an attempt to 'teach poor farmers how to save'.

After the mid-1980s, it became more and more evident that market-based solutions were preferred and required. This led to a new approach that considered micro finance as an integral part of the overall financial system. Emphasis therefore shifted from the rapid subsidized loans to target populations towards the building up of local, sustainable institutions to serve the poor.

This background explains why micro finance has grown substantially since the 1980s. Donors actively support and encourage micro finance activities, focusing on micro finances that are committed to achieving substantial outreach and financial sustainability.

Today, the focus is on providing financial services only, whereas the 1970s and much of the 1980s were characterized by an integrated package of credit and training, which required subsidies.

Most recently, micro finances are being transformed into formal financial institutions that recognize the need to provide savings services to their clients and to access market funding sources, rather than rely on donor funds. This recognition of the need to achieve financial sustainability has led to the current 'financial systems' approach to micro finance.

Back in 1980, government projects, local and international, incorporated in their activities a new branch termed 'micro finance' in order to supplement their activities in developing rural areas. In addition, in the 1990s, new credit and savings schemes were created, to cope with fund mobilization to finance women's activities, construction of residential houses and other equipments.

In rural areas, many local and international nongovernment organizations have started the mass mobilization of people to create their own micro finance institutions using existing credit and savings schemes.

Stakeholders in credit and/or savings can be divided into several categories such as nonprofit associations; credit and savings schemes; national nongovernment organizations; international nongovernment organizations; commercial banks and government projects.

13.3.2 Characteristics

Micro finance institutions clearly belong to the category of financial institutions, but the mission of micro finance is to go for the small ones with all the extra staff and handling costs. They do what normal financial institutions would not do. For example, regular banks prefer to give one loan of €100 000 (in their local currency), rather than a thousand loans of the equivalent of €100 for the cost consideration. Commercial banks typically would not give a loan without adequate collateral, but micro finance institutions concentrate on poor people who have no bankable collateral to offer. Some micro finance institutions even work with the so-called 'negative assets test': 'is this client poor enough to qualify for a loan?'

Micro finance as a 'financial system' is built up on the following rationale and beliefs:

- Subsidized credit undermines development. Poor people can pay interest rates high enough to cover transaction costs and the consequences of the imperfect information markets in which lenders operate.
- The goal of sustainability (cost recovery and eventually profit) is the key not only to institutional performance in lending, but also to making the lending institution more focused and efficient.
- Because loan sizes to poor people are small, micro finances must achieve sufficient scale if they are to become sustainable.
- Measuring enterprise growth, as well as impacts on poverty, cannot be demonstrated easily or accurately; outreach and repayment rates can be proxies for impact.

One of the main assumptions in the above view is that many poor people actively want *productive credit* and that they can absorb and use it. But as the field of micro finance has evolved, research has increasingly found that in many situations poor people want secure savings facilities and consumption loans just as much as productive credit and in some cases instead of productive credit.

Micro finances are beginning to respond to these demands by providing voluntary savings services and other types of loan. It was noticed that large countries like China and India are becoming active in this field as well. The general expectation is that the distribution cost can be reduced in the future through new technology, such as phone banking.

13.3.3 Products/Product Structure

Micro finance activities usually involve:

- Small loans, typically for working capital for micro entrepreneurs
- Loans for home improvement
- Small consumer loans
- Money transfers
- Insurance, etc.

As mentioned, micro finances can be nongovernmental organizations (NGOs), savings and loan cooperatives, credit unions, government banks, commercial banks or nonbank financial institutions. Micro finance clients are typically self-employed, low income entrepreneurs in both urban and rural areas. Clients are often traders, street vendors, small farmers, service providers, and artisans and small producers, such as blacksmiths and seamstresses. Their activities are expected to provide a stable source of income.

13.3.4 International Network

Micro finance is mostly linked to a limited number of countries. There is no international framework or organization for the activities of micro finance. International Development Aid agencies are usually very much interested and involved in these activities.

13.3.5 Risk Management

Micro finance is unique as it is intended for the poor or very poor people and lending is usually on a noncollateral basis. Micro finance is crucial to a sustainable development. As Kofi Annan mentioned: 'Let us be clear: microfinance is not a charity! It is a way to extend the same rights and services (financial services) to low-income households that are available to everyone else.' Commercial viability is thus emphasized and it is supposed to be self-sustaining with income earned from the financial services to cover costs. The income and access to the capital market allow micro finance institutions to grow.

Usually late payments are maintained at a very low level, often below 5% of total lending. There are a few explanations.

First, the concentration risk in micro finance institutions' portfolios is very low (very high number of small loans) compared to big international banks' normal loans. The costs of micro finance are high, because of the high cost of distribution and monitoring. This intense monitoring is probably one of the reasons for the low ratio of nonpayments.

Second, there is usually appraisal of borrowers and investments like normal commercial loans. Although collateral will hardly be possible, collateral substitutes such as group guarantees or compulsory savings are used to reduce possible bad debts. Group guarantees are probably better collateral than the traditional stuff.

Third, borrowers are encouraged to repay on time by access to repeated and larger loans based on repayment performance. These are streamlined loan disbursement and monitoring and secure savings products. Needless to say, donors are providing soft funds to finance portfolios.

SUMMARY

For marketing purposes and also to contribute to risk management, risk mitigation and problem solving in emerging markets, institutional banking will have to consider some forms of specialized finance prevailing in emerging markets. These are: project finance, commodity finance and micro finance.

Project finance is the finance of large-scale industrial (utilities, telecom, oil and gas, etc.) or infrastructure (bridges, railways, etc.) projects, usually for the medium to long term. A special purpose vehicle (SPV) is common for executing the task of building the project. Lending is covered by future cash flow generated by the project itself.

Several risks are to be monitored in such cases: completion risk, operating risk, market risk, currency risk, environmental risk and political risk.

Commodity finance is more often short term and self-liquidating. Finance is provided to commodity traders who have thin capital. Commodity trade as a whole is more transparent than general trade. Commodity finance is a specialized finance that requires the financing bank to have relevant knowledge on the subject.

Micro finance is to provide financial services to low income clients. It is more a development tool for emerging markets. Micro finance activities involve small loans, loans for home improvement, small consumer loans, insurance, etc.

Although lending to low income clients seems to be risky, several factors explain why micro finance may survive: risk is much diversified in terms of number of borrowers and their background; borrowers, who usually do not have access to finance, value this channel of borrowing and are encouraged to repay for future borrowing. Moreover, different forms of collateral are also used to reduce the default risk.

14 Marketing for Emerging Markets

14.1 UNDERSTANDING THE CULTURE AND BANKING PRACTICE FOR COUNTERPARTIES

Marketing institutional banking products in emerging markets has many barriers and difficulties. One barrier can well be the language issue. It probably hasn't escaped your notice that many institutional banking staffs in emerging markets do not speak good English, although they are supposed to do so. In addition to language barriers, we will probably also be aware that cultural differences, which are often less obvious, can be just as big an obstacle to institutional banking business.

Due to the heterogeneousness of the emerging markets in terms of social, political and cultural background, sensitivity to culture emerges in many cases as a crucial or even decisive factor to the success of marketing.

People are different. They are different because they have different cultural backgrounds. We have discussed already that culture consists of specific learned norms based on people's attitudes, values and beliefs. The fact is that cultural differences exist everywhere, in each country and society.

People doing cross-border business – for example, institutional bankers – find that behavioural differences give rise to different business practices in various parts of the world. Understanding the cultures of groups of people is useful because the banking business, like any other business, employs sales to and purchases from counterparties. Banking business is regulated and owned by people.

Before marketing, institutional banking professionals must consider these differences in order to predict and control their relationships and operations. Further, institutional banking professionals have to realize that the accustomed way of doing business may not be the only or the best way. Culture sensitivity entails a built-in instinct for cultural differences.

Besides, when a bank is marketing its products or services abroad, it should first determine whether a typical banking practice in a foreign country differs from that at home. It is not surprising to find the business practice there differs.

Even in a more or less same culture environment such as in Europe, business practice may differ. A simple example can be fee charges of account service in Europe – the British and Germans are used to getting free current accounts but paying for cash withdrawals from other banks' ATMs. The French pay for their bank accounts but expect cash withdrawals across the euro-zone to be free. Italians pay nothing for keeping a current account but are charged high fees for every transaction. It is not certain if these differences are due to cultural factors. But cultural differences can make business practice different. If you do not do as the Romans do, you will be out of the market.

Yet it is not so easy to identify which are 'cultural factors', as culture cannot easily be isolated from economic, political and other factors. Some even argue that culture is influenced by religion. Nevertheless, some aspects of culture differ significantly across national borders and thus have a substantial impact on how business is normally conducted in different cultural backgrounds.

Many examples can be found to indicate that culture has an impact on the marketing of banking products. For one, why is asset management as a product still in its infancy in Asia? Why are unit trusts or mutual funds still not as popular as they are in the US or in Europe, although they are growing rapidly?

To some extent, this is linked to Asian mentality: they do not want to give money to other people to manage. Rather, they prefer to manage their money themselves. If they pay a fee, they want to see a physical return. In Asia, to pay a fee for someone who might lose your money is rarely acceptable. In Europe, people give money to professional fund managers. And to share profits with these professionals is quite fair business practice. This will enable the owner of the money to have more free time to follow other life targets.

In terms of pricing, one private banker also noticed the cultural difference. In Asia, private bankers price their products linked to performance rather than total volume/turnover (of assets). Many customers of private banking in Asia are self-made millionaires who care very much about their hard-earned money, whereas some rich clients in Europe inherited wealth from their parents and their attitude towards wealth can thus be different.

An interesting phenomenon – although not tested – in Asian culture, particularly among the Chinese, is the instinct to take risk or simply the instinct to gamble. A colleague from a Taiwanese bank mentioned that the stock exchange in Taiwan is one of the places in the world which has the highest turnover of stocks (to buy and sell stocks in order to lock in profits), although there is no empirical evidence of this. People will say that they 'invest' so much in stocks or foreign exchange. Even if they are unsuccessful they are not willing to give their money next time to a professional. This is because if they do, they will lose the fun of 'gambling'. In this cultural context, for asset management, an (income) guarantee product is definitely more attractive.

Another aspect of culture are individualism and group activities. The Japanese are recognized as having low employee turnover. They are extremely loyal to their company and advancement is primarily based on longevity with the company, although this is definitely changing. Employees usually also enjoy considerable after-work socializing. Working more as a group and having a bottom-up consensus for decision making are favoured among Japanese workers.

Culture influences behaviour and business practice. For many years, Japan has enjoyed nearly zero interest on deposits, but the saving rate has still been very high. Such a phenomenon can only be explained by cultural factors – the attitude towards borrowing. In the field of mortgage loans, the same principle works. In Asia, a mortgage is usually linked to periodic payment on principal and interest whereas in Europe there are schemes that allow you to pay only interest without paying principal until the end of the mortgage contract, when your principal will be paid by your parallel investment.

There are more examples of differences in banking practices in different parts of the world – letter of credit has been of less significance in some markets (like Latin America) whereas eastern Europe/CIS, Africa and mainly Asia remain regions where clients traditionally ask for the establishment of letters of credit to protect themselves.

These examples, and possibly others as well in our further discussion, certainly help to explain the point of view that cultural difference among countries is something worth considering in marketing products and services for institutional banking.

14.2 UNDERSTANDING THE NEEDS OF YOUR INSTITUTIONAL CLIENTS

Marketing serves clients needs and can also do them favours. To research these needs therefore is an important step.

Institutional clients in emerging markets may indeed have various needs, some of which may differ greatly from those of developed market clients. For the purpose of marketing, the needs of your institutional clients can be classified into several categories: liquidity and cheap funding, banking know-how, special support, external support for their strategic development (e.g. branch/product expansion), special products (UPAS, remittance business, etc.).

14.2.1 Cheap Funding for Liquidity Purposes

Many of the emerging market banks need money market lines from their correspondents as a source of cheap funding. Before Basel II, the price of such money market lines was determined by the lending banks and usually the margin was thin and the borrowing was thus relatively cheaper.

Money market limit is a name for lending with nothing as collateral. This is an attractive relationship product because not every bank can get such a money market treatment due to a relatively low credit rating for the country or a low credit rating for that specific borrowing bank in an emerging market.

In institutional banking, such a need for a money market is evident. This need for cheap funding is especially strong for overseas branches of emerging market banks, as these overseas branches do not have a retail network to support a cheap source of funding via deposit taking.

Money market lines can be offered in a package for other related, more profitable but less risky business, such as foreign exchange business, trade finance business, derivative business and structured fixed income business.

14.2.2 Banking Know-how: Specialists and Skills

Many banks from emerging markets need banking know-how. Competition among banks is usually one of human capital and management skills.

Some of the emerging market banks develop very fast in hardware but there is lack of exposure to complicated products and complicated banking management practice. These banks need to absorb the skills and banking know-how from their correspondents when they are evolving into developed markets or catering for more sophisticated banking products.

To achieve this, one way is to buy knowledgeable and experienced people in the market. It is understandable that these banks often offer international competitive salary packages to recruit banking brains for many key positions. But it is neither necessary nor possible to hire all the required staff in the international banking market. To offer training to emerging market banks, therefore, is a very important marketing instrument for institutional banking.

To provide training is not only to 'help' emerging market banks. It is not a one-way 'favour'. On the contrary, training can be offered to achieve the goals from two ends: to transfer banking know-how to emerging market banks and to educate the market for offering banks' future products. Training offered will enable your institutional clients to have full knowledge of your history, your brand and your product. The second function tends to be ignored by some banks but is important. The institutional clients will only be interested in your product when they really understand what it is about and how to use it.

Training can take several forms: seminars, internships, on-job training, study (survey) tour, etc.

Seminars

Seminars are usually given on some special topics which the host bank is good at. Thus the knowledge is delivered in a short period with relatively lower costs.

Specialists may also go all the way to an institutional client's home base to organize such a tailor-made seminar. A successful seminar, however, is not easily achieved. The host bank needs a thorough understanding of the interest, the concern and the professional level of the participants. Here the language issue is quite essential. If the trainer can speak the language of that country, it will greatly help the communication during the training period. If the trainer cannot speak the language, a qualified interpreter is crucial to the success of such a seminar.

It happens very often that an interpreter is hired and although they may speak the language beautifully they have hardly any knowledge of the subject matter. As a consequence the audience could either be confused or bored.

Box 14.1 offers an outline of what can be expected in a three-day seminar.

Box 14.1 Seminar for Commercial Banking and Risk Management in Banking

Outline

Training Course Risk Management

Objective:
Risk control is increasingly recognized within the banking sector as an important aspect of banking management. This three-day course intends to provide participants with an in-depth overview of the most recent risk identification, measurement and management techniques, in order to implement a risk management strategy in a bank with an international perspective. The course includes extensive real world cases and discussions.

Target participants:
Bank managers with 3–5 years' experience in different fields especially in

- Corporate lending
- Retail banking
- International business, etc.

As the course will involve a great deal of financial analysis, some fundamental knowledge of accounting is a must.

Course content:
Day One
The fundamental task of banks: risk management

- Balance sheet of a bank
- Working environment
- The function of central bank

The importance of risk management

- Asset and liability management
- Liquidity, insolvency and profitability

The categories of risk in the bank

- Credit risk
- Operation risk
- Forex risk
- Reputation risk

Day Two
Company risk

- Assets and liabilities, the concept of bankruptcy
- Five Cs principle
- Four eyes principle

Bank risk

- Capital adequacy guideline
- Major indicators on strength, size, liquidity, efficiency and profitability

Day Three
Country risk

- The definition of country risk
- The methodology of country risk

Risk management in the bank

- Credit limit and the decision of limits
- The supervision principle and mechanism

Internships

Internships are attached to departments in the bank with so-called mentors to guide them. This kind of training gives opportunities for emerging market banks to learn face to face.

The trainees under the internship arrangement sometimes have their own training targets or research topics, such as to establish a back office in their bank. They only wants to see and investigate the practical side in the host bank.

Subjects for an internship can be anything including feasibility of a branch, human resources management (salary and bonus distribution and promotion system), back office function, or experience of product development (real estate, leasing, etc.).

The host bank is willing and ready to accommodate such an internship. The intended internship usually provides some concrete conclusion on the subject to be researched, or the existing conclusion for desk study is to be cross-checked during the trainee's stay in the bank.

On-job Training

On-job training is intensive training in the actual business environment. Trainees are expected to work as employees of the bank.

With exposure to the day-to-day work in the host bank, the trainee will gain knowledge of specific tasks when he/she returns to his/her home bank. A trainee's future function can be as a department head, a dealer, etc.

This kind of training, often on a one-to-one basis, offers a long-lasting impact on mutual relationship and understanding between the host bank and the trainee's bank.

There were many cases where, when the trainees returned to their own bank, a personal relationship was forged and it became easier to communicate with the host bank as a counterparty in daily business. This is why the host bank is encouraged to offer an internship.

The trainee will know exactly the pros and cons of the host bank, and most of them are likely to hold high positions after on-job training. Such a trainee is thus a valuable asset both to the host bank, which provided the training, and to their own bank, which requested the training. On-job training, however, is offered on a small scale and there are other issues to be dealt with such as logistics (of the trainee) and confidentiality of bank data.

Study (Survey) Tour

A study (survey) tour from emerging market banks is intended for a host bank to receive delegations and have in-house presentations on some special subjects.

Such a tour, if organized, focuses on one or more topics which are of interest to the members of the delegation. The subjects range from credit card and human resource issues, motivation systems and IT, to risk management, relationship management and credit norms and rules. In receiving such a delegation, a good interpreter (he/she should know both the language and the content) is again crucial as emphasized earlier.

The costs of training as a marketing incentive or business rebate are usually borne by the host bank. The host banks are motivated to the extent that the relationship can be developed via such training. The institutional clients who receive the training will have a closer understanding with the host bank.

It may sometimes happen that such training is financed by another organization such as the World Bank and regional and international development banks, governments and other institutions like the EU. These institutions have a so-called *Technical Assistance* (TA) budget but do not themselves have the training facility. Under such circumstances, commercial banks can utilize such facilities for their marketing purposes without bearing the costs themselves.

14.2.3 Special Support

In institutional banking, special support can also be required from counterparties, who need such a special support for their strategic development or for some operational issues.

A typical example is that when a bank intends to expand into another country, they will ask a good correspondent to help. Such help includes market feasibility, logistics support, information checking and cross-checking, etc.

Incidentally, a correspondent may also ask you to assist in finding a good lawyer, in case they have a court case with another party in the country where your bank is located.

Banks may also be requested to channel L/Cs to a nominated country where their branch was recently established, in the hope of supporting their branch there. Such branch support is requested on commercial terms (cheaper fees, rebate, etc.).

14.2.4 Special Products

The original purpose of correspondent banking was the need for a foreign agent – you chose a foreign bank when you had some special need for your client but you did not have your own branches there.

Many correspondent banks may need product promotion to the overseas market specially oriented to their own market need. A relevant example is remittance business for overseas workers from some emerging market banks.

As we already know, many emerging market countries count on remittances as an important source of hard currency income. Remittance is a contribution to economic growth and development for the country.

A survey from the *Economist* magazine based on information from the World Bank indicates that immigrants from developing countries were expected to send more than $167 billion back home in 2005 (see Table 14.1).[1] In institutional banking, to facilitate overseas remittance is an interesting task.

These international payment transfers play a crucial role in the wider debate on access to finance for both migrants and their relatives and communities in their home countries.

Table 14.1 Importance of remittances to selected countries (% of GDP 2005)

Haiti	24.8%
Jordan	20.4%
Jamaica	17.4%
Serbia	17.2%
The Philippines	13.5%
Egypt	4.4%
Pakistan	4.1%
Colombia	3.3%
India	3.1%
Mexico	2.7%
China	1.3%
Malaysia	0.8%
Indonesia	0.7%
Brazil	0.6%
Russia	0.5%
Turkey	0.3%

Source: World Bank, etc.

[1] *Economist*, 3 December 2005, p. 102.

Recognizing the high volume and potential impact of these flows, the G8 national governments, regulatory bodies, financial institutions and the civil society have expressed their interest and commitment to facilitate these transfers across the world. In order to maximize the benefits arising from remittances, private and public initiatives are working together, because for remittances to contribute effectively to economic development, private and public forces need to converge. In these efforts, institutional banking can have a definite role to play.

To effectively channel the remittances home, Filipino banks indicate their interest in the tele-money remittance programme, a system of serving the remittance proceeds from foreign exchange earnings of their overseas workers.

This remittance product turns out to be the key element in their correspondent banking For Filipino banks.

Such a remittance programme operates through a network of agents/tie-ups that a Filipino bank establishes around the world and a delivery system that a Filipino bank has set up throughout the Philippines archipelago.

As a correspondent, the foreign bank acts as a foreign agent handling the sourcing and acceptance of the remittances from overseas workers, while the delivery system handles the payment/implementation of the remittance proceeds to the designated beneficiaries. This kind of tie-up helps a great deal to bolster the market share ambition of Filipino banks.

To the correspondent (agent) bank, the motivation is a close relationship with account services and deposit services on top of mark-up earnings in excess of minimum services fees for Filipino banks.

The bank qualified for such cooperation should have an extensive retail network and an interest in such remittance business. As a result, the relationship usually will lead to more spin-off benefits for the agent banks. For Filipino banks, this is a low cost programme for approaching their remittance target clients.

Korean and Indonesian banks need refinance facilities under trade finance. Therefore, refinance has been traditionally a product of institutional banking business.

14.3 THE PRICE ISSUE IN MARKETING FOR INSTITUTIONAL BANKING

The success of marketing depends on quality and price. In marketing for institutional banking, the price issue is inevitable. But to price a product is no easy job and it will in the first place depend on *price objectives* and *price strategy*.

To decide on a price for banking products, like any other products, has several considerations. Cost plus mark-up is a typical way of charging clients.

Here the cost refers to the cost of funding (LIBOR, etc.) plus a risk premium. If it is a commission fee, the cost is for administrating the product. But price can also be demand driven, in which case the price is determined by supply and demand rather than costs.

There are also strategic concerns such as market share, branch development and the importance of the counterparties, as we will see in the following discussion of price objectives.

The basic price objectives include but are not limited to:

- Maximizing profits for the short run: This is especially relevant for some walk-in clients or other one-off relationships.

- Maximizing profits in the long run: This applies to clients of strategic importance – clients with good credit standing, large business volume, etc.
- Expanding market shares: This applies especially to a new market or to a new product where you want to reach some economies of scale.
- Surviving: This applies to a new and difficult market where you are more a price-taker than a price-dictator. You therefore have to accept any price offered to you, if you want to remain in that market.

Apart from these principles, the practical factors outlined below must also be taken into consideration:

- The geographical factor: Usually large banks have branches all over the world. Like it or not, the price offered has to follow the local market conditions. To different branches in different continents or countries (Dutch, Belgian, Asian, European, etc.), different price indications must be given, that is there has to be a differential price policy towards different geographical markets even if the product is the same.
- The benchmark: It is always good to investigate the competitive environment (competitors, bank lending interest rate level, availability of line, nature of the risk taken) for price and set a benchmark. Government bond price is sometimes taken as an indication of a benchmark for country risk.
- The price structure: Like marketing any other products, marketing banking products also needs a sophisticated attitude. The price of a trade finance product for instance is not at all straightforward.

  If your bank adds your confirmation to one bank's letter of credit at the price of 1% pa, but your competitor offers a price of 0.8% for the same risk as the issuing bank, does that automatically mean your price is less competitive? No, not always. What is missing here is the 'price structure'.

  In reality, we notice that the price offered by some banks indeed looks cheaper at first glance, but they charge the fee on a quarterly basis with the condition of 'part-thereof'. This may result in higher total charges.

  In some cases banks may charge a fee for the *confirmation* of L/Cs but so-called confirmation is on a 'with recourse' basis. Under the name of 'confirmation', the risk coverage is different. In other cases some banks may offer a lower price for confirmation but add an extra margin for the discounting period. All this leads to *ad hoc* higher costs to the clients.

  The important thing in marketing is that you have to indicate 'what your price really covers', if you face price competition. Sometimes it is best to sit down and calculate together with the client.
- The relationship with your client: Special arrangements are for different clients based on the total earnings and their importance towards the bank always possible.

  It is not unusual that a company client has relations with several banks. To motivate loyal clients and encourage their volume, arranging a progressive scheme for price (the higher the total volume is, the lower the price that will be charged) turns out to be effective.

  As specialists for bank and country, institutional banking professionals should make joint efforts with account managers of companies to maximize the price including providing them with arguments (such as tight country limit, nature of the transaction, branch, tenor, etc.).

14.4 THE PRODUCT ISSUE IN MARKETING FOR EMERGING MARKETS

We have detailed discussion for products of institutional banking. What is to be discussed here is that these products offered in the menu of institutional banking will have different risk implications for the counterparties.

Not every product is suitable for marketing to each institutional client in emerging markets. Money market limit is a relevant example – it is offered on a much selected basis. Some of the products such as trade finance products are offered with limited tenor considering the counterparty risk. To some countries, project finance is offered under the condition of an *ECA* (export credit agency) cover or the involvement of international development banks. Other products will be offered on a structured basis to redistribute the risk.

Some global market products such as interest rate swap, currency swap, etc. are offered on the basis that *ISDA* or even *CSA* (credit service annex) agreements are signed. For letters of credit, a *silent confirmation* service is offered to some emerging market countries, but to others, it will be forbidden.

It is not unusual that products will be on offer only when a framework agreement is signed between two parties. Since not every product is suitable for marketing to each institutional client in emerging markets, it is necessary to adjust the product structure or develop a new product.

In doing this, usually legal opinion from a local law firm is recommended or required in the bank. Due diligence is nevertheless not limited to this situation. For emerging markets, more important than legal opinions for a new product will be:

- The market practice (how other banks are coping with this kind of product)
- Its pitfalls (negative experience in the past or in other countries)
- Regulator's attitude (how far central bank/monetary authorities can tolerate this product and why)

SUMMARY

Several relevant issues come to our attention when securing success in marketing institutional banking products to emerging markets: an understanding of the counterparty's culture and needs, the price and what products can be offered on what terms and conditions.

When a bank is marketing its products, it must first examine whether the usual banking practice in a foreign country differs from its home country experiences. Culture does have impact on the marketing of banking products. Culture also influences behaviours.

In terms of needs of institutional clients for emerging markets, we foresee the following: cheap funding for short-term liquidity purposes, knowledge of banking management and banking products, special support for overseas activities, and special products for funding and international expansion of business.

The price issue is also important. First, a price strategy has to be determined – to maximize profits in the short or long run, to increase market share or simply to achieve market entrance. Here special factors like geographical difference, the benchmark in a competitive environment, relationship with the client, and more importantly the underlying structure of your price need to be considered.

Not every product of institutional banking can be offered to each and every emerging market client. If they are ever offered, the terms and conditions may vary from bank to bank or country to country. You may have to rely on experienced legal opinion to decide whether you accept a new product or not. Due diligence is necessary as well.

15 Risk Management for Emerging Markets

15.1 RISK MANAGEMENT AND INSTITUTIONAL BANKING

Risk management culture is an important issue for emerging markets. It was emphasized that with the knowledge and experience in emerging markets, institutional banking professionals should bear risk management responsibility – that is they should play a role in identifying, monitoring, mitigating and controlling bank and country risk. Such a risk management role is also reflected – perhaps most importantly – in the situation of so-called 'intensive care', that is problem solving and/or crisis handling.

In some banks, the risk management function as such for institutional banking professionals is not emphasized or even debatable because there are risk professionals working along side correspondent bankers. The argument goes that the risk management function is under the coverage of the credit risk department.

Institutional banking professionals, if motivated, can give important input to risk management. The reasoning is straightforward – institutional banking professionals are at the forefront of risk exposure.

Risk management starts with *risk identification*. In general the risks in emerging markets are identifiable and to an increasing degree quantifiable in terms of underlying factors. We know that some of the risks attached to banking practices are particularly linked to country risk. Others are linked to market imperfections and illiquidity of emerging markets.

As explored in the first part of this book, emerging market economies are often plagued with unsound legal environments implementing poorly defined or enforced legal rights, inadequate and nontransparent information, poor infrastructure for financial market transactions such as custody or clearance and settlement arrangements, inefficient secondary market as well as corruption and fraudulent trading activities.

Hence in emerging markets, risk management is not about blindly following the rules. What will be needed are managers who are risk aware and able to use judgement and common sense – people who understand the environment and who have been entrusted with sufficient authority to act when necessary.

The first stage of the risk management process is the setting of the right risk strategy. In this process correspondent bankers and risk professionals are partners not adversaries. This carries through to the development of a risk framework appropriate to the bank's strategy. That risk framework must be adequately researched so it can operate effectively with a degree of flexibility that will allow it to respond to an ever-changing environment.

As emphasized, one of the prime reasons for the difference between developed and emerging markets is the cultural environment that exists between these two markets. Different backgrounds, different religions, different values and different languages all bring a diversity which has an impact on how people see situations and how they deal with them. In this respect, institutional banking professionals have added value in the framework of risk management especially for bank risk and country risk. This is because understanding other people's points of view is definitely an asset when discussing risk and the ways to deal with it.

15.2 'STOP-GO' POLICY: A DILEMMA?

In the field of risk strategy towards emerging markets, a special discussion is needed for the notorious 'stop-go' phenomenon in many banks.

With the volatility of emerging market banks, some banks in the developed world are following a 'stop-go' policy towards countries and banks from emerging markets. What is a 'stop-go' policy?

A 'stop-go' policy refers to the situation where the bank decides to put a brake on the operation and stop the entire bank limit and/or country limit when some problems occur in that country, that is when there is something wrong, the bank stops the business totally with that country. They take a wait-and-see position.

It goes without saying that, if there are really serious problems in the country, such as a moratorium or civil war, it is indeed necessary to stop all the credit lines to protect the position of the bank. It will, however, hamper the relationship and continuation of business if a bank frequently resorts to a so-called 'stop-go' policy. This is perhaps a dilemma facing many banks, and very often it is a 'me too' phenomenon – 'if our competitors stop doing business there, we should do the same'.

Harmful as it is, such an attitude is unfortunately very common in practice.

The argument against such a 'stop-go' policy is that risk in emerging markets is just like electricity. Electricity will give you light but it will give you a 'shock' as well. The key point here is to understand and control it. It is important to think of risk in a positive light – the corollary of risk is opportunity. The word 'crisis' itself means, in Chinese, both 'dangers and opportunities'. Very often people see only one side of the story. The credit inert being shocked by electricity are motivated to think of risk avoidance rather than risk exploitation. The wisdom, however, lies in the ability of getting the 'light' without being 'shocked'!

It is difficult to sort out reasons for this long lived 'stop-go' policy towards emerging markets. We, however, find that a 'stop-go' policy tends to win favour when there is either lack of professional risk managers/correspondent bankers who are risk aware and able to use sound judgement and common sense by their knowledge and experience, or lack of risk managers/correspondent bankers who understand the environment.

The decision to 'stop' may also occur when internal debate on 'stop or go' lasts so long that people choose 'to stop' as an easy and safe escape. Or it may occur when there are good institutional banking professionals but these people cannot function because they are either not entrusted with sufficient authority to act, or the organizational structure excludes their function at all.

As a competence centre for countries and banks, the institutional banking department can have added value in this field. In close communication and consultation with credit people, institutional banking professionals should evaluate the situation in a proper manner and propose an appropriate policy towards any emergency events in emerging markets.

Sometimes 'to stop' is indeed easier than 'to go' ('to continue'). But risk management is about controlled decision making, not simply risk avoidance. When most of your competitors stop their activities, those institutional clients/correspondent banks that are in difficulties will be impressed if you continue. This needs the unique ability to 'tiptoe' on the risk.

'Tiptoeing' on the risk is a process of fine-tuning your risk management measures and discovering ways to mitigate your risk exposure. It is by no means an easy job and needs the support of management.

When handling difficulties, what does an institutional banking professional need to pay attention to when he intends to 'tiptoe' on the risk and to fine-tune?

- The cultural aspect: In many cultures 'face' is as important as 'money'. When facing difficulties, the basic question is – is the problem/crisis fundamental or temporary?

  Many emerging market countries may experience temporary disequilibrium 'which may be overcome over time'. To push for payment may kill the chance for recovery. Even real sovereign debt default can be rescheduled as a solution.

  A friend in need is a friend indeed. If you are not willing to give face, it may be hard to forget. 'To stop' or 'to go' very much depends on your view of this relationship.
- Product aspect: From the categories of products in institutional banking, we may well notice that different correspondent banking products have different risk factors ranging from 100% financial risk (money market) to very limited or even zero risk such as trade finance guaranteed by or participated with other financial institutions.

  Risk management here is 'fine-tuning' your products' range or 'fine-tuning' the tenor of the relevant deal. That is, you need not immediately stop all the business for a problematic institutional counterparty. You may, for instance, start with shortening the money market (MM) tenor, and end up with perhaps confirming their L/Cs with full cash cover from the issuing bank.

  If the situation is really serious, such as in the Asian crisis, you may still continue with some products, such as L/C confirmation with some risk mitigation measures. The exported/imported goods, in general, collateralized trade finance.

  In many countries, trade finance is given priority for payment by the government even during difficult periods. To continue L/C confirmation on a selective basis (good client, short tenor, creditworthy issuing bank, etc.) is very often recommended and incidentally very profitable during a difficult time – a point to be explored fully later in the discussion on risk mitigation.
- Head office vs local branch: For risk tiptoeing, there are sometimes conflicting attitudes between the head office and the front people at the branch.

  Credit decision in the head office, if based on a media or credit rating agency report, will see the difficulty differently than those who are at the front. To strip out the truth from the media reports is easy to say but difficult to realize. The reports, even though good for their quality, are often on a macro level instead of being tailor-made for your own bank, and there is often a time lag between what is reported and what is happening. On the other hand, local people may lose sight due to their direct exposure and are likely to be misled by the emotional comments there. Judgement and evaluation on both reports and spot communication with front people in the local market are the best.

A bank which chooses to tiptoe during a crisis therefore needs good coordination between the head office and the local branch. It also needs the involvement of skilled people with a record of experience accumulated over many years of crisis in the past, both at the branch level and at the head office level.

15.3 PRINCIPLES OF RISK MANAGEMENT

If we agree with the argument that there is no reason to steer clear of these difficult emerging markets, or to stop the entire business during difficult times, how to manage the risk is then an issue. There is a better return on offer for those that understand and can manage risk effectively and a consistent attitude and policy towards an emerging market country is rewarding in the long run.

Risk management or risk 'tiptoeing' is not gambling with the hope of good luck. Not at all. Risk management is based on systematic principles and the belief that risks can be identified and can, to some extent at least, be priced and reallocated.

First, risk management analysis for emerging markets will require us to have a critical look into the following fundamental issues:

- Asset-backed finance and balance sheet finance
- Debt finance and equity finance
- Short-term and long-term finance
- Financial risk and operational risk

15.3.1 Asset-backed Finance and Balance Sheet Finance

Due to the fact that in emerging markets

- the financial figures are often distorted and delayed
- company governance is less strict and
- there is lack of local, reliable credit rating agencies

balance sheet finance, that is clean lending based on financials of the company, is usually not easy.[1]

As a result most banks are willing to be involved, or more active, in collateralized (asset-backed) finance than in balance sheet finance.

The focus of finance for emerging markets is then *the quality of collateral as well as the control and management of that collateral.*

In institutional banking, trade finance attracts a lot of attention particularly because of its trade background, quick turnover and its self-liquidating nature.

Trade finance is so-called 'bread and butter' business for emerging markets. As it has a trade background, it is usually collateralized, and therefore more secure than pure financial deals.

Collateralized finance can take many forms: accounts receivable finance, warehouse receipt finance, trust receipt finance and pre-export finance.

[1] Of course problems of corporate governance occur also in OECD countries. The notorious cases of Enron, WorldCom, Tyco and many more provide ample evidence on a global scale.

Many of them belong to the sphere of corporate finance where institutional banking plays a marginal role. But institutional banking is directly involved in those bank linked products such as letters of credit, collections and guarantees.

As emerging market countries need to import technology and other industrialized products for their development and to promote their exports to get hard currency to finance their international payments, import and export are quite fundamental for emerging markets.

For banks that intend to manage their risks in emerging markets, trade finance is preferred as it will be put on the priority list for payment during difficult times. This is evidenced in some crisis cases for countries and banks from emerging markets.

To justify the above argument one example is the case of Indonesia. In 1997 during the Asian crisis, the Central Bank of Indonesia officially declared that as of 1 November, 16 Indonesian banks would be liquidated. To handle this banking crisis, foreign banks held a conversation with Bank Indonesia on trade finance transactions with banks under liquidation (17 November 1997).

One of the subjects of the meeting was *Trade Finance Transactions* (TRT) relating to the 16 banks under liquidation. Bank Indonesia was quoted examples of Brazil, Columbia and Turkey to highlight how central banks had found it appropriate to treat creditors with TRT exposure in priority over other general creditors, in order not to disturb international trade flows. It was pointed out that during bank failures in the above countries, TRTs were specially segregated to help facilitate the self-liquidating nature of the transactions.

During the course of discussion with Bank Indonesia, the Bank indicated its willingness to study the issue as a matter of urgency. Eventually, Bank Indonesia, the central bank of Indonesia, did write a 'letter of guaranty' to correspondent banks, which maintained trade finance credit limits towards Indonesian commercial banks:

> Bank Indonesia hereby unconditionally and irrevocably guarantees (the guaranty) the punctual payment of all obligations of each obligor (the guaranteed obligor) now or hereafter existing with respect to any Trade Finance extended by each Participating Maintaining bank to each such guaranteed Obligor on and after the effective date. Bank Indonesia's liability shall extend all amounts that constitute part of the Guaranteed Obligations . . . [2]

Thus, for Indonesia, while trade credit lines from foreign commercial banks did somewhat tighten and pricing for L/C confirmation did increase, trade finance activities nevertheless continued throughout the crisis period and credit limits from commercial banks more quickly returned to 'normal' levels.

Another example of the priority of trade finance in default debt settlement is the liquidation of a Chinese bank.

On 21 June 1998, *PBOC* (People's Bank of China) announced that it decided to close 'Haifa' bank (Hainan Development Bank) by taking back its licences and stopping all its activities.[3] PBOC then set up a team to liquidate Haifa's assets. *ICBC* (Industrial and Commercial Bank of China) was appointed as the custodian to handle local deposit and overseas debt among which payment obligations under letter of credit were explicitly given priority.

---

[2] Interested readers can refer to the letter of the governor of Bank Indonesia (Mr Syahril Sabirin) dated 25 June 1998.

[3] *Hainan Daily* newspaper, China, 21 June 1998.

It was interesting to note the procedure for the repayment of L/C obligations under the L/Cs issued by Haifa bank – trade debt was indeed segregated from other debts. The Chinese authorities made it clear that the trade finance nature of individual transactions should be checked and tested by the relevant authorities.

Foreign banks that had trade finance exposure on Haifa bank – the liquidated bank – were asked to provide evidence on the nature of their debt. *State Administration of Foreign Exchange* (SAFE) – the Chinese authorities for foreign exchange control – then investigated the truth of the trade. If the foreign debt was created by the letter of credit, it should be subject not only to the international requirement of UCP500 but it should also be in compliance with the SAFE regulation. All the relevant documents of the trade background should be provided such as customs declaration and duty certificate, packaging lists and insurance policy related to the transaction.

Despite the fact that it took more than one year to clarify all these details, ICBC on behalf of PBOC did honour the payment under L/C including the delayed interests. Obviously the message PBOC gave was that the Chinese central bank did distinguish between trade finance and other financial obligations and did give priority to the payment of international trade. They wanted to have international confidence in financing trade for Chinese banks.

It is not a general rule that every country honours its trade finance obligations during a crisis. A negative example was the case of Peru, where such TRT priority meetings did not take place. As a result, foreign trade facilities were severely restricted and pricing was increased accordingly.

15.3.2 Debt Finance and Equity Finance

Debt finance and equity finance have different natures. Debt finance, if the obligor has a strong financial position and reliable rating, will give more liquidity to the lender, especially if the lending instrument (syndication loans, sovereign bonds, for example) is marketable. Equity finance may give access to the management but has more involvement in the borrower's daily operation. In the portfolio of emerging market exposure, these different natures will have to be borne in mind.

Some banks have a risk guideline for emerging markets. They prefer debt finance than equity finance.

In general one advantage of international debt finance is that debt finance provides more liquidity in the market. Omni Bridgeway, for example, publishes information on emerging market debt pricing regularly. Issue No. 24 in September 2006 indicated several countries' pricing change for debt. Countries on the list include:

Africa

Angola, Cameron, Central African Republic, Congo, Ethiopia, Gambia, Ghana, Ivory Coast, Kenya, Liberia, Mozambique, Nigeria, Senegal, Sierra Leone, Sudan, Tanzania, Uganda, Zambia, Zimbabwe

Latin American and Caribbean

Argentina, Cuba, Honduras, Nicaragua, Paraguay, Suriname

Eastern Europe

Albania, Azerbaijan, Bosnia, Georgia, Russia, Serbia, Turkmenistan, Ukraine, Uzbekistan

The Middle East

Iraq, Libya, Syria, Yemen

Asia

Cambodia, Laos, Myanmar, Mongolia, North Korea, Vietnam

15.3.3 Financial Risk and Operational Risk

Banks used to look into financial risk and check credit more than the operational risk. But for emerging market countries, the operational risk is very often bigger due to many factors. Alan Craft commented:

> It was not that many years ago where fundamentally bankers had the view that they took credit risk and that was it. Market risk, operational risk and all the other ancillary risks that we now look at quite scientifically were really just simply ignored or considered to be a part of being a business – you had to live with them and that's what capital was for.[4]

Operational risk is now realized as important so that it is mentioned in Basel II as one of the three major risks: market risk, credit risk and operational risk.

Operational risk is real and common. For institutional banking, operational risk under L/C is often a nightmare to many banks.

Although it is known to all bankers that a letter of credit is supposed to be a bank's payment undertaking, it happens, however, that if the goods are still in demand but the price of the goods has dropped substantially before or upon arrival, the buyer's bank will take advantage of the operational mistake of the negotiating bank and will only take up the documents and effect payment if the seller agrees to renegotiate a much lower price with the buyer.

This seems contradictory to the original purpose of letter of credit and people may wonder how that is possible. Some of the issuing banks are even suspected of supporting their client – the buyer under these circumstances, particularly if the buyer has strong influence (e.g. a state-owned enterprise, a big name in the market, etc.) by searching for 'discrepancies' to avoid paying under the letter of credit.

Obviously, all these non payment cases are operation linked. The L/C issuing bank does have the ability to pay but is not willing to do so. One of the ways to achieve this is to find an operational mistake of the counterparty.

In many banks cases are found involving substantial and influential enterprises that have resorted to this practice to force sellers to cut the price of imported chemicals and other commodities. It has become a banking malpractice in certain countries and areas to manufacture 'discrepancies' to escape payment obligations.

---

[4] Comment from Alan Craft quoted in 'Risk insights from an experienced voice', *Global Association of Risk Professionals*, May/June, issue 2005, p. 34.

Common discrepancies include:

- Expiry date and place of the credit.
- Presentation after permitted time from the date of issuance of shipping documents.
- Quantity of the goods exceeded.
- Marks and numbers differ between documents.
- Bill of lading, insurance or bill of exchange not endorsed correctly.
- Weights differ between documents.
- Absence of signatures where required on documents presented.
- Language of document is not the one required on the credit.
- The amounts shown on the invoice and bill of exchange differ.
- Absence of original documents where required on documents presented.
- Shipment made between ports other than those stated in the credit, etc.

There are other examples where correspondent banks may raise unexpected discrepancies:

- US$ vs USD
- Telephones vs telephone
- ABC/DEF vs ABC DEF in shipping marks
- Hongkong vs Hong Kong
- *Qinhai* vs *Qinghai* as ship name, etc.

Such malpractice to search for counterparty's operational mistakes sometimes causes more damage than straightforward nonpayment of the issuing bank. This is because such malpractice is difficult to predict.

As we know, for international trade finance, approximately two-thirds of the time a seller's documents fail to meet the letter of credit terms and conditions upon first presentation to the banks. This will result in delays in payment and occasional nonpayment. Ultimately, most of the problems are resolved through the buyer's/seller's banks' communication.

But such disputes may give negative impacts on both sides: for the buyer, the goods may be delayed, for the seller payment may be delayed. In the meantime, the issuing bank and the negotiating bank must fight with each other. Even worse, unresolved discrepancies may result in expensive litigation.

Such L/C linked operational risk may be prevented on a best efforts basis. The following is the checklist for the purposes of due diligence:

- The issuing bank and its branches authorization: As noticed in daily operation, some branches of issuing banks may have a tendency for delaying payments. L/Cs issued in certain places should be monitored due to smuggling.
- The commercial relationship with the buyer: A good and long lasting relationship will reduce the chance of conflict as both parties are willing to solve problems if any.
- The goods and the market for those goods: Goods that have greater price fluctuations will have more chance of incurring documentary problems.
- The status of the applicant: An applicant with big name or state-owned companies tend to have less motivation for cheating or fraud as their reputation will be at stake if they do so.

- The letter of assignment: When the beneficiary has signed a letter of assignment of receivables to their negotiating bank, they will be more willing to cooperate in case of a problem with the issuing bank since they are in a similar situation.

To avoid losses, document departments have to take precautions and be equipped with necessary measures. Banks are trying to build up core competence in the field of human resources:

- Language equipped staff who may notice minor difference
- Legal knowledge of the country where the L/C was issued
- Relationship with the branch of the issuing bank (good relation with that particular Branch may help reduce the risk of a 'discrepancy' being found)

In the field of trade finance, there are further operational risks for outright fraud:

- Fraudulent bills of lading: To enact a letter of credit against false documents such as pre-dating bills of lading, charterers/exporters pre-dating bills of lading in order to meet letters of credit expiry dates, etc.
- Fake chops

In some Asian countries signatures on documents are not common. The chop is used in all documents to replace a signature and also for authentication purposes. Chops are primitive in design and can easily be imitated. With an easily accessible imitation service, these fakes are as good as the genuine chops.

There is a due diligence checklist recommended by the International Chamber of Commerce[5] to help banks prevent these bill of lading frauds.

For institutional banking, good relations and communication with correspondents are understandably important in identifying fraud.

15.3.4 Short-term and Long-term Finance

The issue of tenor is regarded as a risk management consideration because the time horizon does have an impact on the evolution of risk.

It is generally believed that longer-term finance will at least present more uncertainty. The probability of default is therefore higher over a longer period.

It is very common for credit people to give tenor limit on emerging market deals, and short-term self-liquidating deals will be given more priority.

To achieve this time factor in risk management practice for emerging markets, lending on a revolving basis or a deal (e.g. interest rate swap) with options for obligations to expire is

[5] Press release of the International Chamber of Commerce due diligence checklist for banks document no. 6641021e.

1. Containerized cargo:
   a. Are the container numbers stated on the bill of lading
   b. Does the total weight of the cargo exceed the capacity of the containers?
   c. Is the issuer of bill of lading the physical carrier of the cargo or has it been issued by nonvessel owning common carriers (NOVV)?
2. Does the bill of lading have contact details for the issuer of the bill of lading, that is address, telephone and fax numbers?
3. Should there be a problem with credit transaction, is there sufficient information on the bill of lading so that you may exert control over the cargo?

not unusual. Accordingly, the longer-term risk is very often compensated by a high mark-up in price.

There are exceptions to the common sense approach noted above. In several crisis cases, short debts in emerging markets did face immediate liquidation which resulted in loss of asset value, whereas those longer-term debts not yet due paid off better in the longer term.

This is because the obligor had survived the crisis and recovered the repayment ability after the crisis. To manoeuvre the time horizon therefore is not simply to conclude that short-term finance is always better than long-term finance.

Using a revolving option to replace long-term commitment may turn out to be a good strategy if you want to handle the time horizon in an effective way. But a sound judgement on short term vs long term is never easy. It requires possession of sufficient hard data, knowledge, experience, long lasting records and a very careful and sophisticated study of the individual case. Sometimes data are available but there is always room for interpretation. Admittedly, there is always an element of speculation involved, particularly when the decisions must be made quickly to avoid losing the opportunity.

15.4 COUNTRY RISK MANAGEMENT: COUNTRY LIMIT AND ITS RELATED ISSUES

One measure used to manage the lending risk is to set a limit to a borrower. This is the same for a country. Banks typically set maximum exposure allowed for a particular country, so that their potential losses will be limited.

The setting of a country limit is the management of country risk. It indicates the maximum the bank is willing to be involved for that specific country.

In Part I, we discussed in detail the concept of country risk.

When a domestic company is unable or unwilling to repay a loan, a bank as a claim holder may get access to legal action using bankruptcy courts to recoup at least a portion of its original lending. By comparison, a foreign company may be unable to repay because the authorities of the country prohibit payments or limit the payment due to foreign currency shortages or political difficulties. Sovereign borrowers, that is governments themselves, may face insolvency in terms of foreign currency due to country difficulties. These events will have an impact on the balance sheet of a bank.

For such a rationale banks usually estimate the counterparties, that is the countries they are doing business with, and set a limit. Sovereign risk rating is used as a reference for decision making on country exposure and monitoring it thereafter.

Setting country limit is an important task. Understandably, decision errors may occur when the rating system predicts that a country will get into difficulties whereas in fact it does not, or the rating system predicts that a country will stay clear of difficulties whereas in fact it ends up in trouble. These will lead to (potential) losses of earnings or losses of business opportunities for banks.

In country risk evaluation and assessment, we already discussed the practice of evaluating country risk. It was mentioned that a country risk committee will be organized and usually an institutional banking department will be involved as the country expert. In many banks the same team will be responsible for deciding the country limit.

Country limits are established on several considerations:

- Assessment of the country risk: There should be an assessment of the country risk based on country risk rating, economic and political development, market information, etc. This is the base for a country limit decision.

  Banks rely on a country risk committee where marketing and credit professionals for the country sit down with country risk analysts and senior management in order to arrive at a consensus on country risk.

  Countries are divided into categories according to their internal and external credit rating, and other related information. The discussion on country limit is based on this assessment of the risk.

  According to the rating of country risk, a 'cap' called as MCR (maximum country risk) is given to limit the maximum amount of credit allowed to that specific country. To have a limit above this 'cap' needs more discussion. Sometimes it may need a 'strategic decision' from top management. This extra country limit may be given under certain conditions (restriction on tenor, product, counterparts, etc.).

  Country risk discussion talks about not only the amount of total exposure, but also the country risk strategy. Therefore country limit, if established, may further be divided into short term or long term. Conditions like maximum tenor allowed and specific products to be booked under the limit will be mentioned.

  Some banks divide the country limit into 'commercial limit' and 'financial limit'. Commercial limit is used for confirming L/Cs, etc. Financial limit refers to exposure to other banks under the financial strength of the counterparty (such as MM limit, financial guarantee, etc.).
- Strategy of the bank towards the country: Even if the consensus towards country risk turns out to be pessimistic to countries with a low country risk rating, that is high country risk, banks may still consider a limit due to strategic considerations.

  Strategic considerations may come from a specific position of the bank towards that country such as historical relationship (ex-colonies, etc.), existence of core clients in that market, intention for expansion and existence of strategic alliance, subsidiary or branch, etc. Under these circumstances, banks are willing to take the difficult risk merely because country limit is a must to realize the bank's strategy.
- Commercial motivation: Even if the country is not on the strategic priority list, banks may also wish to establish a limit to acquire this part of the market if there are business opportunities or an understanding that business opportunities may exist there. But overall the return on the potential exposure should be attractive enough.

  It was emphasized that a rational and scientific assessment of country risk is no easy job and a country credit rating system has its fundamental limitations despite best efforts. In fact any risk analytical techniques 'use historical benchmarks and historical time series which cannot adequately capture risk when they go beyond these parameters'.[6]

  A consensus on the assessment of the country default risk is difficult for a financial institution, let alone the decision on a country credit limit according to the ranking.

  The success of a country credit committee lies in the wisdom of the coordinator (chairperson) who must be able to bring together as many different, often conflicting, viewpoints as possible, and take the best of each by balancing the credit consideration and the commercial motivation. The chairperson may not necessarily be the country expert but must utilize the best expert to assist.

---

[6] Henry Kaufman (2000), president of Henry Kaufman & Company Inc., *The Future of Banking*, p. 163.

The best expert must have enough risk awareness and sufficient country experience as well as sharp commercial sense and product knowledge. Such a team meeting may take a long time but the discussion itself helps each of the members in one way or another.

It is interesting to notice the conflicting viewpoints in the team. The representatives from the country may underestimate the country risk and the economist will emphasize the 'theoretical risk'. Business managers tend to focus on business opportunities, estimated earnings and competition. Such role playing may change if one of the team members changes his/her position – moving from credit to commercial, for example. He/she may change his/her viewpoint on the country accordingly. Through such a meeting, the country representative, or 'country manager' as he/she is sometimes called, will see more of the strategy and global policy of the bank towards that country. The business manager may be more alert to the (aspect of) risk he/she perhaps would have ignored. The economist, or country risk analyst, may see the real life of the country and the gap between rating and fresh information. Thus the bank as a whole will benefit from active discussion. If such a meeting becomes a routine, it tends to be a bureaucratic game.

It happens sometimes that some banks may leave the task of setting country limit either to credit managers or to commercial managers. The consequences may therefore be either loss of business opportunities (too strict from credit) or loss of money (too aggressive from commercial).

It is not uncommon that people tend to say 'no' to 'emerging market' deals. After all, emerging markets are markets where risks come first and then opportunities. The discussion on country and bank limit determination to emerging markets is one full of conflicting concepts – nuisance or useful, colour blind or warning signal, policeman function or value added. The skill thus lies between recognizing risk and rational and decent mitigation of the risk.

Once a limit is set, all the business lines within the bank will have to make sure that their exposure will not exceed the approved country limit.

15.5 COUNTRY RISK MANAGEMENT: COUNTRY RISK REGISTRATION

To evaluate a country risk and set a limit on it is not easy. Neither the risks nor the returns are clearly definable. To register the exposure to a country is, sometimes, even more challenging in many banks. In practice, which (lending) credit risk belongs to which country risk category can present some complications.

One example is *off-balance sheet items* (OBIs). Derivatives are OBIs. The principle is that, all activities that contain a direct or indirect credit risk that can be localized in the country concerned are eligible for admittance to the calculation of country risk. Derivatives are off-balance items, whose credit equivalent is eligible for admittance to the gross base of calculation. But the question is should a gross amount or a proportion be registered.

Another example may be lending to a Western bank located in an emerging market. How to register a bank's lending to HSBC in Malaysia, for example, may invite some discussion if there is no clear-cut guideline in the bank.

Covers in the form of guarantees, insurances and other securities can decrease the country risk in a certain risk country, but they also can increase the country risk in another risk country.

Investments and/or participations fall outside the country risk registration in some banks. These investments will often be done out of strategic considerations. Furthermore it is necessary to perform country risk reporting on a consolidated basis, as a result of which the foreign claims of a foreign office, insofar as these are nonlocal currency, are already enclosed in the gross liabilities. The balance of claims and outstanding debts with a foreign office remain a part of the gross liabilities, because there is a transfer risk involved.

Besides pure country risk as defined above, there are other risks that relate to a country and need to be registered, controlled and monitored. In banking practice, these risks will be further known as *country bound risks*.

Initially the default value for the country performance risk and the country transfer risk is the country of residence of the borrower. This is because in most cases the country of residence is also the country from which payments are made (transfer risk) and from which performance has to be made (performance risk).

Sometimes the delivery of the repayment may have to be made from more or other countries than the country of residence. Several country risks have to be registered on a percentage basis.

In some banks, at most three countries can be mentioned in terms of percentage of their share in the performance risk. The total sum of these percentages has to be 100.

In calculating the transfer risk, the ability to repay a credit facility can depend on one or more different countries than the country of residence. This is possible if there is an economical dependence on other countries. At most three countries can be mentioned in terms of percentage of their share in the transfer risk. The total sum of these percentages has to be 100.

To precisely quantify and properly register the risks, especially in the case of emerging market countries, are very important. This explains why in many banks a *risk-weighing method* is introduced, to avoid over-reporting of country risk.

The purpose of risk weighing is to give a realistic and actual picture of country exposure. Some of the nominal exposure may be over-reported on its own. This is due to the fact the exposure of products booked under country limit may indicate a *different degrees of risk* to the bank.

Money market exposure, for example, is calculated at 100%. Failure of the borrower will lead to the full amount of loss to the bank. Trade finance, discussed earlier, may offer some chance of recovery if the issuing bank goes bankrupt. Sight of an L/C may give an even bigger chance as the goods under L/C may be available as collateral before the title documents are released.

The degree of risk for derivative products such as, repo transactions may also vary, as mentioned as an example in the early part of this chapter. A bank may have real risk if a derivative counterparty fails to fulfil the margin calls, or collateral under repo is going far beyond its market value which was estimated earlier.

For a small bank whose capital will not allow a huge country limit, it is quite essential to have a realistic registration of country exposure. Risk weighing will enable the bank to prevent overestimation or underestimation of its exposure to a difficult country.

Overestimation (too big exposure registration) may lead to less capacity for good business, whereas underestimation may lead to a nasty surprise when the country in question suffers a serious crisis.

15.6 BANK RISK MANAGEMENT: BANK LIMIT AND ITS RELATED ISSUES

Similar to the establishment of country limit, banks set limits to their institutional clients, that is their correspondent banks.

The establishment of bank limit is based on bank risk assessment, strategy of the bank towards that specific correspondent bank and commercial motivation, that is risk return estimation from market information.

Institutional banking is often involved in setting the bank limits in cooperation with credit colleagues. Usually the institutional banking department initiates the proposal for a limit with its arguments, and the proposal is supposed to be approved by credit. The format of such a proposal was presented in Part II.

A number of practical issues linked to bank limit may emerge in this procedure:

- Unrated banks: It is usually difficult to get bank limit approval for some new or unrated banks. But the development of any bank has its life cycle and the initial contact is important as it is the beginning of a long-term relationship.

  A newly established bank has limited correspondents and will value your initiative in helping them. However, if the credit colleagues are not in a position to approve a limit, it is rather awkward to develop a relationship. The following may give insights into solutions under circumstances where bank limit is not possible, or the existing limit is full.

  If an unrated bank interests you, you can follow its development. Study the local media for that bank. Check the attitude of the regulators towards this bank to research on the management and shareholders' background and its competitive advantages, and listen to the market – all this may enable you to formulate a strategic view on this bank.

  If a bank, with the above-mentioned data, turns out to be potentially interesting, it is the task of institutional banking to persuade credit for a line. If credit insists on a credit rating, it is possible that a rating company does the rating for you on a fee basis.
- Input of market prevailing price: Information on bank limit is usually internal and confidential. It is sensitive to ask your correspondent how large is the limit for a bank. But market reaction is relevant to the approval of bank limit. When a bank is not rated, market price is at least a source of evaluation.

  One of the spin-off benefits for risk participation which will be discussed in the next chapter to see how other banks evaluate this bank. It is very interesting to see the price change in the market when news is announced for certain banks. Therefore price information on the bank is the vote from the market for the risk of that unrated bank.
- Speed of approval: Another issue linked to bank limit is the speed for credit to approve a limit.

  Credit people need a set of information including series of financials, business plan and management background of the bank. Some of them may not be readily available or not available in English, for example. It happens, however, that an important client of the bank may need a deal to be approved (e.g. confirming an L/C issued by a bank unknown to you) but bank limit is not yet in place.

To have a certain 'short-cut' procedure established in the bank is necessary either for the *ad hoc* approval of a bank limit, or for a temporary excess to accommodate one deal. Delay of approval may end up with loss of business opportunities.

This 'short-cut' of approval is especially important for commercial reasons. Competent people should be authorized to approve bank deals exceptionally with, of course, limited amount, without the need for lengthy meetings. This quick approval should not be beyond credit discipline.

SUMMARY

Risk management is one of the important tasks for institutional banking. Although institutional banking works side by side with credit professionals, their added value to risk management is quite important for emerging markets because emerging market economies usually have an unsound legal environment, nontransparency of information, inefficient secondary market, corruption, fraudulent trading, etc.

Institutional bankers are involved in risk strategy setting, risk identification, risk mitigation and problem solving. This is because of the institutional banking professionals' knowledge and understanding of both bank and country risks which they are supposed to have. This is also due to the fact that they are relationship managers of countries and banks.

Regretfully many banks follow a 'stop-go' policy which disrupts the continuation of business with countries and banks in emerging markets. This perhaps can be explained by the fact that there is a lack of professionals in the banks for the specific environment or a lack of professionals experienced enough for the country. To avoid this you have to 'tiptoe' on the risk, that is fine-tuning the risk management measures and finding ways to mitigate the risk exposure.

There are some basic principles of risk management for emerging markets. In general you have to rely more on asset-backed finance because financing, if any, is based on underlying collaterals. Several country or bank crises show that trade finance, collateralized by underlying trade background, is a more secure way of financing for emerging markets. Debt finance is preferred as it provides more liquidity in the international secondary market. In emerging markets operational risk gives as many, if not more, problems, and short-term finance gives you more flexibility in case of difficulties.

Country limit is established to control and monitor total exposure of the bank towards that country. The establishment of a country limit will have several considerations such as an assessment of country risk, a bank's strategy towards that country and commercial motivation, etc.

After the establishment of country limit, to register the risk precisely and realistically is also important in country risk management. A couple of practical issues must be addressed.

Especially for a bank with a small capital base, which cannot afford a large counterparty limit, over-registration of country risk exposure may block business opportunities. Risk weighing will play some role in indicating a realistic and actual situation of country exposure. Risk weighing intends to have the precise calculation of risk, that is the nominal exposure vis-à-via the real exposure. Nominal exposures are supposed to be recalculated by the nature of the deals booked under the limit. Some exposure will thus be 'discounted' in percentage terms for the booking.

Bank limit is established to control the exposure to one single correspondent bank. The institutional banking department is usually involved in setting the limit. However, in practice, some unrated banks may have difficulties to get their limits from correspondents. Bank limit for them, if necessary, will be established based on information available and evaluation of the institutional banking department. Here market price for bank risk is an important indication of market evaluation on the bank. Sometimes speed of approval inside the bank for some *ad hoc* deals is crucial to business development.

16
Risk Mitigation for Emerging Markets

16.1 RISK MITIGATION: PRINCIPLES AND PRACTICE

Banks are handling risks. Banks are trading risks as well.

Risk management is about controlled decision making towards risk. When a risk is identified and evaluated, the next thing to do is mitigate the risk. Risk mitigation is especially important for emerging markets as they are supposed to have more risks.

Risk mitigation starts with *risk identification* and *evaluation*. Sometimes risk mitigation is mistakenly understood as risk avoidance. As Daniel Riordan said:

> Mitigating risk frequently has the connotation of avoiding risk. While this notion may be appropriate for some hazards, it is for the most part an impractical strategy for those engaged in trade and project development in emerging markets. A notion of risk avoidance denies the macroeconomic and geographical trends that are occurring and the prospects they present.
>
> For many businesses, success in the future will hinge on embracing the opportunities that globalization and privatization offer to them. It will also depend on partnering with entities that have the experience and specialization to understand the risks of new markets and the expertise to effectively manage the political and trade risk they entail.[1]

When 'tiptoeing' on emerging market risk, the skill of mitigating risk is essential if you want to avoid a 'stop-go' policy.

The subject of risk mitigation has long been a topic of fascination. The discussion here is an attempt to cover a small piece of this complicated ground. Specifically, we intend to discuss *risk redistribution*, *risk diversification* and *risk restructuring*.

In fact the essence of risk mitigation is linked to measures taken to *convert unacceptable risks into acceptable risks*. This process therefore starts with the questions *why*, *who* and *how*.

If the risk is not acceptable to your bank, you have to ask *why*. By asking *why* you understand more of the risk. Sometimes the reasons for declining a deal are not the right ones or not the major ones. This will lead to a re-examination of the decision. If finally the reasoning confirms a 'yes' conclusion, that is the risk is unacceptable, you then ask *who* may be interested in taking it. You have to search for such counterparties, and you have to have an external risk taker. The last question is, if you have found the party who is willing to take it, *how* can the risk be transferred to that targeted counterparty?

The importance of this answer to *how* is sometimes underestimated. The reliability of the targeted party to whom the risk is going to be transferred is important, as in many

[1] *'Confronting risks in emerging markets'* by Daniel Riordan at Zurich's Emerging Markets Solutions Group. *Trade Finance* magazine, April 2004.

cases banks think that their risks are 'mitigated' by that 'third party' but eventually they are not – either because the third party, who is also vulnerable, eventually cannot honour their obligation, or, although the third party is financially solid, the legal documents are nevertheless not watertight to protect you. Either way you will lose. And you will only find that out at the very last moment when default really occurs.

To make risk mitigation possible, there must be a common 'risk language'. The people involved should have a clear understanding of the difference between risk tolerance, risk appetite, risk reduction and risk transfer. Some examples of risk mitigation are discussed as follows.

16.2 STRUCTURED MITIGATION: PRACTICAL CASES

Certain risks can be structured for redistribution purposes. A relevant example is a pre-export facility to finance a producer in an emerging market. A structured deal for the Baha (an emerging market country's name artificially created for the purpose of discussion) Cocoa Board (Cocobod) is one of such cases.

Cocobod is the public entity in charge of Baha's cocoa industry and its exports. Baha is the world's third largest producer and exporter of cocoa.

Understandably, a large clean lending facility to Cocobod could be difficult given the low ranking of country risk for Baha.

Classic risk chain analysis for such pre-export finance transactions for Baha Cocobod will at least identify the following risks:

- Country risk of Baha: If Cocobod can deliver the cocoa and has received payment from the potential buyer, will the Baha government allow free payment flow especially when the country is in macro 'disequilibrium'?
- Performance risk of Cocobod: Can Cocobod really deliver cocoa as required in the contract? Can its delivery meet the requirements defined under the contract?
- Financial risk of Cocobod: If it delivers cocoa as required, can it use the incoming cash flow to repay the facility?

The risk mitigation structure thus plays a role in changing the picture (see Figure 16.1).

<u>Lending facility</u>

\> Risk *diversification*: syndication

By selling part of the lending exposure to the interested parties, the lending risk to Cocobod is transferred into the risk of participating parties. In case of default, the participating parties are supposed to honour the payment.

\> Risk *restructuring*

The lending party would ask for a pledge of the export contract. Repayment of the lending facility not only depends on the financial capacity (balance sheet) of the obligor but is restructured so that part of the risk is backed by receivables (export contract signed by off-shore buyers to be assigned to the lenders).

Figure 16.1 Risk diversification and risk restructuring

Although the obligor of the facility is located in Baha, the country risk of which is high, the lending is so structured that risk is mitigated by the receivables from reliable buyers outside the country and that the facility itself is syndicated by several banks.

Syndication limits the country risk exposure of each participating bank. The facility is supposed to be used to finance the purchase of cocoa beans for the 2005–2006 season secured by the assignment of cocoa export contracts signed by buyers who are located in developed countries. The assumed worst case scenario of nonperformance of Cocobod and the sovereign risk of Baha are mitigated by the fact that the lenders may control the underlying goods of the offshore buyers. Several banks are therefore mandated to arrange this facility by structuring it with receivables.

The intrinsic quality of the transaction's structure plus the established 12-year successful export performance track record for Cocobod, which raised over US$4.5 billion including this kind of facility in the market, made the difficult risk attractive.

The market appetite for this turned out to be enthusiastic. The facility was oversubscribed by almost 25% with a total of 25 banks joining the syndication. The oversubscription was partly scaled back while the launch amount was also uplifted from US$500 million to US$550 million.

Similar risk mitigation cases are found for production facilities to finance a prepayment to a producer in lieu of future delivery of products.

The general rationale is: we assume that the obligor is not qualified for such a facility for his own financials, or the borrower does not have strong financials to justify a substantially clean lending, especially for longer-term lending.

Since risk of a clean advance on his balance sheet is not acceptable, the total risk is to be redistributed to different but involved parties. Such risk mitigation by redistributing can also be used for longer-term financing in emerging markets where a correspondent bank is involved.

Take another example of lending to an emerging market commodity producer and examine how risk is redistributed and reallocated and the role of a correspondent bank.

A facility is granted to this commodity producer and the maturity of the transaction is 36 months with a certain grace period. Repayment will be over a 34 month period for amounts in accordance with minimum delivery units and agreed deductions.

Under such a deal, a risk chain analysis is the basis for lending. The focus is always on the flow of collateral. The credit facility is based on security over the physical products in the form of a local law pledge. The buyer in this deal, who is called an *off-taker*, is also a party for risk mitigation. The money is lent first to this off-taker.

The key point is that receivables arising under the export contracts for the products are to be *assigned* to the bank.

The risk chain analysis will identify a couple of risks involved in the transaction among which the major ones are:

- Supplier performance risk: Can the producer produce such a volume of commodity? This is the key question as the commodity is the basic security of the total facility.

  A good correspondent bank in the country of the supplier can help. This correspondent may produce a *performance guarantee* and promises to refund the lending if the supplier does not deliver.
- Buyer/off-taker risk: If the mitigation to the first risk is acceptable, the next is the creditworthiness of the buyer or the off-taker of the products. This is because the risk off-taker will pay back part of the money in case of the nonperformance of the supplier. Upon delivery of the product, the lender will revert to full 100% payment risk on the buyer.

Apart from these two major risks, there are other related risks such as:

- Operations risk: When the products are delivered, control of the title documents (bill of lading and/or warehouse receipt) is important. It happened that due to the loss of control on title documents, products change hands without the permission of the lender, who finally suffers a loss.
  A good correspondent bank may help in controlling the flow of goods.
- Quality risk: Even if you do have control of the goods but the quality of the goods is less than expected, the value of the collateral will be lower.
- Price risk: If the price of the product under the subject contract changes but not in favour of the lender, the collateral value will deteriorate. Some hedge arrangement is deemed necessary in order to avoid this.
- Policy risk: This refers to the risks of potential changes, that is government changes its policy for trade, for raw material export and for dealing with foreign companies.
  The change can also be linked to production subsidiaries, etc. These changes may have an impact on the value of the collateral.
- Legal risk: This refers to the right the lender has at this moment. When the legal environment changes, what was agreed under the arrangement may change as well.

Moreover, there are further risks linked to the deal such as transportation risk (transport of the product to the port), organizational structure risk (change of ownership of the factory), raw material risk (energy, alumina for alumina, iron ore for steel, etc.).

If all the risks are analysed and mitigated and relevant documents are studied (e.g. contracts, etc.), the impossible lending will become possible when a correct and suitable structure is developed and the right partners (producer, buyer, banks, etc.) are brought together.

Unlike the previous case where Cocobod itself has international reputation, the commodity producer itself, though influential in the local market, is not good enough for a facility of a large amount. The idea is to unload the (unacceptable) risk to an acceptable counterparty especially an offshore party, where possible, over which you have more transparent control. But first you have to find a risk off-taker which is usually the buyer of the final products (see Figure 16.2).

Figure 16.2 Risk-restructuring

The function of institutional banking in this risk mitigation is to take over some of the risks. Institutional banking plays a role here because risk mitigation may involve a correspondent bank who is in a position to take over the risk.

Thorough estimation of the production capacity – the performance of the producer – now and in the future, is the starting point in mitigating performance risk. But for a foreign bank, it is difficult to follow up day-to-day operations. This risk is thus being mitigated if one of the correspondent banks in that country knows the supplier and is confident in its production capacity. By receiving a 'performance guarantee', the performance risk of the supplier changes into the bank risk of guarantee issuing bank to the lender (see Figure 16.3).

Dear Sirs

You have concluded on (date) with (company) a contract No. (xxx) for the delivery of (products) at a price of (amount). As security for the due performance of the delivery, an indemnity by a bank shall be furnished.

At the request of (company), we (bank) registered in (place) herewith unconditionally and irrevocably undertake to pay you on first demand, irrespective of the validity and the effects of the above mentioned contract and waving all rights of objection and defence arising from said contract any amount up to (amount) (USD amount) upon receipt of your written and duly signed request for payment and your written confirmation that (company) has failed to deliver the ordered merchandise, or not delivered such merchandise as specified in the above mentioned contract.

For the purpose of identification, your request for payment and your confirmation hereunder have to be presented to us through the intermediary of a first rate bank confirming that the signatures thereon are binding for your bank.

Our indemnity is valid until (date) and expires in full and automatically if your written request for payment and your written confirmation together with a first rate bank's confirmation of your signatures are not in our possession on or before that date.

This indemnity is governed by (law) place of jurisdiction is (location).

Yours very truly

bank name and the representative's signature

Figure 16.3 Performance guarantee

16.3 INTERNATIONAL MITIGATION – RISK COVER BY NATIONAL AND MULTILATERAL FINANCIAL INSTITUTIONS FOR DEVELOPMENT

Risk mitigation often involves foreign parties. But *international mitigation of risk* refers to risk cover by development agencies, that is national and multinational financial institutions for development.

In the chapter on 'products of institutional banking', we detailed the function of syndication. Syndication is used in many banks as a *leverage for handling a large portfolio without large exposure under both country lending limit and bank lending limit*. As a matter of fact, syndication is a way of risk mitigation because it redistributes the existing risk portfolio to other parties.

Therefore when country limit is not enough or not available at all, to sell to other banks and institutional investors, including these development banks, is a good if not the only solution.

For institutional banking, however, the difficulty is that under many circumstances, banks have similar credit policies and credit limits. A difficult lending for one bank to realize is also a difficult lending for others, and very few correspondent banks may be able to take it. You need an extensive network to realize the syndication purposes. Price is also an issue here.

When a bank does not have a limit at all but an important client needs to have a deal done, the bank has to search for solutions through its international network. Institutional and multinational development institutions now come into the picture.

As discussed, to some emerging market countries that lack ready access to market-based finance provided by commercial banks, *official development assistance* (ODA) remains the most important source of external finance. Other capital flows and nontraditional sources of foreign exchange-workers' remittances, grants from nongovernmental organizations, and aid from middle income countries will play a role as well.

In institutional banking business for emerging markets, contacts with multilateral financial institutions are interesting for risk mitigation purposes. Multilateral financial institutions here refer particularly to the World Bank and other regional development banks such as the African Development Bank, Asian Development Bank, Inter-American Development Bank and European Bank for Reconstruction and Development. Multilateral financial institutions may also include organizations funded by the European Union, the United Nations or the government of an individual country. FMO, the Dutch finance company for development, is one such national development bank.

The target of these development banks is poverty alleviation. These multilateral financial institutions are involved in business (especially project finance), in energy (oil, gas, coal, electricity), agriculture and ago-industry, finance and manufacturing, transport, education, urban development, water supply, sewerage, etc.

The interest of institutional banking in development banks is twofold.

First, the mission of these development banks is different from those of commercial banks. These multilateral institutions focus specifically on long-term finance and corporate investments in emerging market countries both of which are not easy risks to commercial banks.

The services of these development banks consist mainly of long-term financing initiatives in risky environments especially for the development of the private sector of the country. Their project loans always involve an element of *co-financing*. In many cases, additional sources of finance are sought and commercial banks can join such financial deals.

Second, these development banks may have a closer relationship with the authorities of the government and are more influential in negotiating with government when in difficulties. To encourage commercial banks to finance these difficult markets, they offer opportunities to co-finance, or they play the role of guarantor.

Apart from financing long-term projects, one of commercial banks' business activities is to provide short-term trade finance facilities. EBRD, for example, and other regional development banks offer a short-term trade finance facility to support some difficult emerging markets.

The following is a list of such a EBRD syndication arrangement:

Rank	**participant bank**	**Country**
1	Raiffeisen Zentralbank Österreich AG	Austria
2	HVB Group	Germany
3	FMO (The Netherlands Development Finance Company)	Netherlands
4	Standard Bank	United Kingdom
5	ING Bank NV	Netherlands
6	Citibank NA	United States
7	Cordiant Capital	Canada
8	Commerzbank AG	Germany

9	ABN AMRO Bank NV	Netherlands
10	CALYON	France
11	Dexia SA	Belgium
12	Nordea Bank Sweden AB	Sweden
13	Erste Bank der öesterreichischen Sparkassen AG	Austria
14	Natexis Banques Populaires	France
15	Fortis Bank NV/SA	Belgium
16	BNP Paribas SA	France
17	Société Générale	France
18	West LB	Germany
19	Raiffeisenlandesbank Niederösterreich-Wien AG	Austria
20	State Bank of India	India

Source: www.EBRD.com

The banks mentioned here joined EBRD for financing trade-related facilities.

16.4 MARKET MITIGATION: POLITICAL RISK INSURANCE

Since risks can be priced and relocated, there is a market for them. *Political risk insurance*, for example, comes into the picture for country risks if and when necessary and if it is profitable.

When country limit is not available or is full, but the client is important, or the business is interesting, one solution is to cover the exposure under political risk insurance.

Coverage details must be reported to the country limit credit managers for their approval. The exposure will still be registered but with zero real exposure as the risk is (supposed to be) covered under insurance.

For emerging markets, country risk is the foremost risk in most cases. Political risk insurance is thus a major insurance form for mitigating emerging market risks. This will either support the deal, or give extra room for business which the institutional banking business department intends to develop but the credit policy in the bank will not allow.

Political risk insurance policy coverage varies from one insurance company to another. It is available to cover, typically, new or existing cross-border transactions designed to protect the insured against losses that result from:

- Confiscation, expropriation and nationalization.
- Currency inconvertibility and nontransfer: Government controls that prevent the purchase or transfer of currency for dividend or loan payments or other remittances such as the remittance of profits.
- Political violence: This coverage usually includes war, terrorism, seizure of property by government forces or rebels and civil unrest that result in physical damage to property or substantial disruption of a business operation.
- Breach of contract: This involves a host government's breach or repudiation of a contract for which there may be no protection under an investment treaty. It is usually tailored to specific circumstances and in some cases it has been possible to obtain cover for up to 10–15 years on a noncancellable basis.

Political risk insurance provides strong protection for financial institutions and multinationals that are doing business in emerging markets. But the coverage is specific and it is no replacement for sound business practices. It has become increasingly apparent that the safety of a company can have has much to do with risks of loss as it can with the change of the political climate in which it operates.

There are, however, some unique points worth discussing as far as political risk insurance is concerned.

First, there is the cost concern. Under many circumstances there simply aren't enough margins to be paid to the insurance company for the coverage of political risk insurance.

The price of the policy is the insurance premium. There are various ways to calculate the premium and the broker will choose the way that suits the client best. But it is different from the way a bank would calculate its pricing. The price of insurance is sometimes difficult to compare with the charges from the banks' risk coverage.

Second, there is usually a grace period involved when making a claim. In most cases, to claim the loss will take some time. This 'waiting period' under political insurance is used to see if during this period the claim situation changes, or that an alternative solution can be found to solve the problem. During this period the financing costs are borne by the client.

Normally in the case of default the insured would have to wait anywhere between nine months to two years to get its money back. Under many circumstances, the interest for this waiting period will not be paid during this grace period.

Third, the terms and conditions are important and specific, and risks covered are defined in the insurance policy. Like any kind of insurance, you have to study what risks you want to cover and make sure that they really are covered.

The insurance policy very often has specific definitions of the risk it will cover as well as specific conditions to claim the cover. What is not covered is usually not explicitly mentioned. It is not unusual that when problems arise, you are informed that you are not covered by the insurance policy.

Fourth, diversification is the lifeline of insurance. An insurance broker may ask to cover a package of risks rather than one specific deal for one country. It is often easier to find cover and competitive premiums when the underwriter is presented with a basket of risks rather than a standalone risk. The underwriter favours a balanced portfolio rather than just one really bad risk.

Political risk insurance has a *brokerage system*. We know that not each and every risk can be covered. Nor can every country risk be covered. Political risk insurance, especially those for special risks, will often be done via an insurance broker. The company looking for political risk insurance informs the broker about the risk it is looking to cover.

To estimate, the insurance broker needs details such as tenor, value at risk, type of goods, etc. The insurance broker will contact a range of underwriters to get an idea of coverage possibilities in the market, pricing, market capacity and type of cover available. This is the estimation stage. On the basis of this information the broker will contact the bank/company and advise them of the possibilities, which can either be 'yes' or 'no'.

If there is indeed a market appetite for country risk, it is then up to the bank and/or the company to decide if the insurance broker is interested in pursuing a particular *non-binding offer* from an underwriter. The broker will be asked to fill in a *proposal form*, which is the basis for the insurance cover. The insurance broker will then proceed to close the transaction with the underwriter(s), and the insurance cover is then in place.

There are two types of political risk insurance, *CEND* (confiscation expropriation nationalization deprivation) and *CFI* (contract frustration insurance).

CEND cover is generally used to secure goods and assets when located in a particular country against intervention from the national government, which in fact deprives the owner of the free use of his goods/assets. Contract frustration insurance provides cover in case contractual obligations taken on by a national government (entity) are not carried out according to the contract, and the client is not delivered the goods/assets he has paid for or they are to be delivered under a servicing contract.

The insurance policy is a document negotiated between the client and the underwriters, with the broker as a go-between. As emphasized earlier, the policy will state specifically which risks are covered as well as what the client needs to show when claiming a loss under the policy.

Political risk insurance coverage is one of the ways to mitigate country risk especially when there is lack of country limit, or country limit is not sufficient for the deals. It is different from other risk mitigation measures for banks.

16.5 COUNTRY RISK SOLUTIONS – HANDLING DISTRESSED SOVEREIGN DEBT FOR EMERGING MARKETS

Whatever a country limit is or how nicely it is established, it has no impact on the negative development of a country.

Once problem debt occurs for sovereign credit, and the loss, partially or fully, is definite, it is very unfortunate. But there are still several solutions such as *debt equity swap*, *debt rescheduling* or sale of *distressed debt* in the secondary market.

Finding solutions as such is an important added value of institutional banking. Although these solutions do not guarantee full recovery, they will offer the chance of partial recovery of the exposure.

16.5.1 Debt Equity Swap

Debt equity swap is the sale of distressed debt to parties that are optimistic or have a special link/interest to that specific defaulting country. These parties are in a position to engage in long-term equity or real physical investment in those debtor countries. The attractive part of debt equity swap as a solution to distressed debt is that it allows international currency loans (e.g. dollar loans) to be swapped for local equity in certain priority investment areas.

In the case of Mexico in 1985, such equity debt swap made it possible for Mexican dollar loans to be swapped into Mexican equity in the motor, tourism and chemical industries. The American Express Bank exploited such opportunities of a debt equity swap programme and built seven hotels in Mexico. This is also a face-saving measure to the borrowing government.

Countries that have employed debt equity swap programmes include many emerging market economies such as Argentina, Brazil, Costa Rica, Jamaica, Mexico, Uruguay and Venezuela.

The lending bank can also sell directly to potential buyers for this distressed debt. Institutional banking is active in this market, the volume of which is estimated to be more than $10 billion. Commercial banks are active both as sellers and as buyers.

16.5.2 Debt Rescheduling

Debt rescheduling is also called *debt rearrangement.*

If a country is unable to keep up its payment on a loan and the lending bank is willing to consider maintaining the loan on its balance sheet rather than selling it or swapping it for equity, the loan and its contractual terms will be rescheduled under a multi-year restructuring agreement.

South Korea, for example, reached such an agreement in January 1998 with its major creditors. South Korea had huge external debt during the Asian crisis. Upon the request of South Korea, the major creditors for different considerations agreed with the rescheduling, with a decent interest income on the rescheduling.

The rescheduling negotiation usually takes place with representatives of the creditors and a rescheduling proposal is offered during the process.

It is not surprising that some of the banks involved in negotiation may insist on repayment without a willingness to reschedule. Under such circumstances the relationship with the obligors may suffer of course, and it will take quite some time to recover such a relationship when the country starts to recover.

Institutional banking professionals are usually for international business and are therefore involved in negotiation and rescheduling. But the legal department of the bank plays an important role in checking the procedure and documents of the rescheduling of the debt. Together they have to evaluate the pros and cons for accepting/declining such an arrangement.

The considerations include, first, the chance of the repayment in the future, that is the estimation of repayment ability in the future upon the new maturity date. Other motivations include the potential extra income such as extra interest, fees, etc. On top of that, relationships with the country become a concern.

Rescheduling is sometimes a package of debt rearrangement. Its purpose is not only to postpone the repayment, that is extension of the maturity date, but may include some of the following:

- Lowering the interest rate
- Waiving or lowering the deferred payment of interest
- Conditional forgiveness of debt
- Unconditional forgiveness of debt
- Possible consideration of conversion debt into equity
- Possible consideration of conditional new lending

16.5.3 Debt Sale and Debt Collection

There are other solutions to distressed sovereign debts.

Some debt agents (including some investment funds) may buy 'bad' debt either as final investors or trade it in the secondary market.

The motivation for them to purchase is to collect the bad debts and finally to recover through their own ability or via special debtor collection agents.

If a sale is ever possible, it will understandably be at a discount. Any difference between the real debt and the recovered part of the debt will be booked as a loss to the bank. Sometimes it is possible to claim a tax refund.

The motivation can also be that the investors (investment funds), after buying it at a good discount, keep the debt and wait. They expect some (political) changes for the obligor of the debts in the future, which raise the hope of the repayment of total debts or part of it.

There was a sharp appetite in the mid-1990s for the bad sovereign debts of North Korea, as people expected that North Korea, once it opened its door to South Korea, might follow the 'open door' reform pattern of China to reintegrate its economy into the world economy. Similarly, there is also a growing interest in the sovereign debt of Cuba.

When trading, the debt agents assist in the monitoring and managing of the transaction including the conduct of negotiations with the investors and asset traders and the repackaging and/or securitization of debts to facilitate the sale.

If the decision of the sale of distressed debt is made, there are issues to be discussed and agreed upon by relevant parties. For example, whether the procedure should be confidential or not, that is can it be released to the third party or even to the public. The confidentiality terms will be made to clarify the commitment of relevant parties. The original loan agreements will be carefully studied.

A key issue here is to see if this debt can be transferred according to the original lending terms.

If the loan agreement specified that the loan would not be allowed to be transferred, the buying party may only offer a solution on a 'participated' basis, with all the future administration remaining in the hands of the selling bank. There are also issues of tax, etc. The bank may get some refund from local tax authorities for part of the loss.

The sale of distressed debt will enable the lending banks to remove the debts from their balance sheet. This will create room under country limit for new deals. The sale of distressed debts will also provide immediate cash to the bank.

Once the selling price is determined and the selling contract is signed, the nightmare of bad debt will be out of the file of the bank. No argument, no renegotiation – out of sight, out of mind.

But not every deal is saleable – either because of lack of any suitable buyers, or because legally the debt is not allowed to be transferred to another party. If the decision of the sale of debts is not the best anyway, another option then is to appoint the debt solution agency to collect the debt on your behalf.

Debt collection, on the other hand, takes time and you will be constantly engaged for the whole period. Return on debt collection is also uncertain, although it may be higher than the direct selling price.

Debt collection typically involves assets tracing. Litigation is often a must. Any debt collection agency must have experienced lawyers and country specialists available, who have both knowledge of the country and a high level contact for effective debt repayment negotiation. They will thoroughly analyse the debt in question, so those relevant professionals will be appointed.

As bad debts can occur anywhere in the world, a good debt collection agency should have an efficient international network of lawyers or law firms, who offer services from a local perspective. Alliance with local professionals including local lawyers is crucial to the success of the collection, as these local professionals will eventually act as real debt collectors. This is also the reason to choose the right debt collection agency for the specific bad debt. OMNI Bridgeway, for example, is very active in emerging market debts including distressed trade debt issued or guaranteed by a government or by a bank, distressed direct bank loans, and distressed corporate and project-related debts.

Final recovery of bad debts is very often through the use of legal remedies. It is important to identify and trace attachable assets in favourable worldwide jurisdictions, to ensure that the judgements obtained can actually be enforced.

For debt handling companies, all these debt solutions start with an assessment from the debt trading agents.

The assessment includes information on the debt – the name of the debtor, amount of the debt, the currency used, applicable interest, etc. It is important to control the payment instrument: letter of credit, promissory notes, and bills of exchange or straightforward loan agreement. The debt trading agent usually also wants to be informed of the latest communication with the debtor, any legal measures, etc.

16.6 BANK RISK SOLUTION: RISK PARTICIPATION

Similar to country risk solutions, there are solutions to deals linked to banks when no bank limit is available or the limit is full. *Risk participation* is one of them.

16.6.1 Risk Participation and Syndication

Risk participation is often mixed up with *syndication*. In certain institutional banking departments, the risk participation desk is even called the 'syndication desk'.

At the first glance, it indeed looks the same – selling exposure to third parties. But in fact there are obvious differences.

Risk participation aims at reallocating some risks, which cannot be accommodated inside the bank under the existing bank limit, to other parties, either because the nature of the risk is unacceptable in the eyes of bank credit, or because the existing exposure exceeds what is allowed. Syndication, on the other hand, may also reallocate risk but for larger and longer-term deals. The syndication procedure therefore takes longer period of time. Moreover, a risk participation contract very often is only a legal contract between two parties – one party reallocates the risk with a price, the other party accepts the risk terms and receives the earnings. Sometimes such a legal contract exists even without cash flow among parties involved during the lifetime of the transaction, except for the payment of risk participation fees. This is called 'unfunded risk participation'.

Syndication is a kind of *club loan* – joint lending to the same party. Risk participation is to share the default risk towards some special financial instruments like letters of credit.

16.6.2 Risk Participation and Reciprocity of Institutional Banking

There is a conventional volume of business in the institutional banking market whereby there is unfunded risk participation in both letters of credit as well as bills/notes exposures. Under these circumstances, the house bank offering risk participation has a corporate exporter and seeks to provide *nonrecourse finance* but may be short of capacity either on bank or on country limit.

To institutional banking, looking for an institutional client to take over the risk or to share a risk from a correspondent is commonplace (i.e. to participate in each other's trade portfolio). This can be on a bilateral basis, as well as using the specialist forfaiting market.

A practical concern is, because the inviting party of risk participation is only offering an 'appetite', that is a business opportunity to you, it can cause problems inside the participating bank when one's own corporate bankers wish to have country limit reserved for their own deals. They do not want to see the scarce capacity (country limit and bank limit) for an emerging market country disappearing out of the door to a correspondent who may appear to be a competitor bank. This will bring risk participation initiatives of the institutional banking department into conflict with internal needs of the corporate finance department. The country or bank limit, once occupied by the deal for risk participation, cannot be used for direct business from a direct client who may offer a higher return on the same limit.

To avoid such an internal conflict, skilful estimation of country/bank limit utilization is important. On the other hand, such a conflict, even if it does occur occasionally, may be comforted partially by the conventional interest in such a risk participation market – there is an expectation of reciprocity, that is the invited party may invite the offering bank in return for future risk participation.

From the perspective of an institutional bank, such expectation of reciprocity and enhanced cooperation will be obvious.

A strong domestic regional bank may have international exporters as its clients, but is concerned with its inability to provide nonrecourse finance due to lack of country limit in emerging markets. Another bank may have strength and corporate knowledge in the markets into which such exporters sell. Risk participation with each other thus fits into the *complementary principle* of institutional banking.

As known, in the institutional banking department, country limit to emerging markets may often limit business volume needed to support a client. A central bank may enforce provisioning when a certain limit is exceeded. Nevertheless, banks may still wish to service their corporate clients in an emerging market where capacity is in short supply. By performing risk participation the principle of reciprocity can work because room for business can be created via a risk participant bank, which has its country limit idle for one reason or another.

In late 1990s, there was a growing need for providing nonrecourse finance (confirming L/Cs issued by Chinese banks) to exporters doing business with China. With a conservative attitude towards Chinese risk, some banks were short of country limit whereas many Middle East banks and branches of Japanese banks in Europe had empty country lines for China. Risk participation had provided a good platform to fill in the gap: it gave room to European banks active in Chinese business and gave earnings to banks in the Middle East, which could hardly gain access to this part of Chinese business.

Risk participation can provide other spin-off benefits, which are often ignored – the capacity to gather market information.

During crises or difficult times, contact with risk participating counterparties is a very useful source of information for your peers. Your network of risk participation contacts may properly inform you if there are market scandals or defaults of large deals. This will enable you to prepare for the unexpected event for your own exposure. In case of default, you may release the fact of participation by mentioning the names of participants, with the consent of the participating banks, so that your negotiation power towards the issuing bank will be reinforced.

16.6.3 Risk Participation Master Agreement

A very important infrastructure in risk participation is the so-called *risk participation master agreement* which defines the privileges and obligations of both parties – the inviting (offering) party and the invited (participating) party.

As the master agreement is a binding document to both parties, internal or external lawyer(s) will be involved in preparing this document. A closer look at this document will enable us to have a better understanding on risk participation as a solution to bank risk.

As usual, a risk participation agreement will include some basic parts of a legal agreement among banks, such as names and addresses of relevant parties, key terminology definitions, applicable laws in case of dispute, and the technical details of the transaction including definitions of

EURIBOR
Expiry date
LIBOR
Maturity date
Offer
Participation percentage
Relevant currency
Tenor, etc.

But the essential part in the master agreement will include the following:

- The categories of transactions for risk participation: Risk participation is more an instrument for bank risks in trade finance deals. It usually includes:
  (a) Confirmation of letters of credit or stand-by letters of credit issued by other banks.
  (b) Negotiation of documents or acceptance of drafts drawn by the beneficiary under L/Cs.
  (c) Refinancing of sight payments under L/Cs.
  (d) Discounting of trade-related documents or drafts in favour of a beneficiary either drawn on accepting banks, or guaranteed for payment by any bank at maturity.
- The conditions for claiming: For the offering bank, risk participation is intended for covering the said risk when default occurs. This is a core part of the agreement, as the definition of default will be given. A definition which is very protective to the offering bank (and not so favourable to the participating bank) can give rights to the offering bank in case of nonpayment.

  'Default' means any nonpayment or any other nonperformance by the relevant party of its obligations under or with regard to any transaction whenever they fall due, causing any defaulted amount to be present, including without limitation to any payment by the Recourse Party in a currency or at a place not specified in the terms governing the relevant transaction.

  Here the *risk-offering bank* may claim as long as that bank does not receive payment from the relevant party – due either to the willingness or to the ability to pay.

  A participant bank, in its position, may ask for specifications of conditions and exclude dispute on the definition. They may ask for the right to decline the reimbursement if the nonpayment is due to something that is out of their control – fraud and operational mistakes, for instance. This is because the participating banks usually do not handle documents and they have no contact with the applicant or with the beneficiary.

In practice, the inviting bank may tend to cover all the risks linked to nonpayment. The participating bank, on the other hand, intends to recover only the nonpayment from the bankruptcy of the (issuing) bank or sovereign default. This creates a gap between the understanding and definition of nonpayment.

Due to these sensitive issues, the negotiation of a master agreement may take years. A practical solution is to sign a one-off agreement first so that a relationship can start. Another solution could be using a third party agreement, which is applicable to both buying and selling. This will ensure that the clauses are neutral to buying deals and selling deals.

It is also noticed that an experienced participating bank may insist that the inviting bank take a certain percentage of the deal. This is to ensure that the inviting bank will make the best recovery effort in the worst case scenario as the inviting bank is in the same boat – the inviting bank will commit to the recovery because interest of the inviting bank is also involved.

- The ways of handling recovery: The master agreement is supposed to outline the ways of handling recovery of default. Here the offering bank and the participant bank must cooperate closely and stay in constant touch with each other.

  In the event of any actual or threatened nonpayment, the offering bank shall consult with the participant bank as to the steps to be taken. In general no legal action or any measure or decision, which may reasonably have the effect of abandoning or in any other way substantially restraining or affecting the rights or interests of the participant bank, shall be taken without prior consultation, expressly without prejudice to the offering bank's authority to enforce whatever right deemed necessary by it (at its discretion) to be performed as a matter of urgency.

  Any reimbursement claim under any participated transaction shall be presented to the recourse party by the offering bank in the name of the offering bank, but for the account and at the risk of the participant bank, pro rata to its participation percentage.

  As long as any money is still owing to the offering bank by the relevant recourse party, the participant bank will not undertake itself any acts, steps or proceedings for the purpose of recovery of any amount due from the recourse party, either by way of subrogation or in any other manner whatsoever, without the offering bank's express prior written consent.
- The possibility for participant bank to resell: Considering the short duration of transactions for trade finance, the general practice is that the participant bank shall not be authorized to sell, assign or transfer to any third party any of its rights and/or obligations arising out of any participation without the express prior written consent of the offering bank. The purpose is to limit the complication of the risk participation in case of claiming (too many parties involved). This is another difference vis-à-vis syndication loans where reselling sometimes is allowed.
- The confidential nature of such an agreement: As mentioned, a trade finance deal may be risk participated by a correspondent bank, which could be a competitor. Therefore, most master agreements will insist that the deals be on an 'undisclosed basis'. The participant bank shall not disclose the deal, any participation, or any particulars relating to any participated transaction to the recourse party, any bank or any other third party. Disclosure is exceptionally allowed under certain circumstances:

  (a) Disclosure is required by any applicable mandatory law or by any governmental authority having jurisdiction.

(b) The participant bank was invited to participate in the related transaction on a disclosed basis according to the terms of the related offering bank.
(c) The offering bank has explicitly agreed to such disclosure by the participant bank in writing.

16.6.4 Risk Participation Procedure

Risk participation goes through several stages. The following list outlines the major ones:

- Risk appetite checking: When the offering bank intends to sell a deal due to shortage of country/bank limit, it will apply appetite checking, that is check with other banks known to them to see if these correspondent banks have country/bank limit available and further if they have an interest in participating. This is called *appetite checking*.

  Appetite checking will give an overall view of the feasibility of selling the deal and its cost. Appetite checking is often done through telephone conversation. The general characteristics of the deal will be mentioned including (in case of L/C) the issuing bank, the amount of the L/C, the currency, the underlying transactions (applicant and beneficiary) and tenor. Sometimes the potential participant bank itself may need more time to prepare the bank limit (in case it does not have the limit itself but thinks the deal is interesting), or to increase the existing limit if they consider participating.

  The competence test of a risk participation desk is linked to its ability to reallocate a 'difficult risk'. This is not easy to achieve as risk has its rating and ranking. Most banks may have the same or similar 'appetite list' for risks. A nuisance risk may mean the same to all parties. It is not surprising that the risks on sale in the market are trouble-some to most banks. Even if you offer a rewarding price, there will be limited appetite in the market for that risk. You have to search for those potential partners that may have a unique ability to accommodate that risk.

  In practice, a clue to the success of finding a risk participant is to see which banks are most familiar with that risk. For example, some small banks in Bangladesh may not be known to your bank but you have good correspondent banks in Pakistan for which you have room under bank limit. You may well invite these Pakistani banks to participate. This may turn out to be beneficial to both parties.

  On the other hand, it is sometimes a disappointment that not every potential participant becomes a target.

  When a participant says 'yes' to you, you are, however, not in a position to accommodate that participant. This is because you must have an estimation of the participant itself and have a bank limit available for that participant to whom you intend to transfer the 'unacceptable risk'.

  The principle is that the participating bank you are looking for preferably has a better rating than that of the risk to be sold, or at least not lower than the risk you want to sell. This will enable you to achieve risk improvement (participating bank risk is better) or at least risk diversification (participating bank has the same rating). In the above case the Bangladeshi risk turns into a Pakistani risk if they agree to take it. In case of default you have to claim to that Pakistani bank.

  Similarly, some of the new and unrated small East European banks may present difficulties to the credit of the bank for a line. But you may invite another East European bank, for which you have a line, to participate.

People many wonder why is this possible? Due to their day-to-day operation, some of these East European banks may have access to some deposits from these small banks and therefore they are in a position to take that risk. Some forfaiting companies are especially active to take these risks as their market niche.

- Risk participation invitation: Once the 'appetite' is confirmed, the inviting bank shall send an official invitation mentioning the terms and conditions of the deal including the amount, the applicant, the beneficiary and other particulars of the deal. This invitation comes under the framework of *risk participation master agreement*.

  If no master agreement was signed, there should be a one-off agreement to cover the obligations of both parties. Future disputes, if any, will be referred to this one-off agreement.

  The risk participant has the right to raise detailed questions vis-à-vis the nature of the deal. It is the inviting bank's obligation to provide relevant information for the purpose of the due diligence of the invited bank.
- Risk participation confirmation: When all the questions are answered and terms and conditions including price and participation percentage are negotiated and agreed, the participating bank will sign the participation agreement to conclude this risk participation. The inviting bank will check the authorization of the signature as the signed document is in fact a contract between two parties.
- Risk participation settlement: Once the risk participation contract is signed, both parties will follow the development of the transaction. Unless there is a default, the *participating bank* will receive the risk participating premium on the maturity date when the inviting bank receives the payment. The *inviting bank* will then 'release' the participant by written notice.

  If a request of extension of the deal is presented, the inviting bank must ask the participating bank for permission of the extension. If the participating bank insists on nonextension, the inviting bank may either take the risk back or decline the extension accordingly.

  When default unfortunately does occur, the inviting bank must immediately inform the participating bank and discuss possible measures to reduce the losses. If the loss is definite, the participating bank, after being shown the evidence and after the procedure defined in the master agreement has been followed, must pay to the inviting bank an amount agreed upon in the agreement.

  It happens that nonpayment does occur but negotiation is ongoing for a settlement. The participating bank will still have to pay the inviting bank, even if both parties know the problem is temporary. Sometimes the inviting bank may not request the payment as they know the payment will finally come. But the inviting bank will reconfirm their right of claim in writing.

  A dispute may occur when nonpayment is due to some operational argument. In most cases the participating bank will not pay as the inviting bank is supposed to handle all the aspects of the operational side. Nevertheless, if the master agreement defines 'default' as a form of nonpayment, then even if nonpayment is not linked to illiquidity/insolvency of the bank, the participating bank will have to pay.

  This is a point to watch and many participating banks would like to make it clear at the very beginning that nonpayment due to documentary arguments, fraud, etc. should be excluded for the participating bank, as indeed these are out of their control.

16.7 OTHER SOLUTIONS TO BANK RISK

There are other alternatives as solutions to no-limit situations for trade finance deals, when risk participation is not possible or not preferred. The following are some of them:

- Confirmation by an acceptable bank: When you receive an L/C issued by an unacceptable bank and risk participation is not possible, occasionally a solution can be found by having another acceptable bank, usually in the country of the issuing bank, to add its confirmation. Better still, such an acceptable bank reissues the L/C on behalf of the original issuing bank that is unacceptable to your bank.

  Under such circumstances, the tested L/C telex should explicitly mention not only the applicant but also the applying bank. The payment instruction should also explicitly mention that the confirming or the reissuing bank (not the applying bank) is responsible for the payment as payment should be drawn on that reissuing bank.

  This kind of solution for *no-recourse finance* can be acceptable if the issuing bank that is unacceptable to you is willing to cooperate by providing information on which banks may be willing to add their confirmation to its L/Cs, or may be willing to reissue its L/C via them. There must be some pre-arrangement among them for reissuing their L/Cs (such as deposit cover, etc.), if the issuing bank knows that their L/Cs may encounter problems in the international market.
- Cash cover pledge: In some cases, the obligor of the debt is really beyond consideration for credit. You cannot accept the risk at all, nor can you find any participant in the secondary market. Then cash cover is a solution because credit is only possible with their cash cover.

  Under these circumstances, a *letter of pledge*, to be discussed later, is structured to ensure that the cash in the account covers the bank risk.

  It is understandable that such an arrangement is interesting to the creditor as their risk is supposed to be covered under pledge agreement. At least legally the bank has the right to control the assets in case of need. The question is why is it also interesting to the obligor whose L/Cs are not acceptable? What is the motivation for them to provide cash cover for their L/Cs?

  Institutional banking practice reveals the fact that such arrangement could be interesting and attractive to many emerging market banks that issue the L/Cs. These banks have their capital in foreign currency, which needs to be deposited somewhere anyway. A cash cover arrangement will allow them to take the advantage of long-term deposit interest but the facility offered based on a pledge agreement can meet their liquidity needs for their day-to-day operation including confirming their own L/Cs. Many eastern European banks were involved in such arrangements, which help them to maximize their foreign exchange position.
- Risk sharing with clients: *Risk sharing* with the client (the beneficiary) in the field of trade finance can sometimes play a role as a solution on certain occasions. This kind of arrangement becomes necessary when non-recourse finance is declined.

  Risk sharing is to confirm and discount an L/C not on total face value but on a percentage basis, that is 50% to 50%, or 30% to 70%, etc. If the issuing bank defaults, the loss under letter of credit will be shared according to a predetermined percentage. These terms and conditions must be defined and agreed upon on formal documents.

The solution as such is exceptional and is offered to very important clients. During crisis periods, most banks stop confirming and discounting letters of credit issued by banks from a crisis country. Some exporters are willing to consider this risk-sharing proposal for two reasons.

First, they may have some finance (cash flow) from the bank. Second – and perhaps more importantly – by accepting this risk-sharing arrangement, they will have their bank backing them up in case of difficulties.

As we know, the institutional banking department of a bank has knowledge and expertise vis-à-vis the difficult country, whereas most exporting companies do not. Risk sharing can give comfort to the exporter (beneficiary) for handling difficulties as the interests of both the bank and the beneficiary are shared.

- Trade finance facility from development banks: In other cases, some of correspondent banks' limits may not yet be in place, either because country line is limited or because the analysis does not allow a limit anyway. But these businesses must be accommodated for the needs of banks' core clients.

  To support trade finance business with these small or new banks, some regional development banks establish trade finance facilitation funds. These can be utilized for commercial banks' trade finance business.

  A good example is the EBRD (European Bank for Reconstruction and Development) which provides trade finance funds. These funds are not available to all, however. To utilize such trade finance facilities, arrangements between the commercial bank and the regional development bank, such as EBRD, should be made beforehand. The issuing bank and confirming bank should be on the registered list. Every transaction is to be reconfirmed by EBRD for the availability of the credit limit.

  Figure 16.4 is a recent list of issuing banks and confirming banks under such a framework for the clients to choose from.

  Importers and exporters may have already benefited from the programme. So are the commercial banks which are not in a position to confirm these L/Cs under their own credit criteria.

  In many cases, importers and exporters under such arrangements may not even realize that their business was financed by an EBRD guarantee because only the issuing and confirming banks are direct partners with the EBRD.

  To secure finance for an import or export transaction, contact an issuing bank in the country you are trading with to request support for your transaction. Finance is subject to approval by the issuing and confirming banks, and the EBRD.

  The trade finance facility as such is not free. Development banks like EBRD are offering such a facility on a commercial basis. These deals are under commercial terms and EBRD charges a fee called the *country/bank risk premium*. The guarantee is usually 'undisclosed' to save the face of the issuing bank, but very often people know the information in the market.

  The trade finance facility as such is not unlimited either, even if you are willing and able to pay. EBRD covers the (non-) payment risk as long as the remaining part of the funds is in place, and this remaining part of the facility is enough for the requested booking. This is on a 'first come first served' basis.
- Sale of distressed debt for banks: Like the selling of distressed sovereign debt, the sale of distressed debt for banks is also a market practice. It will enable the banks to remove the debts from their balance sheet. This will offer country limit room for new deals. But

Albania
American Bank of Albania
Banca Italo Albanese

Armenia
Anelik Bank Co. Ltd
Armenian Import Export Bank CJSC
Armeconombank
Agricultural Cooperative Bank of Armenia
Inecobank

Azerbaijan
Azerigazbank
Bank 'Respublika'
Joint Stock Bank Azerdemiryolbank
Joint Stock Commercial Bank
'Bank of Baku'
International Bank of Azerbaijan Republic
OJSC UniBank

Belarus
Belvnesheconombank
Priorbank
Belgazprombank

Bosnia and Herzegovina
Raiffeisen Bank d.d. Sarajevo
UniCredit Zagrebačka Banka
(former Universal Banka d.d.)
UPI Banka d.d.

Bulgaria
CB Unionbank AD
United Bulgarian Bank

Georgia
Bank of Georgia
TBC Bank
United Georgian Bank

Kazakhstan
ATF Bank
Bank Caspian
Bank Center Credit
Halyk Savings Bank of Kazakhstan
Kazkommertsbank
Temirbank
Turan Alem Bank

Kyrgyz Republic
Demir Kyrgyz International Bank
JSC Bank Inexim
JS Commercial Bank Kyrgyzstan
Kyrgyz Investment and Credit Bank

Lithuania
Nord/LB Lietuva

Macedonia
Eurostandard Banka AD
Export and Credit Bank
FYR Macedonia
Stopanska Banka a.d. – Skopje
Tutunska Banka

Moldova
Banca Sociala SA

Figure 16.4 EBRD Trade Facilitation Program Issuing Banks
Source: www.EBRD.com/apply/trade/comfort/issue_pdf

Moldincombank (MICB)
Victoria Bank

Romania
Banca Comerciala Romana SA
Banca Transilvania
OTP Romania (former Robank)

Russia
Absolut Bank
Center-Invest Bank
Chelindbank
Commercial Bank 'Asia-Invest Bank'
Credit Bank of Moscow
International Moscow Bank
NBD Bank
Orgresbank
Commercial Bank Petrocommerce
Probusinessbank
JSCB Promsvyazbank
Rosbank
Russian Standard Bank
Savings Bank of Russia (Sberbank)
Joint Stock Commercial Bank for Scientific, Technological and Social Development
Joint Stock Bank Transcapticalbank
UralSibBank
Uraltransbank
Vneshtorgbank
Yugbank
ZAO Westdeutsche Landesbank Vostok

Serbia & Montenegro
Eksimbanka a.d. Belgrade
Euromarket Banka a.d.
Poslovni centar Krusevac
HVB Banka Jugoslavija a.d.
Opportunity Bank a.d.
Raiffeisenbank a.d.
Bank Eskhata

Tajikistan
Tajprombank (Tajik Joint-Stock Commercial Industrial Bank for Reconstruction and Development)
OJSC Tajiksodirot Bank
Open Joint-Stock Company AgroInvestBank
Senagat Bank

Ukraine
Joint Stock Post Pension Bank 'AVAL'
First Ukrainian International Bank
Joint Stock Commercial Bank 'FORUM'
HVB Bank Ukraine
Kredyt Bank (former WUCB)
OJSC Kreditprombank
Nadra Bank
Closed Joint-Stock Company ('ProCredit Bank')
Raiffeisenbank Ukraine
JSC Bank for Social Development Ukrsotsbank

Uzbekistan
Asaka Bank (Specialised State Joint-Stock Commercial Bank)
National Bank of Uzbekistan (NBU)
UzDaewoo Bank
Uzjilsberbank

Figure 16.4 (Continued)

not every deal is saleable, either because of lack of any suitable buyers, or legally as it is not allowed to transfer the debt right to another party.

If the sale is possible, like the selling of distressed sovereign debt, the selling price is usually at a discount of the *face value* of the debt. Any difference between the real debt and the recovered part of the debt will be booked as a loss to the bank. It is also possible to claim a tax refund if the relevant tax regime allows.

16.8 TOOLS FOR RISK MITIGATION

Under many circumstances, finance in emerging markets is asset-backed finance. A fundamental point in risk mitigation for emerging markets is *control of the collateral*. This is because by getting hold of the rights on the assets, the counterparty risk is supposed to be mitigated. The art of risk mitigation thus becomes

- what to control and
- how to control

In fact, proper control of the underlying collateral for the transfer of right needs to be monitored.

The transfer of right on collateral has legal dimensions. Legal considerations from lawyers and proper legal structure are important to know how to reinforce banks' position in worst case scenarios. Hence it is worth mentioning some of the legal tools used for such purposes.

16.8.1 Letter of Assignment

In trade finance, a bill of lading under an L/C is the title document to control goods. As long as the issuing bank does not pay, the beneficiary still holds the right to the goods.

Letter of assignment is often used in so-called 'silent confirmation'. In institutional banking business, foreign banks may add its confirmation to endorse the issuing banks' payment risk. But the confirmation can be an 'open' one where the issuing bank requests such a confirmation and the confirming bank knows the confirmation. The confirmation can also be a 'silent' one where the issuing bank did not request a confirmation and the confirming bank simply adds confirmation upon the request of the beneficiary.

Whereas under 'open confirmation'[2] circumstances the confirming bank has the right to claim, under a silent confirmation structure, the confirming bank is not direct in the legal framework of an L/C. The right of claiming payment for the issuing bank is in the hands of the beneficiary.

Confirmation to L/Cs, be it 'open' or 'silent', is regarded as a nonrecourse product in institutional banking for trade finance. Nonrecourse means that the confirming bank should pay the beneficiary under the conditions that (a) the issuing bank does not fulfil its obligation, (b) the issuing bank goes bankrupt, or (c) the country where the issuing bank is located has difficulty in allowing payment.

Confirmation, however, covers only the political risks and the risk of insolvency of the issuing bank. Under certain circumstances, the confirming bank may have the right to claim

[2] 'Open confirmation' is usually mentioned in the text of the L/C. The issuing bank would say: 'Please add your confirmation'. In the case of 'silent confirmation', the confirmation instruction would be 'without'.

to the beneficiary. These circumstances under which the confirming bank may have the right to claim should be defined and agreed upon under this letter of assignment.

Some of the typical difficulties in international trade may prevent issuing banks from paying, for example fraudulent documents, discrepancies in the documents from the part of the beneficiary, legal attachment which is effected by the applicant of the L/C, or a court order/court injunction, or any other legal hindrance which is issued by the applicant of the L/C or any other third party.

For the purpose of proper control of this right in case of legal dispute and default risks that are mentioned above and that are not supposed to be covered by the confirmating bank, the bank must arrange to request the beneficiary to transfer the right to the confirming bank and define the conditions of recourse in case of nonpayment by the issuing bank. A legal document – the letter of assignment – is thus produced for the obligations and privileges of both confirming bank and the beneficiary.

The letter of assignment is an important agreement between the confirming bank and the beneficiary. The beneficiary assigns all the money that is or may become due and payable to it under an L/C. The beneficiary assigns its claim on the issuing bank.

As banks only handle documents with 'reasonable care', the situations mentioned above are out of the control of the confirming bank. The confirming bank is therefore not liable even if the finance is regarded as nonrecourse finance.

The letter of assignment will therefore clarify this:

> the confirming bank should have right to claim already paid money in case the goods delivered were not in accordance as specified under the commercial contract. As a result, legal actions were taken that prohibit the issuing bank to effect payment under the L/C.

16.8.2 Letter of Comfort

Letter of guarantee is often used to convert a difficult risk into a conformable risk – the issuer of the letter of guarantee, the eventual obligor, is assumed to be financially stronger than the direct borrower. In institutional banking, the case can be a subsidiary bank with small capital base being guaranteed by its parent bank.

Sometimes we may encounter a situation where a guarantee is hardly possible either because of the time restriction or due to a complicated administration and regulation environment. Eventually, it may happen that you cannot get a letter of guarantee. Instead, you get a *letter of comfort*.

Just imagine a small bank that is a subsidiary of a big bank issues a letter of credit. Within the existing bank limit to this subsidiary bank it is difficult to accommodate this letter of credit. However, you have a good understanding and relationship with the parent bank and are confident about its strength. Hence you will request a letter of comfort from the parent bank with almost the same wording as the letter of guarantee but without the same legal enforcement. The following is an example:

> We were pleased to confirm our full knowledge of the letter of credit transaction L/C number xxx, which was issued by our wholly owned subsidiary xxx on xxx and which will be confirmed by your good bank according to the request of the beneficiary of the above mentioned L/C.

We are aware of the fact that this confirmation is made by your esteemed bank because we control directly or indirectly xxx Ltd (name of the subsidiary).

We confirm that we shall maintain our shareholder in xxx (name of the subsidiary) until the above transaction is fully settled and xxx (name of the subsidiary) is released from all the obligations of the letter of credit.

We also confirm that we shall take all appropriate measures to ensure that the financial position of the subsidiary is such that it is at all times in the position to meet its liabilities to you under above transaction.

A letter of comfort does not have legal enforcement. A relevant question to ask will be: in what sense can it help for the purposes of risk mitigation?

True that such a letter of comfort cannot be used as a legal instrument to secure your position. Nevertheless, such a letter of comfort gives awareness of the transaction from the perspective of the parent bank and thus makes the parent bank alert to the transaction.

Understandably, the letter of comfort will not allow the confirming bank to claim directly to this parent bank. But at least the subsidiary must report the transaction to its parent and has to be disciplined in its internal credit norms and regulations. In case of default of the subsidiary, the parent bank is at least taking reputation risk if it chooses to let the subsidiary fail without any rescue measures.

16.8.3 Pledge Agreement

In institutional banking business for emerging markets, collateral cover to secure a position is frequently used. This cover position is secured by a *pledge agreement*. The following is an example:

The undersigned
1. ABC Bank

And XYZ Bank, established at xxx (place), hereunder referred to as xxx bank

Have agreed as follows:

To secure the payment of all present and future indebtedness of the bank to XYZ bank, in whatever regards, the bank hereby pledges to XYZ bank, and ABC bank hereby accepts such pledge, all assets, documents of title and other securities which are in the possession of XYZ bank or of a third party on behalf of XYZ bank from or for the benefits of the bank in whatever regards, including all sums standing to the credit to any present or future account of the bank with XYZ bank, hereafter also referred to as the 'bank balance'. The bank herewith authorizes XYZ bank as its attorney to pledge to XYZ bank the 'bank balance'.

The pledge will be established by notification to ABC bank hereof. This document shall serve as notification of such pledge to XYZ bank. The following terms and conditions shall govern the pledge:

If insofar as the bank balance shall appear to be subject to one of more prior changes, a pledge in favour of ABC bank shall nevertheless exist, without prejudice to the rights of XYZ bank as a consequence of the bank's default.

XYZ bank is entitled to block the bank balance. In the event the bank wishes to transfer your bank balance or part of it, XYZ bank shall only release the bank balance or part of it in the event that the remaining of the bank balance offers, in the opinion of XYZ bank, sufficient cover for any and all claims ABC bank has or will have on the bank.

The bank shall require the written consent of XYZ bank to establish an instruction of charge, or pledge in respect of the whole or part of the bank balance other than that in favour of XYZ bank.

The pledge shall include all dependent and accessory rights attached to the bank balance.

If XYZ bank calls in a present or future debt, arriving from whatever reasons, of ABC bank, XYZ bank shall have the right at all times to set off the bank's debt to it against the bank balance. XYZ bank is authorized to administer the bank balance on another account number without prejudice to the pledge established by this agreement.

The bank hereby irrevocably relinquishes its rights to demand that if XYZ bank decides to execute the pledge, other assets belonging to the bank that have been given to XYZ bank by way of security shall also be included in the execution and shall be sold first.

ABC bank, if so requested, is solely obliged to give a written declaration of waiver of the pledge if the bank in the opinion of XYZ bank is no longer in debt to XYZ bank and all relations between XYZ bank and ABC bank have been terminated.

Subject to proof to the contrary, a duly signed extract from the records of XYZ bank shall be conclusive evidence of the bank's indebtedness to XYZ bank. The bank shall at no time be entitled to suspend its obligations pursuant to this agreement, not even by disputing the indebtedness.

All reasonable legal and other expenses incurred by XYZ bank in order to excise and retain its rights hereunder shall be borne by ABC bank. The bank shall indemnify XYZ bank for any and all claims from other parties on XYZ bank which arise from the excises of the rights of XYZ bank pursuant to this agreement.

This agreement shall be governed by and contracted in accordance with the laws of xxx (the country). Disputes between ABC bank and XYZ bank shall be brought before the court in place or any other xxx (country) court.

Signed in twofold

Name title, place and date

Of course, when *collateral management* in handling risk in emerging markets is emphasized, we have to avoid over-reliance on collateral.

The term *pawnshop mentality* is used in this respect. Pawnshop mentality refers to an over-reliance on collateral at the expense of credit analysis that examines cash flow and financial conditions, to secure and justify a lending. Under the pawnshop mentality, collateral is more or less the sole criterion in the decision regarding whether or not to lend. Good credit management should not consider collateral to be a substitute for creditworthiness, which is the existence of cash flow adequate to repay the loan. In this view, collateral merely provides an additional ambition/comfort of protection for a lending that is already acceptable. Taking security interest in collateral does not ensure that the loan will be repaid and the forced liquidation of an asset frequently erodes the value of assets substantially.

Because of these considerations, we often have counterparty agreements in place for claiming their collaterals. For global market transactions, one such agreement is called *CSA* – credit service annex to the general framework of ISDA.

SUMMARY

Risk mitigation is not simply avoiding risks. It is risk redistribution, risk diversification and risk restructuring. The fundamental purpose is to handle difficult risks and to covert unacceptable risks into acceptable risks.

Structured mitigation is to analyse the risk chain and to distribute the risks, so that the risk is not solely the borrower's. Part of the risk is transferred to another party such as a correspondent bank which issues a performance guarantee.

International mitigation is to have the risk covered fully or partially by a national or international development bank. The rationale is that these development banks have a special mission towards emerging markets and are often in a good position with governments despite the fact that they work on a commercial basis as well. Risk mitigation also includes political risk insurance. This is because risk can be priced and reallocated. When good prices are paid, some party in the market will take it over.

When bad debt does occur, there are solutions to reduce the loss. Solutions include sale of debt and debt collection, debt equity swap and debt rescheduling.

For bank risk mitigation, risk participation is often used. Risk participation is to reallocate some risks which cannot be accommodated inside the bank to other parties. Risk participation is organized under a legal framework which is called a master agreement for risk participation. Such an agreement will define which transactions are supposed to be covered, conditions for claiming, how to handle recovery in default, the possibility of reselling, etc. From appetite checking to the settlement of a transaction, risk participation presents a platform for institutional banking to cooperate in trading bank and country risk. It may also incidentally provide market information to the inviting and participating bank.

For bank risk solutions, confirmation by an acceptable bank, cash cover from the issuing bank, and risk sharing with the client are also solutions used occasionally.

Risk mitigation is the control of the title (right) to collateral. Special tools of interest in this field are letter of assignment, letter of comfort and pledge agreement.

17
Problem Solving for Emerging Markets

17.1 PROBLEMS: HEADACHES TO BANKS

The development of business, especially for business in emerging markets, is usually beset by problems. Problems are headaches to banks.

First, the costs associated with problematic exposure can easily wipe out the hard earned bank profits. Added to that are the potential attorneys' fees, time spent and opportunities lost.

The best problem solving therefore is problem prevention. Survivors in emerging markets will often be those that hope for the best but prepare for the worst. We have covered most of this subject in previous chapters. However, when all has been said and done, problems may still come despite various efforts.

If we look at the problem from any perspective, success in business depends on the ability to solve problems.

Problems occur more often in emerging markets. Debts are unpaid due to foreign exchange shortage, operational mistake, bank failures, fraud, etc.

As a relationship department, institutional banking will be involved, indirectly or directly, in solving problems under all these circumstances. In fact, this problem-solving ability can well be regarded as a test of the value of the institutional banking department.

There are two crucial elements in securing the success of repayment of problem debt. One is an honest and thorough appraisal of the case and the counterparty. The other is a good communication line with the counterparty, not only with senior level decision makers but also with persons at the operational level of the counterparty.

Once a problem of payment occurs, the fundamental rule is to get yourself organized as soon as possible. This is because the longer you wait in addressing a problem the more serious a problem may become.

17.2 PROBLEM ANALYSIS

Solution comes from good and thorough appraisal of the case and the counterparty. You can hardly expect a solution acceptable to both parties if you are not sure that you have the answer either to 'what went wrong?' or to 'why don't they pay?'

Very often the reasons given for delayed payment/nonpayment on paper are only superficial. Under a letter of credit, for example, discrepancy argument is very popular as a trade finance problem. Banks are arguing for 'discrepancy' to defend their nonpayment attitude. But the fundamental causes could well be price of the underlying goods, quality of goods, or any commercial conflict between the buyer and the seller.

For solving such problems it is imperative to talk to the counterparty frequently, and all the lines of communication with the counterparty should be open. You have to know promptly all the relevant facts including legal requirements and procedures.

To analyse the problem, you need (professional) knowledge and contact with your operating colleagues in your own bank. Their first-hand information will give you access to the problem. However, sometimes your colleagues may be emotional or may interpret circumstances in their own way. To approach a problem with an unbiased attitude is necessary – it is always better to study in depth similar cases in the past, the banking practice of your counterparty and the legal environment (the origin and evolution of the legal system in the country of your counterparty, etc.).

A careful review of the case and relevant documentation files will give you a better understanding of what is happening and why. Reading detailed correspondence between your bank and the counterparty and reading between lines may give you more clues to a solution. There you will find sophisticated change of attitude, major basis of argument, potential steps your counterparty may take etc.

Before communicating with external departments, first talk to internal departments including the legal department. The advice of your attorney, internal and external, can be fundamental because they may be in a position to point out different scenarios when you progress further into negotiation.

Needless to say, relationship is always important in the mind of institutional banking professionals. Any consideration should take into account future relationship. A good relationship is supposed to generate more business for you. Sometimes the relationship is overwhelmingly important that you have to consider more on waivering the debt. On the other hand, even for your most important relationship bank, what is right and wrong should also be maintained for fair business practice. Internal coordination will also make the case more transparent. Different colleagues may add value to your final solution.

17.3 NEGOTIATION AND COUNTERPARTY'S POSITION

Once you have an appraisal of the case, you can start your negotiation.

In cases of disputes banks often start negotiation by arguing who is right and who is wrong. This can be very misleading. Many (Western) banks are too brutally frank and too quick to propose a legal solution, and the negotiation will easily end up with 'seeing each other in court!'

As a matter of fact, negotiation, if any, is in the first place for the purpose of recovering your money rather than saving face. You will have time afterwards to sort out who is right and who is wrong, or perhaps the question will become irrelevant altogether.

The settlement can be 100%, 50% or less. This is down to your negotiation skill and it depends on how strong your position is and how good the relationship/understanding between your bank and the correspondent is.

During the course of negotiation, it is better to identify quickly how decisions are made in the hierarchy of the counterparty. It may happen that one of the persons at the operational level is a key person in the process. Decisions are of course taken by the senior decision maker but the operational staff may give input.

From time to time banks adopt an up-looking attitude for negotiation – try to push payment by approaching top management of the counterparty, which is not always effective. Payment, if any, must be made by the proposal of the operational department. Moreover, contact with the operational staff will give you useful information on the background of the problem, so that you will know what really went wrong – the starting point of your negotiation.

The institutional banking department of your counterparty can be neither on the operational side nor on the decision-making (management) side. However, institutional banking staff are very often ideal sources for a 'map' of organizational structure of the counterparty, so that you can reach either the operational staff or the senior decision makers.

17.4 PROBLEM-SOLVING FRAMEWORK

After you identify the real cause(s) of the problem and the position of your counterparty, you then work out a problem-solving framework, or a plan of action.

You will decide either to comprise, or to take legal action. One obvious benefit for negotiating an agreed settlement is maintaining a relationship that may generate future business opportunities – the ability to earn profits and serve the needs of customers in that emerging market. The perspective is an overall estimation of the entire relationship rather than a one-off deal.

In the problem-solving framework, the cultural issue is relevant. Almost in all cultural contexts, legal action is at least unpleasant. If you have to go that far, you should clearly indicate that you are being pushed by the counterparty for this legal action, but even at the last minute you are still willing and ready to listen to what they have to say, and that the legal action, though unpleasant, is not necessarily unfriendly. The message should get across to the counterparty that the door for communication is always open.

Even if you are sure that you are morally and legally competant, to 'give face' can always better serve the purpose. To send a telex saying that 'your bank is one of the best banks in your country . . . ' gives comfort to the counterparty without costing you anything. The following is an example of such a face saving/amicable approach:

> Dear Mr xxx
>
> We, at xxx bank, have made seamless endeavours to build our bank a reputable and trusted name in the financial industry helped by long-standing cooperation and generous encouragement shown to us by other distinguished institutions, notably your own. Xxx bank has consistently been a pioneer in the development of the xxx (country) banking industry, despite severe competition.
>
> With regard to the recent troubling L/C matter between us, we would like to express our sincerest regrets. May we ask, however, that you understand that we are making our best efforts to resolve this dispute? In line with that, our trade finance department will send an inquiry to ICC asking them to mediate in this matter with full cooperation from your good bank.
>
> Again, we are most grateful for your unfailingly supportive cooperation, and we hope that this unfortunate incident will not deflect the course of our joint pursuit of mutual prosperity. We will therefore pay the L/Cs as promptly as possible once the ICC decides that we should. In the meantime, may I request that you take account of possible differences in interpretation?
>
> Best regards,

A point of interest is that if you notice other banks with a similar nonpayment problem, you can contact other banks for information and joint action, especially in large-scale defaults.

Practice in the past indicates that collective negotiation is often more effective than an individual one. If possible, creditors' meetings are advisable. If not, other creditor banks should be contacted so that you may exchange information, views and strategies.

Whether your bank should assume a leadership position among all creditor banks will depend on various issues. A seat in a steering committee will help your future position in the country and reinforce your contact with the regulator and the government. But a leadership position itself does not guarantee any priority for payment. Usually a big and influential bank assumes the leading position in collective negotiation.

There are advantages and disadvantages for this collective approach. One of the advantages is that it will definitely give more pressure to the defaulted party, but to repay all the debts could be more difficult for the defaulted party. To pay one party without paying the other could be awkward to the debtor. To pay all is sometimes impossible. Moreover, coordination among all the creditors could be a time-consuming task.

17.5 ACTION PLAN

If no settlement is reached after negotiation, there are options for various actions.

Strangely, perhaps, to take no action could be one of them. If the fundamental problem is the regulation on foreign exchange control of the country, or a legal injunction from a local court, in most cases you cannot expect an immediate solution unless you can influence or persuade the regulatory authorities or the court. The solution therefore is to wait until the paying bank is allowed to pay.

Indeed in certain difficult cases, the real problem turns out to be that the counterparty needs time to sort out their internal problem. The solution then is simply to give time but insist that their commitment for payment is in place. To push for immediate payment could force the counterparty into deadlock.

Occasionally, a payment problem may cure itself, given time. This, however, does not mean that you just sit back and hope. In the case of a legal court injunction, for example, you cannot take any action but you still have to follow the development in the court. Sometimes a steering committee is working on general solutions but you may have to provide different documents to the authorities. Ignorance of a deadline may have a consequence on your legal right.

A creditor bank may also search for collateral to secure its position, even though the final settlement may depend on legal action. The creditor bank can also offset some deposits it may hold of a defaulting borrower, if a pledge agreement does allow that (see the discussion on letter of pledge).

In some cases, further lending could be a possible action. A case to be discussed later indicates clearly that it was even effective. But several conditions must be met:

- This new lending may give the defaulted party more time to sort out problems and to weather the immediate crisis.
- The lending should give momentum for a dynamic motivation, that is new income may be generated if and when the new lending is in place.

This action of new lending must be carefully weighed as it should be secured in a way that assures that you are paid (e.g. control of collateral, secured flow of future income, etc.).

For emerging market banks, new lending should be linked to hard currency income as off-shore income is important for emerging market debtors. If possible, the new lending should have a senior position among all existing outstanding loans. There should usually be restrictions to the utilization of the new lending, as it should only be used in places where new income can be generated.

17.6 LEGAL ACTION AS LAST RESORT

Out-of-court settlements are usually preferable to legal actions. The fact that legal action is not preferred can be explained for a couple of reasons.

It usually takes a very long time from 'writ serving' to 'scheduling the date of hearing'. Sometimes it may even take years. Legal documents usually need to be translated into the local language and different countries may have different legal procedures.

Admittedly, the professional level varies greatly from bank to bank. Even certain law firms, which do have good reputations, may not have in-house law specialists in specific fields and/or in specific countries.

Legal action can be a source of embarrassment and usually can result in bad publicity to both parties. There are also complications linked to foreclosure. The relevant assets must be carefully identified and their location known.

Last, but not least, it is difficult to predict the result of a court decision. Some banks lose cases due to negligence of legal procedure rather than plain facts.

Legal action should be taken as a last resort and only after careful deliberation – a number of issues should be addressed before court:

- Does the counterparty have means to pay? If not, the court decision only gives you the comfort of who is right and who is wrong. Of course, the case may serve as a model for similar cases in the future.
- Is the relationship with the counterparty important enough that you have to think twice before taking legal action, to avoid cultural harm to the relationship? It is not unusual that when two banks are preparing a court file, the business relationship becomes frozen. This is not necessarily good for both parties, unless you definitely do not want the counterparty as your business partner.

  It is good practice to separate an individual business dispute from the overall business relationship. A phenomenon worth noting is that when two parties are under legal settlement procedure, the chance for 'business accidents' will be less as both parties are on the alert. The institutional banking department as relationship centre will have to bear this in mind and try to minimize the cultural harm to the overall relationship.
- How certain is the result of the court? The result of the court is difficult to predict, an estimation is, however, possible. Nevertheless, do not rely on this estimation. Logic and common sense may not always work in court.
- Is there any similar alternative for a solution such as third party arbitrage?[1] Sometimes alternatives used in similar cases, in the past, which turned out to be quicker and cheaper, should be taken into consideration.

[1] Howard Palmer in his *Bank Risk Analysis in Emerging Markets* mentioned his principles. Legal action can work if:

- The debtor has money or saleable assets
- The debt is acknowledged
- The law is agreed
- Exchange control formalities are in order
- There is reasonable certainty about the law; and
- Exchange reserves are available for repayment

- How do you facilitate the post-solution relationship? There are a number of cases in which dispute and conflict create great emotions and both parties finally become, unnecessarily, 'enemies'.

Handle the relationship carefully whether you win or not. Under many circumstances, your efforts for a positive relationship will be rewarded in the end.

If both parties agree to go to court, there are still other things to consider:

- Is the judgement of the court enforceable to the other party? If the verdict of the court is not enforceable, the verdict is only a judgement of who is right and who is wrong.
- Which court suits your interest most? If there is no mention of an applicable law in the agreement, what has to be considered is that the same facts may lead to different judgements due to the applicable law. A typical example is the discrepancy argument among banks. Under certain circumstances, some courts may give favourable judgements if material conformity is evident despite documentary irregularities.
- Which law firm is the most specialized in this regard? Usually large law firms may have law experts available in different fields. But some law firms may be particularly strong in the field to which your case is relevant – strong not only in the subject matter but also in cultural and network peculiarities of the country of the counterparty. Relationship counts in emerging markets, even in court!
- When to file the complaint: Sometimes a counterparty may insist on the solution of the court and try to file the case first. This will complicate the legal process. In many cases, if the counterparty files a legal action in the national jurisdiction first, it could be more difficult for the other side to get their national court (the New York court, for example) to rule on this first judgement.

It is worth mentioning that some companies offer a special service for litigation of 'distressed debts' in emerging markets as an alternative. These firms could be well experienced but you have to check:

- Their price (very often they will charge 50% of the debt)
- Their way of charging ('no cure no pay' or hourly basis like law firms)
- Their country experience and record

17.7 PROBLEM SOLVING: CASES

17.7.1 Case 1 Compromise and Face-saving

There was an L/C dispute with a bank in Asia. The alleged 'discrepancy' was used for the bank to delay their obligation. The real fact was that the bank lost their collateral and wanted to delay or escape the payment.

However, we noticed that the bank itself had funds available. An *ICC docdex solution*[2] was proposed for the alleged 'discrepancy' as the counterparty used the 'discrepancy' as an excuse.

---

[2] Docdex is a special agency under ICC for arbitraging letter of credit disputes among banks.

The L/C issuing bank nevertheless did not accept the ICC as a solution. It was then decided to present the case to the court. In the meantime, ICC's opinion was provided to them, together with:

- The evidence from the beneficiary (the exporting company) that he had performed his duty under the contract
- The comments of our lawyer
- Conclusions of similar cases in the past

After being patiently confronted with all these evidences, the L/C issuing bank was contacted for a settlement.

To avoid pushing the counterparty to an expensive and time-consuming court solution and to give face as well, a compromise of giving up some of the delay interest was offered as a gesture.

Under the pressure of future court ruling, the counterparty accepted a settlement without legal procedure. The bank got 100% principal plus €10 000 as a 'voluntary payment'. The case resulted in full payment without cultural harm to the relationship.

In fact even if both parties agree to choose legal action as a solution, you may still continue your contact and negotiation. In one case with an Asian bank, when the ICC did give the opinion but the counterparty still insisted their position, court litigation seemed to be the only solution. But a facing-saving solution was still offered – a reduction of the total claim by $5000. The counterparty accepted this reduction and paid. The court hearing was avoided at the last moment.

In fact this reduction amount was compensated by legal fees saved.

17.7.2 Case 2 New Lending and 'Old Debts'

Case 2 is linked to a nonpayment from a Latin American bank which had owed several million (the 'old debt') since 1980s.

First, an effort was made to let them acknowledge the nonpayment of the debt. After several meetings in their capital city, the defaulted bank agreed on the debt fact and accepted the figures. For the very first time, the defaulted counterparty officially recognized their debt vis-à-vis the lending bank.

A proposal was then made. The internal credit committee approved the proposal which was presented to the counterparty for settlement. Under this proposal a new pre-export loan of $5 million was made in favour of the debtor with the condition that 50% of the new money would be retained by the bank to reimburse itself in connection with the 'old debt'.

There was internal discussion as the new loan would increase exposure to the country rather than immediately reduce the 'old debt'. Finally, all the parties accepted the proposal.

The new loan enabled the counterparty to produce and export. The 'new production' was exported to a French trader – a client of the bank, and the deal was successfully completed. The new deal did reduce the 'old debt' by $2.5 million. Such a result encouraged both debtor and creditor to continue. The experience was replicated applying the same procedure and structure to new loans. Finally this arrangement enabled the bank to recover most of the 'old debt'.

17.7.3 Case 3 General Manager vs Operational Staff

This case was for a nonpayment under a letter of credit from an Asian bank. All the relevant evidence had been provided. Repeated contacts and negotiation did not, however, make any progress. The facts were plain and straightforward. The only solution seemed to be legal action.

The communication with the operational staff of the counterparty, however, gave a hint that a 'stubborn' general manager insisted his nonpayment position because he did not want to book the debt under his department. When this 'key person' was confronted with the 'writ' of the lawyer, he did change his position and effected the payment.

17.7.4 Case 4 Who is Right and Who is Wrong?

A dispute under letter of credit delayed the acceptance of the documents. Payment was delayed as well.

After investigation it turned out that the real cause of delay was the drop in the price for the underlying goods. The applicant intended to use 'discrepancy' as an argument to force the beneficiary for a compromise for the price of goods.

The negotiation started but it was intensive and took a long time. Finally the goods arrived at the port. To avoid the extra cost of demurrage charges, which may make the case even more expensive, both applicant and the beneficiary reached an agreement for a 10% price compromise for the goods. The advising/discounting bank, however, insisted that an ICC opinion be given and the deduction of 10% of payment should be settled after ICC opinion.

ICC finally gave its opinion that the alleged 'discrepancy' was not valid. When it was clear who was right and who was wrong, the advising/confirming bank claimed back the 10% early reduction.

SUMMARY

Problems in emerging markets are not exceptional and they are headaches for banks. Problematic exposure may develop into nonpayment and thus cause losses for which a bank must use its hard earned profits to compensate. Problem solving is thus very important and is a test of the competence of institutional banking.

Problem solving needs problem analysis in the first place. You have to understand what happened and, more important, why it happened.

You then negotiate with the counterparty for a possible solution. Here, being too quick to propose a legal solution, especially when you have not yet prepared for this, is harmful.

Once you identify the real causes of the problem and the position of your counterparty, you can work out a problem-solving framework. Step by step, you move forward, but bear in mind the key words: relationship and 'face'.

If no settlement can be reached after persuading and negotiation, you may still have some options including legal procedure. But, in general, legal action is not preferred as it will take a long time and a lot of money. It will also hurt the relationship. Moreover, the outcome is difficult to predict.

Before you take a legal action, several questions must be asked and the answer to these questions must be carefully examined. Even if the decision is made on court litigation, you have to check several points to ensure your chance of winning the case.

Practical cases highlight some of the principles of problem solving – thorough understanding of the ins and outs, face-saving, being creative, and focusing on the settlement rather than the argument are all relevant for a good solution.

Conclusion

Much of this book has dealt with issues in institutional banking for emerging markets. When the discussion comes to an end, there usually follows some predictions in this area.

Making predictions about institutional banking for emerging markets, however, is a doubly dubious affair as the subjects of both 'emerging markets' and 'institutional banking' are dynamic by nature. But the question of how emerging markets will develop is relatively simpler – some will definitely disappear, to be replaced by others. Nevertheless, for the next decade at least, BRICT countries (Brazil, Russia, India, China and Turkey) – the focus of this book – seem to remain for the attention of those who are interested in emerging markets. Accordingly, the discussion on principles for those emerging markets will remain of relevance.

Emerging market is a competitive landscape but one with enough room to accommodate many competitors. The *Economist* magazine correctly pointed out:

> Developed countries that are quick to abandon declining industries and move up market into new industries and services will fare the best as the emerging market economies come of age. Those that resist change can loom forward to years of relative decline. Those that embrace it can best share in the emerging economies' astonishing new wealth.[1]

In my opinion, it is inevitable that a greater number of financial institutions will invest in resources to enhance their franchises for emerging markets in order to capture a larger share of growing opportunities in this part of business.

Globalization and consolidation will also bring emerging market as an inevitable subject because no bank can really be everywhere in the world. John Bond:

> We think we need to be in countries where we can make sense of it for our shareholders and where we can make a contribution to the host economy . . . that means that you're unlikely . . . to see a truly global bank. If global is 225 countries in the world, we are only in 80, but HSBC is as international as any financial institution in the world today.[2]

On the other hand, institutional banking, given its cross-border business nature, is expected to undergo changes to serve the overall strategy of the bank towards emerging markets.

---

[1] *Economist*, 'Emerging economies: coming of age', 21 January 2006.

[2] *The Future of Banking* by Henry Engler and Jamse Essinger, Person Education Limited Reuters Series, p. 12.

Institutional banking as a business is not equal to an institutional banking department in a bank. The way each financial institution organizes its institutional banking department will differ greatly, depending on entrenchment of each institution under the context of globalization. But institutional banking as one line of business is indispensable for each global player.

When we review the history of institutional banking, we notice that nowadays this business line is more oriented to the profit target of the bank as a whole rather than to serve the needs of internal clients in foreign countries. Thus the concept of institutional banking covers more than traditional correspondent banking. The history of institutional bankers functioning as 'cocktail bankers' seems to be over. Relationship is not only for the sake of relationship. Relationship must have added value and is more for generating future flow of business. Institutional banking as a business line is expected to generate business and serve the needs of both other business lines internally and institutional clients externally.

There is hardly any disagreement about banking being a risky business. But in the business for emerging markets there are more risks or risks are more complicated. As a result, to earn profits there is as 'easy' as to suffer losses. One mistake made in emerging markets can wipe out a year's profits or more. Hence two key factors, among others, are emphasized throughout this book – the importance of the concept of *risk* and *reward* and the understanding of culture.

Bankers venture into the emerging markets and they find risks which hardly exist in the developed economies. Balancing risk and reward is critical to maintaining profits and reputations, and operational independence as well. To face the challenges of an emerging market is to face its risks. To face the challenges of risks there need to be creative ways of mitigating the risks, instead of avoiding them. In this field both principles and practice will expand.

In emerging markets, bankers cannot rely on the implicit guarantee of efficient supervision and probably bail out or rescue difficult banks, which is common in developed countries. Management ability is the key to much of the bank risk and management ability must be discovered from available information.

On the culture side, we foresee that the importance of culture with its fascinating perspectives will persist for all aspects of emerging market business. Competence in culture, however, cannot be obtained overnight and culture expertise cannot be trained in classrooms – they can only be learned from real life exposure.

The future of competition in institutional banking will focus on building up the capacity of competence of culture in different and individual markets. Insights into cultures will enable banks to be more effective when interacting with people in other countries. If understood and applied properly, cultural awareness will reduce the level of frustration and anxiety, and increase the chance of making successful deals – this kind of edge in understanding culture will translate opportunities into more successful results. Principles and practice in this field will develop as well.

The subject of institutional banking for emerging markets has been discussed in this book from principles to practice and from practice to principles. It is believed that people's practical experiences add knowledge to a subject and business practice demands more principles. After all, both principles and practice will merge into one simple fact – eventually the success of institutional banking for emerging markets will depend on how you play with culture and on how you play with risks.

Like any other businesses for emerging markets, institutional banking will present its colourful perspective and offer brilliant opportunities to those who are willing to *adapt* to the changing environment, who may have the *brainpower* to analyse what is really happening, and who can be *creative* for solutions to difficulties and risks.

A Chronology of the Asian Crisis, 1997–1999

1997

January Korea
Hanbo Steel, a large chaebol, collapses with $6 billion in debts – first bankruptcy of a leading Korean conglomerate.

March 3 Thailand
First official announcement of problems in two finance companies, and a recapitalization programme.

March–June Thailand
Sixty-six finance companies secretly receive substantial liquidity support from the Bank of Thailand. The baht currency is hit by a massive attack by speculators who decide Thailand's slowing economy and political instability mean it is time to sell. This causes significant capital outflows.

April Malaysia
Bank Negara Malaysia imposes limits on bank lending to the property sector and for the purchase of stocks.

June 29 Thailand
Operations of 16 finance companies suspended and a guarantee of depositors' and creditors' funds in remaining finance companies announced. The Thai central bank orders the companies to submit merger or consolidation plans.

July Korea
Korea's third largest car maker Kia suffers credit crunch and asks for emergency loans.

Early July Indonesia
Pressure on the rupiah develops.

July 2 Thailand
The Bank of Thailand announces a managed float of the baht and calls on the International Monetary Fund for 'technical assistance'. The announcement effectively devalues the baht by about 15–20%.

July 8–14 Malaysia
Bank Negara Malaysia intervenes aggressively to defend the ringgit; efforts to support the ringgit are abandoned; ringgit is allowed to float.

July 11 The Philippines
The central bank says in a statement that it will allow the peso to move in a wider range against the dollar. The IMF backs the move.

July 11 Indonesia
The rupiah starts to be affected. The central bank widens its rupiah trading band to 12 from 8%.

July 13 Korea
The market is saddled with billions of dollars of bad loans in the wake of a series of bankruptcies. Several Korean banks are placed on negative credit outlook by international rating agencies.

The Central Bank of Korea intervenes and defends the won by selling dollars from its foreign currency reserves.

July 24 Korea
All currencies melt down. Severe pressure on rupiah, baht, ringgit and peso.

August 5 Thailand
Thailand reveals austerity plan and complete revamp of finance sector as part of IMF suggested policies for a rescue package. Operations of 42 finance companies suspended.

August 14 Indonesia
Authorities abolish their system of managing the exchange rate through the use of a band and allow it to float. The rupiah immediately plunges.

August 20 Thailand
Three-year stand-by arrangement with IMF approval.

August 25 Korea
Government guarantees banks' external liabilities. The withdrawal of credit lines continues.

October 14 Thailand
Financial sector restructuring strategy is announced. Financial Sector Restructuring Agency and Asset Management Company are established.

October 24 Thailand
Emergency decreed to facilitate financial sector restructuring.

October 31 Indonesia
The International Monetary Fund announces a $23 billion multilateral financial package which involves the World Bank and Asian Development Bank to help Indonesia stabilize its financial system. Sixteen commercial banks close and other bank closures are expected to follow.

November 19 Korea
Widening of the daily trading band for the currency to 10% from 2.25%. The won falls sharply. Most regional currencies also fall sharply following the fall in the Korean won.

Mid-November Thailand
Change in government. Significant strengthening of economic reform programme.

November Korea
Korea Asset Management Corporation's (KAMCO) nonperforming asset fund is established.

December 3 Korea
All the currencies, won, rupiah, baht and ringgit, are each sent crashing to an all-time low against the dollar.

December 4 Korea
IMF approves three-year stand-by arrangement of $57 billion but rollover of short-term debt continues to decline.

December 8 Thailand
Fifty-six suspended finance companies are permanently closed.

December 10 Korea
Korean foreign-exchange reserves have run dangerously low.

Mid-December Indonesia
Deposit runs on banks, accounting for half of banking system assets.

December 18 Korea
New government is elected; commitment to programme is strengthened.

December 24 Korea
The IMF, the United States and 12 other countries pledge to speed $10 billion in bailout money to Korea to support its embattled economy. Foreign private bank creditors agree to maintain exposure temporarily.

December 29 Korea
Legislation passed strengthening independence for Bank of Korea and creating a Financial Supervisory Commission.

December 31 Thailand
Bank of Thailand intervention in a commercial bank; shareholders' stakes estimated.

December Korea
Fourteen merchant banks are suspended and two large commercial banks taken over by the government.

1998

January 5
All Asian currencies plunge as investors returned to the foreign-currency markets and heavily buy the dollar.

January 15 Indonesia
Second IMF-supported programme announced. Suharto signed to dismantle the monopolies and the family-owned businesses. Indonesian Bank Restructuring Agency (IBRA) established and blanket guarantee announced.

January 20 Malaysia
Bank Negara Malaysia announces blanket guarantee for all depositors.

January 23 Thailand
Bank of Thailand intervenes in two commercial banks. As a consequence the shareholders are eliminated.

January 27 Indonesia
Indonesia announces new reforms to restore confidence in its banking sector, guaranteeing commercial banks' obligations and allowing overseas investment in local banks.

January 29 Korea
South Korea's government and global creditors agree to exchange about $24 billion of Asia's short-term debt for government-guaranteed loans in a deal expected to end Korea's liquidity crisis.

January 30 Korea
Korea closes a third of its 30 merchant banks, in the first significant step towards a restructuring of the nation's ailing financial industry.

February 10 Indonesia
Southeast Asian currencies skyrocket against the US dollar in Asian trading indicates that Indonesia may peg the value of its currency to the dollar.

February 15 Korea
New president and government take office.

March 11 Thailand
Foreign strategic investor purchases a commercial bank.

March 31 Thailand
New loan classification and loss provisioning rules introduced.

March The Philippines
Three-year stand-by arrangement agreed with IMF.

End of April Korea
Four of 20 merchant banks' rehabilitation plans rejected. These banks are closed.

Mid May Indonesia
Rupiah depreciates which intensifies the deposit runs. Bank of Indonesia must provide liquidity.

June 5 Indonesia
International lenders and Indonesian companies agree on corporate debt rescheduling.

June 29 Korea
Five small commercial banks are closed by the government. Two merchant banks are closed and two are merged with commercial banks.

June 30 Korea
New loan classification and loss provisioning rules introduced.

June Malaysia
An asset management company, Danaharta, is established.

August 14 Thailand
Comprehensive financial sector restructuring plan announced, including facilities for public support of bank recapitalization.

August Malaysia
Bank restructuring and recapitalization agency, Danamodal, is established.

September 30 Indonesia
Plans announced for joint government–private sector recapitalization of private banks.

Bibliography

Calverley, J. (1990) *Country Risk Analysis*, 2nd edition. Butterworths, London.

Chacholiades, M. (1990) *International Economics*. McGraw-Hill.

Chye, K.H. and Gerry, C.K.L. (2002) Data mining and customer relationship marketing in the banking industry, *Singapore Management Review*, 24(2), 1–27.

Czinkota, M.R. (ed.) (2000) *Marketing: Best Practices*. Dryden Press Harcourt College Publisher.

Daniels, J.D. and Radebaugh, L.H. (1998) *International Business – Environments and Operations*, 8th edition Addison-Wesley.

David, J. (1995) *Asia Pacific Communications*. Kodansha International, New York.

Dufey, G. and Giddy, I.H. (1987) *50 Cases in International Finance*. Addision-Wesley Publishing Co.

Ellis, S., McCullough, J.M., Wallendorf, M. and Tan, C.T. (1985) *Cultural values and behaviours: Chinese within geographic boundaries*, in E.C. Hirschman and M.B. Holbrook (eds) *Advances in Consumer Research* 12, 126–8. Provo, UT, Association for Consumer Research.

Engler, H. and Essinger, J. (2000) *The Future of Banking*. Person Education Limited, Reuters Series.

Fung, K.T. (2004) *Leading Court Cases on Letter of Credit*. ICC Publishing SA.

George, A.M. and Giddy, Ian H. (1983) *International Finance Handbook*. John Wiley & Sons, New York.

Ghatak, S. (2003) *Introduction to Development Econmics*, 4th edition. Routledge Taylor & Francia Group, London and New York.

Glenn Hubbard, R. (2004) *Money, the Financial System and the Economy*, 2nd edition. Addison-Wesley, Columbia University.

Graham, J.L., Kim, D.K., Lin, C.Y. and Robinson, M. (1988) Buyer–seller negotiation around the Pacific Rim: differences in fundamental exchange processes, *Journal of Consumer Research*, 15, June.

Hofstede, G. (1980) *Culture's Consequences: International Differences in Work Related Values*. Sage Publications, Beverly Hills, CA.

Hofstede, G. (2003) *Culture's Consequences Comparing Values, Behaviours, Institutions, and Organizations across Nations*, 2nd edition. Sage Publications, Newbury Park, CA.

Hofstede, G. (2004) *Cultures and Organizations: Software of the Mind: Intercultural Cooperation and its Importance for Survival*. McGraw-Hill, New York.

ICC Crime Bureau (2000) Guide to the prevention of money laundering, published by ICC Commercial Crime Services, ICC Publications No. 585.

ICC Crime Bureau (2002a) Preventing financial instrument fraud, published by ICC Commercial Crime Services, ICC Publications No. 648.

ICC Crime Bureau (2002b) Trade finance fraud, published by ICC Commercial Crime Services, ICC Publications No. 643.

ICC International Maritime Bureau (1996) Special report on China trade – the risk factor, prepared by the ICC International Maritime Bureau.

James, D. (1995) *The Executive Guide to Asia–Pacific Communications*. Kodansha International.

Kincaid (2001) *Principles of Practices of Marketing*, 3rd edition. McGraw-Hill, Berkshire.

Kindleberger, C.P. (2001) *Manias, Panics, and Crashes: A History of Financial Crises (Wiley Investment Classics)*, 4th edition. John Wiley & Sons Inc, New York.

Kingman, P.R. and Obstfeld, M. (2003) *International Economics: Theory and Policy*, 6th edition Addison-Wesley, Boston.

Knop, R. (2002) *Structured Products – A Complete Toolkit to face Changing Financial Markets*. John Wiley & Sons, Ltd, Chichester.

Koch, T.W. (2000) *Bank Management*. Dryden Press.

Krugman, P.R. and Obstfeld, M. (2003) *International Economics*. Addison-Wesley Publishing Co.

Levi, M.D. (1996) *International Finance*, 2nd edition. McGraw-Hill.

Lewis, M.K. and Davis, K.T. (1987) *Domestic and International Banking*. Philip Allan.

Madura, J., Tucker, A. and Chiang, T. (1990) *International Financial Markets*. West Publishing Co.

Maudra, J. (2003) *International Financial Management*, 7th edition. West Publishing Co.

Meier, G.M. (2005) *Biography of a Subject on Evolution of Development Economics*. Oxford University Press.

Mishkin, F.S. (2005) *The Economics of Money, Banking and Financial Marekts*, 7th edition. Addition-Wesley Publishing Co.

Olsson, C. (2003) *Risk Management in Emerging Markets*. Pearson Education.

Palmer, H. (1998) *Bank Risk Analysis in Emerging Markets*. Euromoney Publications.

Redding, G.S. (1993) *The Spirit of Chinese Capitalism*. Walter de Gruyter & Co., Berlin and New York.

Saccone, R. (1999) *The Business of Korean Culture*. Hollym International Corp., USA.

Saunders, A. (2003) *Financial Institutions Management – A Modern Perspective*, McGraw-Hill, Irwin.

Trompenaars, F. (1997) *Riding the Waves of Culture – Understanding Cultural Diversity in Business*. Nicholas Brearly, London.

Watson, A. (1995) *Finance of International Trade*. The Institute of Bankers.

Zsolnai, L. (ed.) (2004) *Ethics in the Economy: Handbook of Business Ethics*. Peter Lang, Oxford.

WEBSITES

http://www.bankofengland.co.uk/
http://www.cbr.ru/eng/analytics/bank_system/bank_laws_e.htm
http://www.cbr.ru/eng/today/status_functions/print.asp?file=law_e.htm
micro-finance
http://www.cgap.org
http://www.themix.org/en/index.html
www.imf.org
www.federalreserve.gov
www. fincrisi.narod.ru
www.worldbank.org/poverty/scapital/library

www.economist.com/countries/
http://www.icc-ccs.org/main/index.php
http://www.ecb.int/home/html/index.en.html
http://www.accion.org/micro_order_our_pubs.asp?PUB_SRC=M

Index